Rethinking Job Security

'This monograph provides a timely and sophisticated contribution to scholarship on comparative labour law, examining the evolutionary trajectories of dismissal protection in Australia, the United Kingdom and the United States. Its arguments are engaging, rigorous and perceptive. It will be widely read and influential in the field.'

Professor Alan L. Bogg, *University of Oxford, UK*

This book critically examines the proper role of the law in protecting job security in the contemporary workplace. It provides a historical, theoretical, practical and comparative perspective on this under-researched, but fundamentally important, legal mechanism at a time when the pressure to deregulate and dilute worker-protective laws has taken on increased importance. The volume critically analyses both statute and case law from three advanced industrialised liberal democracies with a common law foundation, the UK, Australia and the USA, to understand the extent to which job security is realised. By applying a common approach and a conceptual framework that emphasises the complex relationships between law, the economy and society to analyse a series of national studies, the book is also designed to draw upon the insights of comparative analysis to deepen our understanding of the limits and possibilities of legal regulation of job security. The national case studies are supplemented by research that focuses on how supra-national organisations have sought both to develop and disseminate new legal norms around the practices and processes of dismissal. This study critically analyses and assesses the adequacy of the international regulatory framework for protecting the rights of employees in the dismissal process.

Joanna Howe is a Senior Lecturer of Law at the University of Adelaide and a consultant with Harmers Workplace Lawyers, Australia. Her research is focused on labour law and migration law. She has published on the subject in international journals, book contributions and the national press.

Studies in Modern Law and Policy
Series Editor: Ralf Rogowski
Professor of Law, University of Warwick

Also in the series

Networking the Rule of Law
How change agents reshape judicial governance in the EU
Cristina Dallara and Daniela Piana
ISBN: 978-1-4094-3305-7

Social Systems Theory and Judicial Review
Taking jurisprudence seriously
Katayoun Baghai
ISBN: 978-1-4094-5402-1

The EU Economic and Social Model in the Global Crisis
Interdisciplinary perspectives
Edited by Dagmar Schiek
ISBN: 978-1-4094-5731-2

Constitutional Evolution in Central and Eastern Europe
Expansion and integration in the EU
Edited by Kyriaki Topidi and Alexander H. E. Morawa
ISBN: 978-1-4094-0327-2

Central and Eastern Europe After Transition
Towards a new socio-legal semantics
Edited by Alberto Febbrajo and Wojciech Sadurski
ISBN: 978-1-4094-0390-6

Democracy, Law and Governance
Jacques Lenoble and Marc Maesschalck
ISBN: 978-1-4094-0395-1

Rethinking Job Security

A comparative analysis of unfair dismissal law in the UK, Australia and the USA

Joanna Howe

Routledge
Taylor & Francis Group
LONDON AND NEW YORK

First published 2017
by Routledge

2 Park Square, Milton Park, Abingdon, Oxfordshire OX14 4RN
711 Third Avenue, New York, NY 10017

Routledge is an imprint of the Taylor & Francis Group, an informa business

First issued in paperback 2018

British Library Cataloguing in Publication Data
A catalogue record for this book is available from the British Library

Library of Congress Cataloging in Publication Data
Names: Howe, Joanna, author.
Title: Rethinking job security : a comparative analysis of unfair dismissal law in the UK, Australia and the USA / Joanna Howe.
Description: Abingdon, Oxon ; New York, NY : Routledge, 2017. | Series: Studies in modern law and policy | Includes bibliographical references and index.
Identifiers: LCCN 2016022083 (print) | LCCN 2016023130 (ebook) | ISBN 9781472450579 (hardback) | ISBN 9781315606101 (e-book) | ISBN 9781317064039 (Web PDF) | ISBN 9781317064022 (ePub) | ISBN 9781317064015 (Mobipocket)
Subjects: LCSH: Employees—Dismissal of—Law and legislation—United States. | Employees—Dismissal of—Law and legislation—Great Britain. | Employees—Dismissal of—Law and legislation—Australia.
Classification: LCC K1773 .H69 2017 (print) | LCC K1773 (ebook) | DDC 344.01/2596—dc23
LC record available at https://lccn.loc.gov/2016022083

ISBN: 978-1-4724-5057-9 (hbk)
ISBN: 978-1-138-36355-7 (pbk)

Typeset in Galliard
by Apex CoVantage, LLC

Contents

Foreword

I am pleased to have the opportunity to present and to commend this monograph to its readers, who I feel sure will be numerous and enthusiastic. This book will in my view considerably enrich our comparative understanding of the law and practice of protection of job security in the English-speaking common law world. The author first became one of the leading experts in the development of unfair dismissal law in Australia and the United Kingdom, very well attuned to the convergences and divergences between the two systems as they at different times each and by turns introduced, reinforced or eviscerated their respective enterprises of imposing a framework of fair dealing upon a largely permissive common law contractual regime for dismissal from employment. Upon that comparative foundation, she has now erected a superstructure of further comparison with the corresponding body of law in the United States of America, which from the perspectives of the United Kingdom or Australia is generally understood as representing a radically contrasting laissez-faire regime of 'at-will' employment, untamed, in most of its state jurisdictions at least, by anything corresponding to the unfair dismissal legislation of those latter countries.

This work carefully questions those assumptions, tending towards the view that such a clear contrast might well represent a false or exaggerated perception: the totemic notion of 'at-will employment' is, after all, no more than a default rule or rebuttable presumption of what the contract of employment may dictate, quite frequently displaced by express contracting which subjects dismissal to requirements of good cause and/or reasonable notice; and moreover it is a default rule which is often overlaid by greater protection for employees in the public service and more generally by legislation against various kinds of discrimination in employment, if not by evolutions at state level of recourse for 'unfair discharge'. In the author's view, all this tends towards a greater de facto convergence of outcomes between the national three systems than the traditional narrative admits. The author's critique fully recognizes that such convergence may of course reflect the weaknesses of the British and Australian systems as much as the strengths of the United States system in terms of the protection of job security. The measured but persistent tone of that critique enhances the quality of this important and timely work.

Professor Mark Freedland QC (Hon), FBA,
Emeritus Professor of Employment Law,
The University of Oxford

Acknowledgements

This book had its genesis in my doctoral research undertaken at the University of Oxford. I am profoundly grateful to my supervisor, Professor Mark Freedland, for his encouragement, insight and guidance throughout this project. I also owe a great debt to Professors Alan Bogg, Keith Ewing, Ron McCallum, Paul Secunda and Andrew Stewart, who offered incisive feedback on drafts of this work. My thanks to the Rhodes Scholarship Trust and University of Oxford Vice-Chancellor's Fund for providing me with the opportunity to study at Oxford through generous financial support. I am also grateful to St John's College and my adviser Dr Alexandra Braun for providing me with invaluable support during my time as a doctoral candidate.

After leaving Oxford, I have found a stimulating intellectual home in the University of Adelaide Law School. Here I have profited immeasurably from the munificence of colleagues and friends. In particular, I would like to thank Associate Professor Suzanne Le Mire, Professor Rosemary Owens, Associate Professor Alexander Reilly and Professor Andrew Stewart.

Sincere thanks are also due to those who have given shape to this book in its final form. I am grateful to Kate Leeson for her careful editorial assistance in preparing the manuscript for submission to Routledge. The editorial team at Routledge has been extremely supportive and a pleasure to work with. In particular, I am indebted to Alison Kirk, Senior Commissioning Editor, for guiding me through the process, to Christine Cottone for overseeing the monograph's publication and Jade Lovitt for her invaluable editorial assistance.

In the time it has taken to turn my doctoral thesis into a monograph, I have been supported by a close network of family and friends. My deepest gratitude goes to my mother Fernanda, whose sacrifices and hard work as a single mother provided the best foundation and model, and my husband, James, whose love, friendship and encouragement have sustained me. Thank you also to my in-laws Jim and Miriam, who joyfully and lovingly have helped me care for my children since I began at the Adelaide Law School in 2012.

This book is dedicated to my children, Laura, Jesse and Paige, whose future job security both inspired and motivated me as I undertook this work.

Joanna Howe
University of Adelaide Law School
2016

Cases

Australia

United Kingdom

United States

Legislations

Australia

Commonwealth

New South Wales

Queensland

South Australia

Tasmania

Victoria

Western Australia

United Kingdom

United States

Federal

Montana

International conventions

ILO Convention No 158 on Termination of Employment at the Initiative of the Employer 1982
ILO Recommendation No 119 on Termination of Employment at the Initiative of the Employer 1963
Recommendation No 166 on Termination of Employment at the Initiative of the Employer 1982

1 Introduction

Introduction

Whether legislation should protect employees from arbitrary dismissal remains an open question. There is no universal agreement on the meaning of job security, its importance and how best to achieve it. This book examines the proper role of statute law in protecting job security in the contemporary workplace. It provides a historical, theoretical, practical and comparative perspective on this fundamentally important legal mechanism at a time when the pressure to deregulate and dilute worker-protective laws has increased.

The book begins by considering the two divergent paths to regulating job security undertaken by the three countries under review in this book. In the United Kingdom and Australia, where unfair dismissal laws exist, they are under considerable pressure. The contrasting United States approach of employment at will is controversial and continues to inspire rigorous debate.

The central inquiry of this book is whether, in substance, there is a significant difference in the job security protection afforded by the United Kingdom and Australia's approach on the one hand, and the United States on the other. Although conventional wisdom answers this question affirmatively, is this the whole story? To what extent do the United Kingdom and Australia's unfair dismissal laws provide adequate job security protection? How different is this to the protection afforded under the United States model of employment at will? Undoubtedly, when unfair dismissal law was first introduced, it was a pathbreaking innovation and distinctive in procedure and substance to the employment-at-will model. Its evolution, however, tells a different story – and it is to these divergent trajectories we now turn.

A pathbreaking innovation: the inception of unfair dismissal law

Albeit at different times, a statutory unfair dismissal system in the United Kingdom[1] and Australia[2] was ushered in as part of a promise of a new beginning for

1 I use the term 'United Kingdom' in this book to refer to the common framework of unfair dismissal law that was created for England, Wales and Scotland in 1971.

2 Australia is a federation in which the Constitution divides power between state and federal governments. Whilst a statutory unfair dismissal system was created earlier in some Australian states, the focus of this book is on the introduction and evolution of a nationwide federal

domestic labour law. The traditions of collective laissez-faire and conciliation and arbitration were being replaced, and with them disappeared the old order of protecting workers from unfair dismissal through union strength. Overturning these traditions was no mean feat. The central debate was not over unfair dismissal rights but the entire kaleidoscope of industrial relations. The United Kingdom's Industrial Relations Act of 1971 was a fruit of fierce debate in the preceding decade over the future of the United Kingdom's labour law and an attempt by the Conservative government to replace strife with orderly industrial relations. For Australia, the aim behind the *Industrial Relations Act 1993* was not order but modernisation: to rejig industrial relations so that enterprise bargaining and not the traditional processes of conciliation and arbitration became the central determinant of wages and conditions. As part of both countries' departure from their traditional paths, a statutory unfair dismissal system was canvassed and ultimately introduced as an enhancement of legal protection to working people so as to guarantee a greater degree of job security that was not contingent upon their ability to garner union support for their dismissal claim against their employer. With the shift to a more juridified concept of industrial relations, workers in the United Kingdom and Australia were empowered to challenge an employer's decision to dismiss before an independent tribunal. The notion of job security conceived by each system tended to focus upon providing compensation for unfair dismissal: in both the United Kingdom and Australia it was the exception rather than the rule that unfairly dismissed workers would get their jobs back. Providing a 'cost' to employers for unfair dismissal was intended to bring about the cultural reform of workplaces so that dismissals occurred according to the correct procedure and resulted in fairer outcomes. The idea was to provide an incentive for employers to only dismiss a worker for good reason and according to the dictates of natural justice.

Yet, despite these aspirations, the reality of the unfair dismissal systems of the United Kingdom and Australia was that they afforded only limited protection for the job security of working people. In both countries, from the outset, constraints were placed upon who was eligible to bring an unfair dismissal application. Casual employees, those on fixed-term contracts, and those who were still part of a statutorily mandated qualifying period were unable to challenge an employer's dismissal decision. From the beginning, both countries placed limits on the amount of compensation that could be awarded and, whilst the statutory preference was for reinstatement, tribunals were given significant discretion to award compensation if, in their view, the employment relationship had been sufficiently severed. Despite these constraints of jurisdiction and upon the remedy, working people in both the United Kingdom and Australia began to use their new unfair dismissal rights, so much so that in both countries concern

unfair dismissal system. A description of the state unfair dismissal systems that existed prior to the inception of the federal law can be found in Chapter 4. Where I refer to 'Australian unfair dismissal law', this is the federal labour law system.

was quickly raised about the caseloads of tribunals and the onus upon business of challenging unfair dismissal claims. Common to the trajectory of both the United Kingdom and Australia's unfair dismissal systems was the emergence of a movement towards limiting access to unfair dismissal protection by reforming the jurisdiction according to the needs of business. This reoriented the focus of both unfair dismissal systems from their original anchorage in a primary concern for protecting job security to a new preoccupation with protecting business efficiency and reducing regulatory burdens.

Despite the challenge to the legitimacy of unfair dismissal law in both the United Kingdom and Australia, statutory protection for workers from unfair dismissal still exists to some extent. No political party or major interest group has seriously proposed eliminating unfair dismissal protection altogether. Instead, the statutory unfair dismissal systems of the United Kingdom and Australia have been unravelled more covertly via an argument to reduce the burden of the unfair dismissal system upon business and to ensure that the presence of statutory protection does not act as a disincentive to job creation. This has led to the peeling back of the statutory superstructure governing unfair dismissal law. Whilst neither system has achieved complete deregulation of its unfair dismissal law, recent reform of the unfair dismissal systems in both the United Kingdom and Australia has centred on enabling efficient dispute resolution. The objective of policymakers is to resolve disputes within the workplace and without recourse to tribunals. In the United Kingdom, reforms have been canvassed which replace unfair dismissal law altogether with a system of no-fault dismissal, and there are new provisions that encourage employees to opt out of job security protection. In Australia the case against unfair dismissal law has been made particularly with small business in mind, and various reforms have exempted small business employees from unfair dismissal law, albeit to different degrees.

This story of a general pattern of parallel, diachronic developments between the unfair dismissal systems of the United Kingdom and Australia should not be overstated. Real differences occurred in the emergence of unfair dismissal law in each jurisdiction because of their divergent labour law traditions, with the United Kingdom's traditional labour law culture one of collective laissez-faire, and Australia's culture one of conciliation and arbitration. In spite of these divergent traditions, the United Kingdom and Australia's unfair dismissal laws were introduced in a broadly similar substantive manner, although some divergences remained. For example, although in both the United Kingdom and Australia a new specialist labour court was created and charged with resolving unfair dismissal disputes, in the latter jurisdiction the traditional processes of conciliation and arbitration, whilst out of favour with the direction of Australian labour law more generally, became embedded as the adjudicative process for resolving unfair dismissal claims. In Australia the decision after 1996 to rely on the federal industrial tribunal traditionally charged with resolving collective disputes as the arbiter of individual disputes produced a different unfair dismissal system to the United Kingdom's. The timing of legal change in both countries was also divergent. In the United Kingdom unfair dismissal protection was introduced over two decades earlier than in Australia. Constitutional shackles in the latter jurisdiction played a key role in this delay. These variations and the differences in the design of the unfair dismissal systems adopted in the United Kingdom and Australia in part reflect the different labour law traditions in each country.

Most important of all, however, is to observe from the outset the significance of this introduction of unfair dismissal law in the United Kingdom and in Australia. Hepple and Veneziani, in their study of the transformation of European labour laws, characterise the establishment of individual rights against unfair dismissal as a 'path departure', which they define as 'when a juncture is reached at which substantively different laws and policies begin to be followed'.[3] The establishment of a statutory unfair dismissal system in the United Kingdom and Australia represents a break with the past tradition of resolving unfair dismissal disputes largely through industrial tactics.

An alternative path: the inception and maintenance of employment at will

Unlike almost every other industrialised country and many developing countries, including Australia and the United Kingdom, the United States has never provided employees with a general statutory law protecting against unfair dismissal. Although International Labour Organization (ILO) Recommendation No 119 (1963) and ILO Convention No 158 (1982) developed international norms around the protection of job security, in particular the requirement of a valid reason for dismissal,[4] the United States remained defiant. Instead, the United States adopted the employment-at-will doctrine, allowing for dismissal without good reason or even for no reason at all. The courts apply this default rule when parties in an employment relationship have failed to specify the duration of that relationship.[5]

Just as unfair dismissal law in the United Kingdom and Australia has been diluted over time, the employment-at-will rule has been gradually eroded. Exceptions have emerged which have increased the level of job security protection afforded to American employees. For example, Montana's adoption of a Wrongful Discharge from Employment Act extends unfair dismissal protection to non-unionised workers; collective agreements also typically provide that an employee may only be dismissed for 'just cause', a matter on which an independent arbitrator can be asked to rule; there exists statutory protection against dismissal for

3 Bob Hepple and Bruno Veneziani, *The Transformation of Labour Law in Europe: A Comparative Study of 15 Countries from 1945–2004* (Hart, Oxford 2009) 21.

4 In full, Article 4 of ILO Convention No 158 on Termination of Employment at the Initiative of the Employer states: 'The employment of a worker shall not be terminated unless there is a valid reason for such termination connected with the capacity or conduct of the worker or based on the operational requirements of the undertaking, establishment or service.'

5 Richard Bales, 'Explaining the Spread of At-Will Employment as an Interjurisdictional Race to the Bottom of Employment Standards' (2008) 75 Tenn L Rev 453.

certain reasons, notably those which are based on discriminatory factors such as gender, race or age or which relate to the exercise of collective bargaining rights; and a number of common law exceptions have emerged over time which have eroded the edifice of the at-will rule.

Despite these modifications, the United States employment-at-will approach seems harsh when viewed in light of the contrasting statutory unfair dismissal schemes existing in Australia and the United Kingdom. The United States is also an outlier amongst developed countries more generally. Why United States labour law has taken a vastly different trajectory in regulating job security can only be understood in light of the historical origins of employment at will and the reasons for its introduction – a subject to which I will return later in this book. First, however, I will describe my approach in this comparative study.

The aims, methods and scope of this book

Controversies around legal regulation of job security abound. There is a well-trodden debate between theorists advocating recognition of employees' investment in their jobs by relying on notions of a right to work, job property, employee dignity, industrial justice or citizenship, and at the other extreme theorists justifying the at-will rule on the basis that it permits greater labour market flexibility, resulting in a more efficient, productive economy. Remarkably, there has been little scholarly attention to the ways in which these controversies converge around the different procedural and substantive protection afforded by the employment-at-will approach and the unfair dismissal systems. As such, a central contribution of this book is its in-depth descriptive work on the laws regulating job security in three countries. Although many scholars have observed and critiqued the difference between these countries' approaches, this has tended to stop at a comparison of countries' normative laws as they appear on the books, and not according to how they operate in practice.

I advance the three descriptive country studies using a method of legislative history advocated by Paul Davies and Mark Freedland in their seminal work on the United Kingdom's labour law and public policy.[6] I rely upon policy documents and parliamentary debates as the main source of primary evidence. In relying predominantly on primary sources, my aim is to avoid the errors of law that can be contained in secondary materials, which Watson observes is one of the perils of comparative legal studies.[7] I supplement this with secondary sources, as I recognise that in order to provide a closely grained analysis of the subject and not a broad-brush account, a multiplicity of sources is needed. Of the importance of 'comprehensiveness' for the comparatist, Zweigert and Kotz note that 'the basic principle for the student of foreign legal systems is to

6 For a description of their methodology, see Paul Davies and Mark Freedland, *Labour Legislation and Public Policy* (Clarendon Press, Oxford 1993) 1–7.

7 Alan Watson, *Legal Transplants: An Approach to Comparative Law* (Scottish Academic Press, Edinburgh 1974) 9.

avoid all limitations and restraints. This applies particularly to the question of "sources of law" '.[8] This approach rejects a static conception of labour law and is mindful of Hepple's warning to avoid becoming 'immersed in the ephemeral details of the present' in favour of studying the evolution of labour law across jurisdictions.[9]

This book focuses upon statute law, supplemented by reference to case law, from the three countries to understand the extent to which job security is realised. What are an employee's avenues for review of an employer's dismissal decision? How are alternative dispute resolution techniques such as mediation, conciliation and arbitration used to aid resolution of disputes? To what extent does the existence of qualifying periods limit access to unfair dismissal systems in the United Kingdom and Australia? How does each country's statute of limitations constrain claims? What types of remedies are available? How frequently is reinstatement awarded? Why are larger damages won in the United States compared with the compensation awarded in the United Kingdom and Australia? Are specialist labour tribunals necessary to resolve employment disputes or do ordinary courts suffice? Does the increasing use of 'zero hours contracts' in both the United Kingdom and Australia, which typically do not attract unfair dismissal rights, essentially amount to an employment-at-will situation?

By developing this common set of research questions and a conceptual framework that emphasises the complex relationships among law, the economy and society to analyse a series of national studies, the book is also designed to draw upon the insights of comparative analysis to deepen our understanding of the limits and possibilities of legal regulation of job security.

In seeking to reconsider the normative ideal of job security, I endeavour to make a comparative historical analysis of the trajectory of British, Australian and American laws regulating dismissal. Part of being a comparative labour lawyer is identifying processes of convergence and divergence that develop over time among the labour laws of different jurisdictions. As Kahn-Freund has warned, upon the comparatist 'the gods have bestowed the most dangerous of all their gifts, the gift of freedom',[10] because in comparing labour laws the comparatist is faced with a multiplicity of choices in order to select which jurisdictions to study and which aspects of the law to focus on. I have chosen unfair dismissal law as the subject of this book, and I define this as the legal system which governs the situation when dismissed workers query the fairness of their termination of employment. This encompasses the general law of unfair dismissal but not the specific law of discriminatory dismissal, which involves dismissal by reason of pregnancy, gender, sexual orientation or any other attributed protected from discriminatory conduct by the law. I also exclude the evolution of mutual trust

8 Konrad Zweigert and Hein Kotz, An Introduction to Comparative Law (3rd edn Clarendon Press, Oxford 1998) 35–36.

9 Bob Hepple and Bruno Veneziani, The Making of Labour Law in Europe: A Comparative Study of 9 Countries up to 1945 (Mansell, London 1986) 1.

10 Otto Kahn-Freund, 'Comparative Law as an Academic Subject' (1966) 82 LQR 40, 41.

and confidence, and good faith. These concepts expand the common law of wrongful dismissal and are not part of this book which concentrates upon statutory unfair dismissal law.

The scope of this comparative study is limited to identifying the evolution of unfair dismissal laws in the United Kingdom, Australia and the United States. Zweigert and Kotz caution against unbridled enthusiasm in selecting too many jurisdictions to compare: they state that 'although a selection may be painful, it is unavoidable on practical grounds' and that 'if a selection must be made, a criterion of selection must be adopted'.[11] Whilst mindful of Kahn-Freund's warning that 'nothing is more difficult than to understand from the other side of the Globe systems of industrial relations as subtle and complex as those of Australia and that of New Zealand',[12] I have selected the United Kingdom, Australia and the United States as the focus of this book because these three jurisdictions have many of their fundamentals in common. Legal origins theory recognises that these three countries originate from the same legal family, as Australia and the United States adopted the United Kingdom's common law system.[13] All three are advanced industrialised liberal democracies with a common economic system.

The purpose of this comparative study is not to ask which country's approach is superior but rather to challenge contemporary understandings of how different countries regulate job security. But to stop at a description of the unfair dismissal laws of the United Kingdom and Australia and the employment-at-will approach of the United States would fall short of the vocation of the legal comparatist to expand knowledge: to understand that comparative law is an *école de vérité* which extends and enriches the 'supply of solutions'. Building on its descriptive core, the final chapter of this book is both judgemental and normative – its purpose is to consider how job security laws can be improved by comparison and evaluation. Although there is no panacea to the job security challenge, this chapter considers how the law can deliver meaningful protection of job security in an inexorably competitive market-based polity.

Key themes and ideas

Ideology is a driving factor in the making and remaking of laws regulating job security. Different ideas have been instrumental in prompting or stymie-ing legal change. These ideas are complex and nuanced.

This section introduces the key ideologies examined in this book. Broadly speaking, these can be divided into three categories. A worker-protective normative

11 Zweigert and Kotz (n 8) 42.

12 Otto Kahn-Freund, *Labour and the Law* (2nd edn Stevens, London 1977) 117.

13 Rafael La Porta, Florencio Lopez-de-Silanes, Andrei Schliefer and Robert Vishny, 'Legal Determinants of External Finance' (1997) 52 J Finance 1131; Rafael La Porta, Florencio Lopez-de-Silanes, Andrei Schleifer and Robert Vishny, 'Law and Finance' (1998) 106 J Pol Eco 1113; Rafael La Porta, Florencio Lopez-de-Silanes and Andrei Schleifer, 'Corporate Ownership Around the World' (1999) 54 J Finance 471.

template for unfair dismissal law has been advanced by theorists based on ideas of 'job property', 'a right to work', 'industrial justice' and 'citizenship'. Those who support the idea of protecting employees from unjust dismissal commonly stress the importance of the job to the individual, to the broader community and even the economy. Other theorists, however, criticise laws requiring just cause in dismissal as unduly interfering with the contract of employment. A number of scholars try to marry these opposing views by supporting the concept of unfair dismissal protection but advocating its efficient operation. Each of these perspectives will now be discussed in turn, but I begin by exploring the idea of 'job security', which is a central focus of this book.

Job security

Unfair dismissal law was conceived as a way of protecting workers' 'job security'. 'Job security' is a taxonomy of different ideas and can be analysed from a variety of perspectives. One way of understanding job security is to identify what it is that requires protection. Kahn-Freund observes that 'for the vast majority of people their job is their principle asset. They have invested their skill and their strength in their job.'[14] Or as Reich states, 'a profession or a job is frequently far more valuable than a house or bank account, for a new house can be bought, and a new bank account created, once a profession or job is secure'.[15] The Donovan Commission also recognised the importance of a person's job in its observation that 'in reality people build much of their lives around their jobs' and that 'for workers in many situations dismissal is a disaster'.[16] Thus, inherent in the notion of job security is an acknowledgement of the significant investment that an employee makes in her job and that this investment should not be viewed as subordinate to an employer's investment in the employment relationship.

'Security' is more difficult to define. From one viewpoint, 'security' suggests that a worker ought not to be deprived of her job in the first place, or at least not in a manner which is arbitrary or unjust. 'Security' can be understood in terms of a worker's procedural rights and/or substantive rights in dismissal. The former suggests that fairness in dismissal is satisfied by technical adherence to procedural requirements, whilst formulating a substantive notion of job 'security' is more challenging. 'Security' is not immunity from dismissal. It can be broken down into *ex ante* job security and *ex post* job security. With regard to an employer's conduct prior to dismissal, the concern of job security is to strengthen the safeguards ensuring that dismissal occurs for only a valid reason. With regard to an employer's conduct during the dismissal process, job security is about ensuring

14 Otto Kahn-Freund, *Labour Law: Old Traditions and New Developments* (Clark, Irwin & Co, Toronto 1968) 38.

15 Charles A Reich, 'The New Property' (1964) 73 Yale LJ 734, 738.

16 Report of the Royal Commission on Trade Unions and Employers' Associations (Cmnd 3888, 1969) [526] ('Donovan').

that dismissal occurs according to a valid procedure and for a valid reason. The prevailing view in both the United Kingdom and Australia is that *ex post* job security is about ensuring compensation for unfair dismissal rather than necessarily mandating that an aggrieved employee is allowed to return to her job. The justification for this is that the employment relationship is so broken down by dismissal that ordinarily an employee does not want her job back but wants to be adequately compensated for being arbitrarily deprived of it.

In sum, the term 'job security' is used in this work to reflect the view that an employee's investment in the employment relationship should be protected from being unjustly removed. This protection is best provided by a system that awards a remedy that reflects a worker's loss of property, making it exceedingly difficult for an employer to dismiss unless there is good reason and due process.

Job property

An idea closely related to job security is job property. The argument that the employee holds a proprietary interest in the individual employment relationship provides a potential normative basis for statutory unfair dismissal protection. Frederick Meyers pioneered this concept in his comparative study of dismissal law in four countries where he sought to develop an argument in favour of recognising employees' property rights in their job.[17] Meyers defines the idea of job property as the right to undisturbed possession of a job, which cannot be taken away without due process of law.[18] Meyers conceives the employment relationship as existing between an employee and her job, rather than between an employee and employer. He states that 'short of economic or technological change which may modify the relation, an employer who is party to a collective agreement takes on an employee for life or at the pleasure of the employee'.[19] Thus, Meyers argues that compensation is not an adequate remedy for unfair dismissal. In his view, whilst an employment relationship may have broken down, an employee's relationship with her job might still be intact. Meyers advocates the US model where dismissal rights are protected under collective bargaining, and reinstatement is regularly achieved because 'we have succeeded in separating the job from the employer so completely that the issue of impossibility or impracticability or indeed immorality of requiring continued association is no longer raised'.[20] According to this perspective, where an employee holds a proprietary interest in the individual employment relationship, 'if the job belongs to the employee, he should be restored to it, and to do so in no way impairs an inherent individual liberty of the employer'.[21] Meyers studied the British phenomenon of unofficial

17 Frederick Meyers, *Ownership of Jobs: A Comparative Study* (UCLA Press, Los Angeles 1964).
18 Ibid 1.
19 Ibid 15.
20 Ibid.
21 Ibid.

strikes relating to dismissal prior to 1971 and observed that the willingness of the collective to take industrial action because of an employee's loss of his job suggests that 'British workers are quite willing to invoke their solidarity and economic strength to protect themselves against what they regard as unwarranted loss of employment; and second, that their object is to secure reinstatement, not merely pay in lieu of notice or some other solution implying continued separation from employment'.[22]

The tenability of the job ownership concept rests upon the discernment of an employee's proprietary interest in the job which is acquired during the time spent in employment. The tangible asset being taken away is an employee's labour services which are in an employee's possession, causing income and other property in the job to be forgone. Unlike a physical asset where it is quite clear what is being taken away, with an employee's labour services it is not just an employee's income that he is being deprived of but potentially many other interests too: an employee's dignity, autonomy, livelihood, sense of self-worth, membership of a union and place in the community.

The United Kingdom's development of unfair dismissal law included some recognition of the intrinsic value of a person's job but did not go as far as mandating that employees should receive their jobs back if a tribunal delivered a finding of unfair dismissal. Employers were extremely reluctant to recognise this notion of job property, with the director of the Confederation of British Industry noting in 1964: 'I do not consider myself that a man has any vested interest in a particular job.'[23] The Donovan Commission's final report recognised that while reinstatement would be the ideal remedy, it is more realistic and therefore preferable for compensation to be the primary relief unless both parties elect for reinstatement.[24] While there is no explicit reference to the concept of job property, it is possible to identify the influence of this concept in the Donovan Commission's reasoning. The commission's final report recognised the significant investment that employees make in their jobs and argued that this investment should not be viewed as subordinate to an employer's investment in the employment relationship. A similar perspective, recognising the intrinsic value of a person's job, is echoed by Otto Kahn-Freund in his statement that where a worker is not immune from dismissal, 'a rule of social ethics' requires that the worker be compensated:

> There is something in the analogy between the ownership of tangible assets and tenure of employment. For the large majority of people their job is their principle asset. They have invested their skill and their strength in the job. Just as the Government may, in virtue of its right of eminent domain or compulsory acquisition, for the public good, deprive a person of land and other property so it may be in the public interest that a person may have to sacrifice

22 Ibid 29.
23 Sir George Pollock, *The Times* (London 30 April 1964).
24 Donovan (n 16) 149.

> his job. But in both cases a rule of social ethics requires that he who sacrifices an asset should receive a fair amount of compensation.[25]

While Kahn-Freund recognised the strong similarity between the analogy of property ownership of tangible assets and of jobs, he imposed limits upon the job ownership concept, believing that 'the analogy can be taken too far'.[26] He favoured establishing a theoretical basis for unfair dismissal law in a 'rule of social ethics', which allows for compensation to be an adequate remedy for loss of an individual's job. He does not argue that an employer should be mandatorily required to provide an employee with her job back in the case of unfair dismissal, but rather that there should be an obligation to pay compensation because of the substantial investment the individual had made in the job prior to dismissal. This perspective has greater analytical similarity to the 'industrial justice' theory discussed later in this section, rather than Meyers' job ownership concept. Moreover, it should be pointed out that Kahn-Freund was not merely influential as a theorist but also an actor in the construction of unfair dismissal law because of his key role as a member of the Donovan Commission. His view that property rights in work should lead not to immunity from dismissal but to entitlement to compensation influenced the diluted version of job property that the United Kingdom's unfair dismissal system ultimately adopted.

A significant critique of the job ownership concept has come from Hugh Collins, who sees the idea of an employee possessing a proprietary interest in her job as untenable. Deriving from his own ideas concerning the achievement of justice in dismissal, Collins' fundamental objection to the job ownership concept is that an employee cannot have absolute control over, and possession of, her job.[27] According to this view, a job cannot be 'owned' by an employee, as many factors can dispossess an employee of her job: managerial decisions interpreting market changes, technological advancement and restructuring can destroy and create jobs. Collins argues that the job ownership concept is not only unfeasible but undesirable, as the labour market would be inefficient if an employee could insist on her absolute right to remain in her job.[28] This view endorses the prerogative of employers to manage their staff by allocating jobs to the most productive workers and legitimately discarding idle members of the workforce. Collins states that as well as undermining productivity, ownership of jobs would limit the ability of employers to meet declining demand in the economy and provide

25 Kahn-Freund (n 14) 38.
26 Ibid.
27 Hugh Collins, *Justice in Dismissal: The Law of Termination of Employment* (Clarendon Press, Oxford 1992) 10. Others have also questioned the viability of the job property concept as a normative template for British unfair dismissal law. See Tony Honore, *The Quest for Security: Employees, Tenants, Wives* (Stevens & Sons, London 1982) 9; Bob Hepple, 'Individual Labour Law' in GS Bain (ed), *Industrial Relations in Britain* (Blackwell, Oxford 1983) 408.
28 Collins (n 28) 10.

a disincentive for employees to work productively in their current jobs or to seek new jobs better suited to their skill set. He argues that rejecting a job ownership concept ultimately rewards productive employees with higher remuneration and benefits society as a whole, through more prosperous, competitive markets leading to improved living standards and greater levels of employment.[29]

The essence of Collins' critique of the job ownership concept is opposition to the argument that an employee has an absolute entitlement to remain in her job, put simply: immunity from dismissal. However, Meyers never argued that an employee should have absolute control of her job but advocated that there should be 'effective enforcement of the right to undisturbed possession of a job against the threat of unjustified disciplinary dismissal' which would result in a wrongly dismissed employee getting her job back.[30] This relative right to own one's job means that 'the job is his, for his and its life, irrespective of the will of the employer' unless and until 'he can be shown to be incompetent or have abandoned his equity by improper conduct'.[31] Meyers recognised that employers may have to shed labour due to economic or technological circumstances but argued that a job ownership concept requires employers to keep workforce reductions to a minimum or to transfer 'the equities of employees in existing jobs to newly appearing ones'.[32] He also argued that the decision to make employees redundant should not be made unilaterally by an employer but rather that objective and externally decided criteria should be used to select employees for redundancy.[33] Thus, in the situation of neither disciplinary dismissals nor redundancies did Meyers' theory of job property confer upon employees absolute immunity from dismissal but protection from unjustified dismissal. In a recent analysis of the utility of the job ownership concept in the case of economic dismissals, Wanjuru Njoya states that the emphasis in Meyers' theory on job property and its evolution by other theorists was 'not simply on trying to keep one's job at all costs, but on drawing attention to the true value involved when the job was lost'.[34] She limits the usefulness of Collins' critique to forcing job ownership theorists to 'map the contours of their claim', as beyond this his critique is less relevant considering that both traditional and modern manifestations of the job property case rest on a relative entitlement that does not exclude an employer's right to dismiss workers for incompetence or for economic reasons in a fair manner and according to due process.[35]

Accepting Njoya's view that contemporary theories of job property are considerably more humble than might be initially thought, the enactment of statutory unfair dismissal law in the United Kingdom and Australia cannot be viewed

29 Ibid 11.
30 Meyers (n 17) 5.
31 Ibid 7.
32 Ibid 15.
33 Ibid 15.
34 Wanjuru Njoya, *Property in Work* (Ashgate, Aldershot 2007) 63.
35 Ibid 64–65.

as achieving the normative ideal of job ownership. Whilst in both jurisdictions the enactment of unfair dismissal law did recognise the intrinsic value of having a job for individual employees beyond mere receipt of remuneration, neither jurisdiction genuinely fostered a culture where unfairly dismissed employees were to receive their jobs back after a finding of unfair dismissal. The job ownership concept forces acknowledgement of the real consequences of dismissal for an employee: not just the deprivation of income, but other things too, such as a social network, opportunities to invest in his or her career, a sense of dignity and autonomy, and so on. To the extent that the unfair dismissal legislation of the United Kingdom and Australia recognised that individuals should not be deprived of their jobs unfairly, there is an echo of job ownership theory and a rejection of the American approach of employment at will. Nonetheless, on the other hand, the failure of the legislation in either the United Kingdom or Australia to guarantee or prioritise reinstatement of unfairly dismissed employees is a clear indication that the introduction of unfair dismissal law does not achieve the normative template provided by the job ownership concept. This concept requires that the job be returned to an employee if this is her desire, as an employee's proprietary interest means the job was not an employer's to take away. It is irrelevant that the employment relationship appears broken down, as the job ownership concept draws a distinction between the relationship of an employee and her job, and the relationship between an employee and her employer.

A right to work

Another worker-protective normative template for unfair dismissal law which emphasises the remedy of reinstatement is that of 'a right to work'. If a right to work does indeed exist, a right to reinstatement in cases of unfair dismissal would be an essential component of it, for it would provide an effective remedy for the person whose right has been violated. The remedy of reinstatement would make the right to work practical and effective. In his 1981 essay, Bob Hepple argued that the right to work must encompass a right to be reinstated in cases of unfair dismissal and canvassed the possibility of the unfair dismissal system being used to achieve a 'right to remain continuously employed including the right to re-employment in the event of unjustified termination'.[36] The theory of a right to work has a narrower agenda than job ownership theory, which seeks to give employees relative control and autonomy over their jobs. Instead, a right to work approach hinges upon the extent to which an employee who is unfairly dismissed can insist upon returning to her job.

As I will explore in this book, the introduction of unfair dismissal law in the United Kingdom or Australia cannot be regarded as achieving Hepple's normative ideal that individuals have a right to work. Despite the provision in both

36 Bob Hepple, 'A Right to Work' (1981) 10 ILJ 65. See further, Joanna Howe, 'In Pursuit of a Right to Work Following Unfair Dismissal' in V Mantouvalou (ed), *A Right to Work* (Hart, Oxford 2014) Chapter 14.

jurisdictions that reinstatement is the primary remedy, this has not changed the fact that only a tiny proportion of successful unfair dismissal complainants are reinstated or reengaged. In both jurisdictions employers can oppose reinstatement and usually buy their way out of reinstatement through the payment of a relatively modest additional lump sum. Scholar Bob Simpson has also observed the failure of the United Kingdom's unfair dismissal law to provide for a right to work, arguing that the law reinforces basic managerial prerogative by only attaching a price to arbitrary dismissal.[37] He cautions against overestimating the impact of the unfair dismissal system on improving dismissal standards given the 'retrogressive impact' of the common law origins of many of the terms in the statutory system.[38] He noted that statutory unfair dismissal protection only benefits workers who are 'employees', with 'contracts of employment', who are 'dismissed' and concludes:

> Perhaps more fundamental is the extent to which the traditions of common law thinking have influenced and moulded the shape of much of the new statutory regime. As long as this remains, the potential for creating effective change in labour relations through employment protection legislation remains limited if not illusory.[39]

An interesting question is whether the American model of employment at will provides a greater opportunity for the realisation of the normative ideal of a right to work. Certainly in the union-represented sector, reinstatement is commonly ordered at arbitration.[40] However, even beyond this, reinstatement is a presumptive entitlement for prevailing employees in discrimination and other cases, and courts tend to order pay-outs of significant damages in lieu of reinstatement.[41] Whilst the latter falls short of returning workers to their jobs, it does provide greater recognition of the value of a person's job, as damages can be punitive rather than merely compensatory and no caps exist, unlike in Australia.[42]

Industrial justice

Hugh Collins argues that an industrial justice justification for unfair dismissal law hinges upon two principles: first, that there needs to be a restraint on absolute

37 Bob Simpson, 'British Labour Relations in the 1980s: Learning to Live with the Law' (1986) 49 MLR 796, 804–5.

38 Ibid 804.

39 Ibid 806.

40 See OECD, 'Detailed Description of Employment Protections in OECD and Selected Non-OECD Countries 2008' (2009) 19, <www.oecd.org/employment/emp/42740165.pdf>, stating that reinstatement orders are normal for US National Labor Relations Act and Civil Rights Act cases, but 'almost never made available' in breach of contract cases.

41 Maria L Ontiveros, 'To Help Those Most in Need: Undocumented Workers' Rights and Remedies Under Title VII' (1993–94) 20 NYU Rev L & Soc Change 607, 624 n 118.

42 Samuel Estreicher and Jeffrey M Hirsch, 'Comparative Wrongful Dismissal Law: Reassessing American Exceptionalism' (2014) 92 NC L Rev 343, 460.

managerial prerogative to terminate the employment contract; and second, that the 'interest' being protected by legislative intervention is an individual employee's self-worth, which goes beyond monetary remuneration. Collins' influential work relies upon these two strands to justify statutory unfair dismissal law: 'A respect for the dignity of the individual and an improvement in the conditions of work which are conducive to autonomy amount to a defence of an employee's interest in job security, but not to a property right in a job.'[43]

Collins' concern with untrammelled management power stems from dissatisfaction with the inadequacy of the common law contract of employment to require fair dismissal, as the common law merely requires the payment of notice.[44] There was also an awareness that using industrial action to deal with dismissal disputes was undesirable, as employees in unorganised industries had no recourse to industrial action and because of the inefficiency of using a collective dispute resolution mechanism to resolve individual dismissal disputes. In his distinct work on industrial justice, Selznick also advocated the application of the rule of law to industrial relations so as to reduce arbitrariness in managerial decision making.[45] In his view, while the application of the rule of law to industrial relations initially acts as a constraint upon managerial prerogative, its end result is transformative because it achieves more than the correct exercise of power. With rhetorical flourish he argues:

> The 'progressive reduction of arbitrariness' knows no near stopping-place. The closer we look at that process, the more we realise that it calls for an affirmative view of what it means to participate in a legal order, whether as citizens, judge or executive. In its richest connotation, legality evokes the Greek view of a social order founded in reason, whose constitutive principle is justice.[46]

In the context of unfair dismissal, Collins argues that legislative intervention is justified on the basis that management power needs to be regulated so as to enhance the 'opportunities for people to bring meaning to their lives through work'.[47] He draws upon the writings of Joseph Raz to develop this justification for unfair dismissal law based on the principle of autonomy, arguing that a liberal society should foster worthwhile opportunities for people to pursue their personal goals and become 'the author of his or her own life'.[48] Likening internal management structures to a form of bureaucratic organisation, Collins says that

43 Collins (n 28) 21.
44 Ibid 29–34. For an excellent exposition of the development of English law and the contract of employment, see Honore (n 28) 2–9.
45 Philip Selznick, *Law, Society and Industrial Justice* (Russell Sage Foundation, New York 1969) 12–13.
46 Ibid 18.
47 Collins (n 28) 19.
48 Joseph Raz, *The Morality of Freedom* (Clarendon Press, Oxford 1986) 369–73, 417.

workplace policies and procedures should not constrain individual employees from discovering meaning in their work.[49] Going beyond Selznick's application of the rule of law as the foundation for achieving industrial justice in the workplace, Collins advocates a further restriction on management disciplinary power so that all disciplinary rules which restrict individual freedom in the workplace should be 'shown to be reasonably necessary for the efficient coordination of the work or they will comprise an unjust restriction upon autonomy'.[50] Writing elsewhere, Collins also argues that an industrial justice theorisation of the United Kingdom's statutory unfair dismissal scheme is more appropriate than the 'floor of rights' theory which other writers have favoured.[51] He says that 'this interpretation misses the revolutionary form of legal intervention involved in the legal review of managerial decisions'. In his opinion, by introducing legal regulation and judicial review to managerial decision making in the workplace, the unfair dismissal scheme 'goes further than the floor of rights and has many of the hallmarks of corporatist legislation'.[52]

Collins proposed that the other cornerstone of a theory of justice in dismissal is a concern with guaranteeing the dignity of employees during the dismissal process. This justification hinges upon the realisation that an unfair dismissal not merely deprives an individual of her source of income, but also has the potential to deprive the individual of her self-worth, a social network, others' esteem and even her place in the community. The Donovan Commission's famous statement identifying the job security case for legislative intervention in the area of unfair dismissals outlines the importance of these non-monetary deprivations caused by unfair dismissal:

> We share in full the belief that the present situation is unsatisfactory. In reality people build much of their lives around their jobs. Their incomes and prospects for the future are inevitably founded in the expectation that their jobs will continue. For workers in many situations dismissal is a disaster. For some workers it may make inevitable the breaking up of a community and the uprooting of homes and families. Others, and particularly older workers, may be faced with the greatest difficulty in getting work at all.[53]

Collins argues that this justification of needing to protect an individual's dignity during the dismissal process permits scrutiny of the reasons for the dismissal so as to ensure that no irrelevant considerations were taken into account.[54] Above all, preserving an employee's dignity during the dismissal process requires an employer to have exercised managerial power in a rational manner and with due

49 Collins (n 28) 19.
50 Ibid 20.
51 Ibid 83–84.
52 Ibid.
53 Donovan (n 16) [526].
54 Collins (n 28) 16–17.

regard for procedural fairness, thus permitting tribunal scrutiny of not just the reason for the dismissal but the way in which it occurred.[55]

Collins' normative ideal of justice in dismissal as providing a basis for unfair dismissal law was not without its detractors. Some argued that a focus on justice legitimised the introduction of a statutory unfair dismissal system which has put a price on jobs and undermined the willingness of employees to safeguard their jobs in return for monetary compensation and procedural fairness.[56] Mellish and Collis-Squires argue that the introduction of unfair dismissal law in the United Kingdom was predicated upon a corrective approach which seeks to ensure that disciplinary rules are well known and accepted and that dismissal occurs only as a last resort after management has attempted a series of softer disciplinary measures such as warnings and lesser punishments.[57] They contrast this with the punitive approach, which they see as existing prior to 1971 where employers would often discipline employees through harsher penalties, albeit on a more ad-hoc basis, aimed at deterring the offensive behaviour.[58] While the corrective approach ushered in greater standardisation of dismissal procedures by employers, a number of criticisms can be made as to the extent to which this approach actually achieves the industrial justice justifications of preserving employees' dignity and autonomy. Firstly, the argument could be made that the focus of the system on achieving procedural reform of dismissal practices has merely resulted in the formalisation of rules rather than the substantive guarantee of justice in dismissal. In other words, employers may formalise the process of dismissal and strictly adhere to this process, but this does not necessarily mean the decision to dismiss the employee has been substantively fair, only that the correct process for dismissal has been followed.

A second criticism of the ability of the unfair dismissal system to achieve justice is that it seeks to regulate management's power to dismiss but from 'an essentially managerial perspective'.[59] According to Mellish and Collis-Squires, this focus on a management-oriented view of discipline 'assumes that management has both the will to reform and the freedom of action to do so and that – in this area of discipline and dismissal – unions are passive recipients of such reform'.[60] A related criticism made by Elias is that the yardstick of industrial justice used by unfair dismissal law legitimises management's prejudices and unfair decisions rather than challenging them to more enlightened decision making.[61]

55 Ibid.
56 Michael Mellish and N Collis-Squires, 'Legal and Social Norms in Discipline and Dismissal' (1977) 6 ILJ 164; RH Fryer, 'Redundancy, Values and Public Policy' (1973) 4 IRJ 2; R Martin and RH Fryer, 'The Myths of the Redundancy Payments Act' (1973) 2 ILJ 1.
57 Mellish and Collis-Squires (n 57) 164–65.
58 Ibid.
59 Brian Weekes, John Lloyd, Linda Dickens and Michael Mellish, *Industrial Relations and the Limits of the Law: The Industrial Effects of the Industrial Relations Act 1971* (Blackwell, Oxford 1975) 28.
60 Mellish and Collis-Squires (n 57) 170.
61 Patrick Elias, 'Fairness in Unfair Dismissal: Trends and Tensions' (1981) 10 ILJ 201.

He argues that unfair dismissal law is 'norm reflecting' rather than 'norm setting' because the United Kingdom's employment tribunals judge the reasonableness of an employer's decision to dismiss based upon their perceptions of how a body of employers might behave, rather than how a reasonable employer would behave.[62]

But perhaps the most serious critique of the industrial justice justification of unfair dismissal law is that it has sought to individualise the employment relationship by separating the issue of discipline from the wider issue of control. In other words, unfair dismissal law has legitimated 'the existing structure of authoritarian control and inequality of reward in industry' by diverting the collective's attention from dismissal issues by providing individuals with a remedy that seeks to 'buy them out' rather than return them to their jobs.[63] Mellish and Collis-Squires articulate that an alternative view of discipline is needed based on their study of port transport employees.[64] They argue that discipline can be a collective issue depending on whether the collective can identify with the individual concerned and whether they support or are indifferent to any corrective action taken against the individual by management.[65] They critique unfair dismissal law as seeking to remove the collective's incentive to care about the unfairness of the individual's dismissal even if the dismissal itself reflects a disturbing management trend to increase control over employees' work unjustifiably. Furthermore, they argue that tribunals entrench the individualisation of dismissal issues because the tribunal only has a duty to settle the individual complaint and does not seek to analyse whether endemic problems exist in the bargaining context from which the complaint is derived.[66] In this light, the industrial justice justification of unfair dismissal law, with its focus on preserving the dignity and autonomy of individual employees against unchecked management power, separates this issue from the legitimate trade union concern with the control of jobs by management. The American system of providing job security through arbitration in the unionised sector provides a contrasting approach to statutory unfair dismissal law and will be explored later in this book.

Citizenship

An ideology related to industrial justice is citizenship. The latter includes a number of different ideas but politically the notion came to prominence in the United Kingdom when the Blair government's 'Third Way' began to permeate labour law policy in the 1990s. The Third Way contained many different perspectives but, as

62 Ibid 212–13.

63 Brian Bercusson, 'Employment Protection' in Charles D Drake and Brian Bercusson (eds), *The Employment Acts 1974–1980 with Commentary* (Sweet and Maxwell, London 1981) 33.

64 Mellish and Collis-Squires (n 57) 172–75.

65 Ibid.

66 Ibid 176.

Fredman explains, had several common elements.[67] It rejected both the neo-liberal dedication to free markets and the traditional left-wing adherence to a social democratic state. Third Way writers argued for a balance between the individual and the state within a competitive market economy. The idea of mutual obligation was central to the Third Way, as citizens could no longer be regarded as passive recipients of state benefits. Individuals were seen by the Third Way as having a civic duty to take responsibility for their lives and to enter the labour market. Notions of active citizenship, social inclusion and democracy were intrinsic to the Third Way. Here I make a tentative hypothesis, which will hopefully be borne out in the substantive chapters that follow, that the practical implementation of the Third Way represented a prioritisation of the market over the individual. In the attempt to create a partnership between employers and employees, the needs of the former took precedence. This hypothesis is based on an exploration of the influence of egalitarian liberal ideas on New Labour's Third Way project. Egalitarian liberalism draws upon the liberal faith in free markets, although this is tempered by recognition that some state regulation is needed to achieve economic justice. Davies and Freedland suggest that the New Labour government's (1997–2010) labour law policy can be regarded as 'having subsumed labour legislation and its associated body of social policy into a larger activity or pursuit of labour market regulation in the interests of a free and competitive market economy'.[68]

The ideas of Alan Bogg in his writings on 'civic republican citizenship'[69] and Ron McCallum in his writings on 'industrial citizenship'[70] are a potential successor to industrial justice in providing a new justification for unfair dismissal law beyond that articulated by the Donovan Commission. Whilst their ideas differ to some degree, there is a general agreement between these scholars that notions of community, fair play and freedom from arbitrary power or domination are central to the normative ideal of citizenship. T. H. Marshall's postwar conception of citizenship has left a lasting imprint on the development of social citizenship scholarship.[71] According to Marshall, citizenship is a matter of ensuring that every person is treated as a full and equal member of society. Marshall offers a tripartite view of citizenship, dividing it along the lines of civil, political and social and is concerned with notions of liberty and equality, achievable through civil and political rights which guarantee full and equal membership. Marshall's definition of what social rights come under the banner of social citizenship is fairly sketchy and is limited to the following guidance: 'The right to a modicum of economic welfare and security to the right to share to the full in the social heritage and to live the life of a civilised being according to the standards prevailing

67 Sandra Fredman, *The Ideology of New Labour Law* (Hart, Oxford 2004) 10–18.
68 Paul Davies and Mark Freedland, *Towards a Flexible Labour Market: Labour Legislation and Regulation since the 1990s* (OUP, Oxford 2007) 9.
69 Alan Bogg, *The Democratic Aspects of Trade Union Recognition* (Hart, Oxford 2009).
70 Ron McCallum, 'Crafting a New Collective Labour Law for Australia' [1997] JIR 405.
71 T. H. Marshall, *Class, Citizenship and Social Development* (Anchor, New York 1965).

in the society'.[72] Whilst Marshall does not specify the level, form and content of social rights, he does argue that the purpose of social citizenship is to be a class-abatement mechanism moderating the impact of capitalism upon citizens. In his view, even though the capitalist profits at the expense of the labourer, the welfare state intervenes to certify that a certain standard of living is maintained. In so doing, social citizenship is 'no longer merely an attempt to abate the obvious nuisance of destitution in the lowest ranks of society. It has assumed the guise of modifying the whole pattern of social inequality'.[73]

Marshall's view of citizenship has been criticised for its passivity because of its emphasis on the welfare state which provides entitlements to citizens without any corresponding duty to participate in public life. More recently, Marshall's conception of citizenship as social rights has transmogrified into a new concern with mutual obligation and reciprocity. Different theories have used this new concern and taken up the language of citizenship. For liberal theorists, also described as the 'New Right', the market is viewed as 'a school of civic virtue', as it encourages citizens to be self-supporting rather than passive recipients of welfare.[74] According to this view of citizenship, the focus should be on people's responsibility to earn a living, and markets encourage this through promoting self-reliance, initiative and full membership of society through work. Markets are also said to promote citizenship through their ability to encourage civility. This is the argument that there is a business case for employers to avoid discriminatory hiring policies or discrimination in customer service, as a failure to do so would result in the business being penalised by the market through reduced custom or an inability to access the best labour. This is not the view of citizenship I adopt in this book, as I prefer Kymlicka's analysis that 'the limits of the market as a school of civic virtue are clear. . . . [M]arkets teach initiative but not a sense of justice or social responsibility'.[75]

Ideas of citizenship feature strongly in the Third Way approach to labour law. The idea of a partnership at work between employers and employees and of a balance between fairness and competitiveness in the employment relationship contain an understanding of citizenship as requiring reciprocity. This involves an expectation that an employer manage the business fairly in return for an employee's willingness to work productively and contribute to the organisation's goals. For the unemployed, there is an expectation that as the recipient of unemployment benefits the unemployed person will re-train and apply for jobs in order to contribute to the national economy. This Third Way approach to citizenship can be distinguished from the liberal idea of the market as a school of civic virtue on the grounds that the Third Way sees the need for government programs and assistance to enable the unemployed to enter the labour market and to develop labour market regulation so as to encourage employers to achieve the civic good,

72 Ibid 30.
73 Ibid 37.
74 Will Kymlicka, *Contemporary Political Philosophy* (2nd edn OUP, Oxford 2002) 304.
75 Ibid.

not just the good of business. Examples of this would be the introduction of the minimum wage, provisions outlawing discrimination and the strengthening of unfair dismissal laws.

Other scholars rely on a notion of 'industrial citizenship' in an attempt to justify the existence of protective labour laws in response to the challenges presented by liberal ideology.[76] This notion of citizenship is distinct from the market view of citizenship and the Third Way conception, as there is a more explicit acceptance of the traditional labour law perspective of the inherent power imbalance in the employment relationship. Unlike in the Third Way, notions of a 'partnership' between employers and employees, and of a 'balance' between fairness and competiveness, are seen as ultimately prioritising employer needs and competitiveness over employee needs and fairness. The normative agenda of industrial citizenship has been described as a form of 'aspirational citizenship' because the focus is on 'what would be an ideal labour relations mechanism in which rights would grow and flourish'.[77] This aspirational conception of industrial citizenship justifies the existence of statutory unfair dismissal protection on the basis that an individual employee is an industrial citizen who can only be deprived of her status as a citizen for a valid reason. At its essence, citizenship's central meaning has to do with membership in a community,[78] and providing an employee with the right not to be unfairly dismissed protects an employee from arbitrary removal from the workplace community. Industrial citizenship perceives this right as inalienable and a legitimate limit upon managerial prerogative and not as an interference with the market mechanism resulting in inefficiency or as a constraint upon the business's competiveness in the economy. Even if unfair dismissal rights result in inefficiencies or uncompetitiveness, this is seen as a necessary by-product of a system of labour laws that achieve industrial citizenship. The challenge for the proponents of industrial citizenship is to differentiate it from theories of industrial justice. As Kymlicka states:

> It is difficult to think of cases where people have defended policies on grounds of citizenship that they were not already committed to on grounds of justice. In this sense, it is not clear whether adopting the perspective of citizenship really leads to different policy conclusions from the more familiar perspectives of justice. It may instead be a matter of putting old wine into new bottles.[79]

76 Ron McCallum, 'Citizenship Theory and Labour Law' (Citizenship at Work? An International Colloquium Theorising Citizenship at Work, University of Laval, Quebec, June 2004); Judy Fudge, 'After Industrial Citizenship: Market Citizenship or Citizenship at Work?' [2005] IR 631, 632; Harry Arthurs, 'Developing Industrial Citizenship: A Challenge for Canada's Second Century' [1967] Canadian Bar Rev 786.

77 McCallum (n 77).

78 JM Barbalet, *Citizenship Rights, Struggle and Class Inequality* (University of Minnesota Press, Minneapolis, 1988); Linda Bosniak, 'Citizenship' in Peter Crane and Mark Tushnet (eds), *The Oxford Handbook of Legal Studies* (OUP, Oxford 2003) 185.

79 Kymlicka (n 75) 319.

Employability and employment security

Some scholars raise ideas of 'employability' or 'employment security' as justifications for protective regimes which go beyond traditional unfair dismissal law as conceived by ILO Convention No 158. They argue that the contract of employment could include a positive duty upon employers to invest in the consistent and meaningful training of their staffs. This translates into making their employees more secure in their current jobs but also with a better chance of securing future employment should they be made redundant. The substantial work by Katherine Stone on what she calls the 'new psychological contract' has led her to argue that long-term employment with a single employer and advancement up a single job ladder is no longer the norm in the 'new economy'.[80] In her view, job security protected through unfair dismissal law is of no help to the contemporary worker embarking on a 'boundaryless career'. She defines this as 'a career which unfolds unconstrained by clear boundaries around job activities by fixed sequences of such activities, or by attachment to one organisation'.[81] Stone says that there is now a new 'job insecurity reality' which can only be addressed through the promise of employability security. In her view, this security is not just created by governments promoting robust labour markets but involves positive obligations upon employers to provide opportunities for their employees to develop their human capital through investment in training and skills development. Even if there are no promotional opportunities available or if their job becomes redundant, then the employee is in a better place to become 'entrepreneur[s] marketing their own human capital in a market place'.[82] Stone advocates the development of a 'model employability contract' by which the firm promises to upgrade worker skills and to help provide new job opportunities should those at the business disappear.[83] In this way, she views the contract of employment, and not the statutory law of unfair dismissal, as a vehicle for providing protection for the worker. Her idea is that the contract of employment could be used to impose positive duties of investment and training upon the employer which would correspond with the employee's duty to become her very best in order to add value to her employer or to subsequent employers down the track.

Another scholar to weigh in on the employability debate is Hugh Collins.[84] He addresses the challenge of low-skilled workers by arguing that the labour force can be divided into three types of employees: the compliant employee, the good faith employee and the flexible employee. For compliant employees who are unskilled or low skilled, job security protection is needed, as there is little avenue for improving their employability. In particular, there may be a case for a minimal

80 Katherine VW Stone, 'The New Psychological Contract: Implications of the Changing Workplace for Labor and Employment Law' (2001) 48 UCLA L Rev 519.
81 Ibid 554.
82 Ibid 570.
83 Ibid 569.
84 Hugh Collins, 'Regulating the Employment Relation for Competitiveness' (2001) 30 ILJ 17.

level of protection against arbitrary dismissal through a statutory right not to be dismissed without just cause. However, for the other two categories of employees, the aim should be to achieve employment security. He argues that the 'good faith employee' – an employee who is generally cooperative with her employer and performs her job according to what is expected under the contract – should seek to become the ideal type, that is, the 'flexible employee'. He notes that 'the flexible employee does not simply work hard at her job but uses all her skills and knowledge to contribute to the process of continuous improvements in quality, efficiency and technological and product innovation'.[85] Like Stone, Collins advocates the contract of employment as the best vehicle for enforcing employability or employment security. As he observes, 'the contract of employment guards against abuse of managerial discretion by constituting and enforcing a job specification, thereby achieving institutional stability in employment relations'.[86] He goes on to write that 'the common law reinforces this institutional arrangement both by enforcing job specifications as express terms of the contract and by placing weak limits on the exercise of managerial discretion through implied terms'.[87] Given this basis, Collins argues that the common law contract of employment could be strengthened in what it requires of employers and employees. Unlike Stone, Collins draws a distinction between employment security and employability. He disregards the latter as too speculative because it is unlikely to provide the assurance needed to the employee to establish stable institutional structures for the flexible employee relation. He says that the employee needs to acquiesce in becoming flexible, that is, the ideal type. The promise of employability due to a higher level of skill, meaning that the dismissed worker has a better chance of obtaining a good job with another employer, is too speculative and insubstantial in the present to be a sufficient motivation for the employee to become the ideal type. Thus, Collins argues that labour law should seek to achieve 'employment security', which is the idea that 'the employment relation will continue indefinitely, but the employee will have to perform different kinds of work, for which training will be required'.[88] Unlike unfair dismissal law, which is conceived as employment protection for the employee but at a cost to the employer, the concept of employment security offers a win–win to both parties to the employment contract. He argues:

> For the employer, this commitment is a crucial long-term strategy for improving competitiveness by means of investment in human capital. For the employee, the commitment to training is an essential component to the promise of employment security and employability that replaces the earlier commitment to job security. Default rules that reflected such an economic model would require the employer to provide worthwhile training opportunities,

85 Ibid 24.
86 Ibid 27.
87 Ibid.
88 Ibid 24.

> including training in general skills, and require the employee to take up those opportunities.[89]

Collins acknowledges that the weakness of his proposals lies in the 'normal defect of private law regulation: its weak sanction'.[90] He suggests that this could be overcome through a mandatory legal right, similar to the right to paid leave, that would enable the employee to take a certain number of days as paid leave to participate in employer-initiated training. According to Collins:

> the reason why a mandatory legal right serves effectively to strengthen the commitment in this case is that the right is self-enforcing: the employee takes the time off work. It does not suffer from the weakness that the exercise of the right requires the threat to take an employer to court.[91]

Neo-liberalism

Another set of ideas explored in this book are those emanating from the liberal tradition. Crouch argues that the term 'neo-liberalism' is a misnomer.[92] He draws a distinction between 'conservatism', which retains a significant role for the state, trade unions and workers' protection, and 'liberalism' or 'libertarianism', which emphasises non-intervention from government and rejects regulation of the market. In this work I argue that the Conservative government (1979–97) in the United Kingdom and the Coalition government (1996–2007) in Australia are of conservative political persuasion in that they sit on the right of the political spectrum but are motivated by liberalism, not conservatism, in their public policy. In particular, I suggest that they are motivated by a particular variant of liberalism, namely neo-liberal ideology, in that they are influenced by the writings of Friedrich Hayek, who argued that employment protection leads to an inefficient operation of the labour market. Hayek suggested that the social goals to which trade unions purport to aspire are in fact misguided and selfish, for 'social justice' is a 'mirage', and the only real justice is that meted out by the unhampered operation of market forces free from collective or other interference.[93] For American scholar Richard Epstein, the very concept of state regulation of employment termination is unacceptable. Epstein argues that such intervention alters the entire fabric of contract law by creating an environment that makes it difficult for the vast majority of good employers and good employees to structure

89 Ibid 40.
90 Ibid 44.
91 Ibid 45.
92 Colin Crouch, *The Strange Non-Death of Neoliberalism* (Polity Press, Cambridge 2011).
93 A useful synopsis of Hayek's view on this is Eamonn Butler, *Hayek* (Temple Smith, London 1983) ch 4.

their relationships efficiently.[94] He says that the whole purpose of the unfair dismissal system is to target the less likely occurrence of a bad employer and thus it is inefficient, as 'it exposes every decision in labour markets to second guessing by either a court or an administrative agency'. In defending the concept of at-will employment, he argues that market forces alone can be relied upon to dissuade or punish arbitrary or unreasonable behaviour, since employers who treat their workforce poorly will be unable to attract or retain good staff and thus will lose ground to their competitors.

This concern with the potential *economic effects* of job security laws is a growing rationale for the deregulation of unfair dismissal systems in the United Kingdom and Australia, and is a subject to which I will return later in this book.

Outline of the book and argument

This book explores two distinct approaches to regulating job security. Despite the United Kingdom and Australia possessing divergent legal cultures, in both jurisdictions there was a convergence upon unfair dismissal law when the traditional labour law culture broke down. This was followed by a striking degree of convergence between the evolution of unfair dismissal law in the United Kingdom and Australia. In both jurisdictions, statutory unfair dismissal law was reformed in a broadly similar, albeit diachronic, manner across the two systems. This evolutionary dynamic of divergence giving way to convergence reveals a high degree of path dependency in the unfair dismissal laws of the United Kingdom and Australia. In contrast, the American system of employment at will has remained resolute throughout this period despite other countries like the United Kingdom and Australia, and international law, developing unfair dismissal protection. Although exceptions to the general rule have emerged, there is still a distinctively American approach of employment at will. As a result, this book is necessarily divided into three country case studies, each comprising two chapters.

In the first chapter of each case study, I address the need for a comparative law work to understand the legal culture and history of the jurisdictions under the microscope. To understand the reasons prompting the introduction of unfair dismissal law (or employment at will in case of the United States) and the time frame that this legal change occurred in, it is essential to understand the institutional context in which it emerged. As Schregle argued,

> [It] is extremely problematical and dangerous to extract from a national industrial relations system a single institution or rule and to compare it with what appears to be the corresponding intuition or rule in another

94 Richard A Epstein, 'The Common Law and the Labour Market' (HR Nicholls Society, 2001).

> country. . . . Institutions must be considered within the general context of the industrial relations system of which they are an integral part.[95]

Or as Theret puts it, 'one must not compare elements but relations between these elements'.[96] The aim is to understand the shift from the labour law tradition in favour of statutory intervention by developing 'case-intensive knowledge'.[97] Accordingly, each country case study consists of an initial chapter which focuses on an in-depth exploration of the country's labour law tradition, followed by another chapter examining the subsequent evolution of laws regulating job security.

For the United Kingdom and Australia, I seek to uncover the drivers of legal change in favour of statutory intervention to safeguard unfair dismissal. This intervention represents a 'path departure', as it amounts to a transformation of the traditional labour law system into a new structure. In Hepple and Veneziani's view, transformation is the identification of path departures.[98] They argue that whilst path dependencies continue to frame the development of European labour law, transformations have occurred and these involve labour law changes not simply in form, but in substance.[99] They cite the introduction of individual rights against unfair dismissal and individualised, juridified procedures for the enforcement of labour laws as examples of path departure.[100] The United Kingdom and Australia case studies examine why this 'path departure' or 'transformation' occurred at different times in the two jurisdictions, and the importance of contextual factors in enabling or restraining unfair dismissal reform. In contrast, no such 'path departure' occurred in the United States, although the employment-at-will approach has been modified over time.

This book explores how the shared common law heritage of the United Kingdom and Australia masks the highly divergent labour law traditions of the two systems. The primary similarity of the United Kingdom's tradition of collective laissez-faire and the Australian tradition of conciliation and arbitration is their common normative ideal of securing industrial peace. This objective was expressed more explicitly in Australia because of the work of Higgins in openly identifying industrial peace as the proper yardstick for decisions concerning industrial relations.[101] Nonetheless, collective laissez-faire in the United Kingdom also sought to achieve industrial peace via voluntary collective bargaining, which provided a forum for the resolution of disputes between employers and unions.

95 Johannes Schregle, 'Comparative Industrial Relations: Pitfalls and Potential' (1981) 120 Int Lab Rev 15, 21–22.

96 Bruno Theret, 'Theoretical Problems in International Comparisons' in Marc Maurice and Arndt Sorge (eds), *Embedding Organizations: Societal Analysis of Actors, Organizations and Socio-Economic Context* (John Benjamins, Amsterdam 2000) 111.

97 James Mahoney, 'Qualitative Methodology and Comparative Politics' (2007) 40 Comp Pol Stud 122, 130.

98 Hepple and Veneziani (n 3) 21.

99 Ibid 4.

100 Ibid 21.

101 Chapter 4 provides an exploration of Higgins' writings.

The long ascendancy of voluntarism in the United Kingdom and conciliation and arbitration in Australia had to be reformed for statutory unfair dismissal protection to be introduced. Both the United Kingdom and Australia accorded individual employees with a statutory right not to be unfairly dismissed when it became clear that the traditional collective labour law systems had stalled and were not achieving the objective of the government to secure industrial peace. Whilst this parallel should not be overstated, in both the United Kingdom and Australia the reforming of traditional labour law produced a convergence over the need for unfair dismissal protection according to a rationale of an individualised notion of industrial justice. This book investigates how the idea of unfair dismissal law was highly challenging to the labour law traditions of both jurisdictions and how, to some extent, a trade-off was made between union security and job security, with the traditional systems prioritising the former. Adverse economic conditions and problems with the operation of the traditional labour law systems increased the pressure on the national governments for labour law reform providing an impetus for the introduction of unfair dismissal law. The divergent timing of the move to unfair dismissal law in the two systems is very much tied up in the demise of the two collective labour law cultures which came under near terminal stress and strain in the periods leading up to the introduction of unfair dismissal legislation. Unfair dismissal law is one of the outcomes of the breakdown of the traditional labour law system in both the United Kingdom and Australia.

Despite the divergent legal traditions, there was a convergent evolution of unfair dismissal law in the United Kingdom and Australia subsequent to its enactment. Whilst both countries have retained their statutory unfair dismissal scheme, there has been a concerted attempt to reduce access to the system and the quality of the remedy that can be awarded. In both Australia and the United Kingdom subsequent to the introduction of statutory unfair dismissal protection, a conservative government driven by liberal ideology was in power for a period lasting more than a decade, affording a unique opportunity for wholesale labour law reform predicated upon liberal ideas. Whilst unfair dismissal law was not the central target of the conservative agenda, as the goal of these governments was broader and focused more on reducing the power of trade unions, in both the United Kingdom and Australia attempts were made to peel back the statutory superstructure governing unfair dismissals. In the United Kingdom the Conservative government (1979–97) developed what Davies and Freedland call an 'argument of principle' against unfair dismissal.[102] The debate about unfair dismissal laws was recast, as the original anchorage of the system in a concern for job security was replaced by new justifications for protecting the profitability of free enterprise, especially small business, and ensuring that regulation was not a disincentive to job creation. A similar theme emerged in the Australian debate over the future of the statutory unfair dismissal scheme. The Coalition government (1996–2007) led a coalition of interest groups which emerged to challenge the validity of protective labour law, in particular what they termed the 'Industrial

102 Davies and Freedland (n 6) 555–58.

Relations [IR] Club' – a term used to deride unions, the Australian Industrial Relations Commission and those of left-wing political persuasion who advocated for employment protection and collective rights.[103] The countermovement arising against the IR Club recast the debate about Australian labour law in favour of deregulation and a minimal safety net topped up by widespread enterprise bargaining. The agenda of the Conservative government's argument of principle and the Coalition government's counteraction to the IR Club was again broadly similar. In the United Kingdom the argument of principle was against tribunal processing of unfair dismissal disputes, as it was believed that tribunals resulted in vexatious litigation, onerous costs and regulation for business and fewer jobs being made available to the unemployed. In Australia the counteraction to the IR Club was largely about the Australian Industrial Relations Commission and the perception that it was too close to the labour movement, resulting in favourable outcomes for unfair dismissal applicants.

Underpinning these comparable legislative efforts, in both jurisdictions there was a desire to peel back the statutory superstructure governing unfair dismissals. This has prompted a tendency towards an efficient, clear and simple dispute resolution process which has diverted emphasis away from the original ideal of Australia's and the United Kingdom's unfair dismissal systems in industrial justice. This original ideal is now being counterbalanced with an increasingly overt preoccupation with the protection of business efficiency and the control of regulatory burdens.

In contrast to the broadly parallel evolution of unfair dismissal law in the United Kingdom and Australia, the case study of the United States reveals a distinctive approach to regulating job security. Although the two chapters on this jurisdiction are significantly shorter, as there was no 'path departure' and therefore no statutory unfair dismissal law to study, their purpose is to identify the reasons for the development of employment at will and to seek to understand the endurance of this approach despite being out of step with developments abroad. This is a terrain many scholars have covered before. Thus, in this book, the utility of the case study is not merely to rehash the story of American exceptionalism. Rather, my purpose is not only to observe and critique the difference between the three countries' approaches, but to question whether there is indeed as much difference as is commonly thought. This is the concern of the final chapter, 'Future Prospects for Job Security', which considers whether the contemporary manifestation of unfair dismissal law in the United Kingdom and Australia is so very different from employment at will in the United States. In this chapter I go beyond a comparison of the countries' normative laws as they appear on the books and consider how they operate in practice. This produces a number of tentative hypotheses that are hopefully borne out in the pages of this work.

103 The phrase 'Industrial Relations Club' was coined in 1983 by Gerald Henderson, a prominent Australian journalist and executive director of the Sydney Institute, an influential policy think tank; Gerard Henderson, 'Industrial Relations Club' *Quadrant* (September 1983).

First, both a historical and an evolutionary perspective is essential to understand the emerging questions surrounding the legitimacy of statutory unfair dismissal law in the United Kingdom and Australia. On the one hand, an understanding of the specific historical developments leading to the enactment and subsequent reform of unfair dismissal law in the United Kingdom and Australia provides insight into the dynamics of legal change; and on the other, an external perspective of the paradigmatic evolution of unfair dismissal law in the two jurisdictions over time reveals why this change is occurring in the form it is. With regard to the former, the movement away from prioritising industrial peace via the conciliation and arbitration system in Australia and the recognition of the inadequacy of collective laissez-faire in protecting job security in the United Kingdom are analogous historical developments occurring diachronically. They both represent the overturning of a particular labour law path in order to bring about statutory intervention. Beyond the minutiae of *how* this occurred, this book explores *why*, through an analysis of the paradigmatic evolution of unfair dismissal law in the United Kingdom and Australia.

Second, the process of convergence displays a similar dynamic in the United Kingdom and Australia. This dynamic is the progressive ascendancy of an 'argument of principle' against tribunal resolution of unfair dismissal disputes and the corresponding erosion of 'job security' as a normative ideal of the regulatory framework. This argument of principle has motivated a trend towards peeling back the statutory superstructure of unfair dismissal law. This deregulation is a deeper current underlying shifts in the political complexion of governments over the period under review. Governments of either political persuasion and in both countries have been active in reforming the unfair dismissal system by scaling back statutory regulation of unfair dismissals and increasing the power of employers to determine the fairness of their decision to dismiss. This convergence upon a deregulated unfair dismissal law to resolve the challenge of job security requires us to revisit the theoretical foundations and core institutions of unfair dismissal law in order to locate their role and function in an increasingly market-driven economy and polity.

Third, although this convergence upon a deregulated unfair dismissal law has much in common with the American approach of employment at will, there is one critical distinction: with the former there is the potential for some acknowledgement by an independent body that an employee should never have been dismissed in the first place. This provides satisfaction to the claimant and, combined with the opportunity for a remedy (however limited), provides an incentive for employers to dismiss workers according to a fair process and with a valid reason. The presence of unfair dismissal law, even if it is diluted and there are opportunities for employees to opt out, provides a check on managerial prerogative and accords employees with a greater sense of security about their jobs. Without unfair dismissal law, or with a system of employment at will, an employee can be dismissed for no good reason and be powerless to challenge an employer's decision. Such an approach obfuscates the more vulnerable position of the employee in the employment relationship in that it is an employee's livelihood that is at stake, whereas an employer can more readily replace one employee with another.

2 United Kingdom – Part I

The journey to unfair dismissal law

Introduction

Much has been written about Kahn-Freund's theory of collective laissez-faire. Recently, Bogg revisited the question of the usefulness of this theory in aiding our understanding of the United Kingdom's labour law and assessed the validity of the main critiques of collective laissez-faire, namely the abstentionist, neutrality and coherence critiques.[1] He concluded that each of these critiques is somewhat misplaced and that 'collective laissez-faire still offers the most compelling theoretical rationalisation of the pattern of auxiliary intervention in the post-war period'.[2] In accepting this proposition I wish to explore a slightly different question: does the theory of collective laissez-faire help explain what Collins describes as the 'apparent tardiness' of the United Kingdom's unfair dismissal system?[3] Or said differently, did the commitment of successive governments to voluntarism in industrial relations and the promotion of collective bargaining delay the development of unfair dismissal protection for employees? Up until 1971 when statutory unfair dismissal protection was introduced, it was thought that the perceived lack of protection for individual employees was best remedied through the voluntary development of procedures within industries and workplaces rather than through providing individual employees with statutory rights. This delay can be largely attributed to the significant influence of the voluntarist tradition upon British industrial relations. As Wedderburn observes:

> Legal enactment has not been the modern method. Voluntary collective bargaining has developed in a system which owes very little to the law, which is covered by very few judicial decisions because it has rarely been brought into any court, and which is controlled by statute very little, if at all. In other countries with comparable economic systems (such as the United States, France, Australia, Sweden, West Germany) the 'collective agreement' and the process which produces it are closely regulated by legal sanction.[4]

1 Alan Bogg, *The Democratic Aspects of Trade Union Recognition* (Hart, Oxford 2009).

2 Ibid 3.

3 Hugh Collins, *Justice in Dismissal: The Law of Termination of Employment* (Clarendon Press, Oxford 1992) 24.

4 KW Wedderburn, *The Worker and the Law* (1st edn Penguin, Harmondsworth 1965) 13.

The state's commitment to voluntarism, as understood by collective laissez-faire theory, has had a significant impact upon the evolution of statutory unfair dismissal laws in the United Kingdom, as we will see in this chapter.

So how did voluntarism become part of the general British cultural heritage in industrial relations prior to 1971? It was primarily due to a view that voluntary collective bargaining provided the best mechanism for securing agreement between the parties. Industrial conflict permeated British industrial relations in the late nineteenth century in the form of strikes, lockouts and picket line violence between hired strike-breakers and unionists. A Royal Commission on Labour was established in 1891 to examine the causes of this conflict and to propose solutions. The Royal Commission reported in 1894 and identified collective bargaining as an effective system of regulating industrial relations. The commission recommended that the government use its powers to support voluntary agreements between unions and employers and provide conciliation mechanisms to help resolve disputes and achieve industrial peace.[5] This was followed by the Whitley Committee's First Interim Report in 1917 which recommended 'the establishment for each industry of an organisation representative of employers and workpeople, to have as its object the regular consideration of matters affecting the progress and well-being of the trade from the point of view of all those engaged in it'.[6] According to Clay, this amounted to a 'public and official recognition of trade unionism and collective bargaining as the basis of industrial relations'.[7] In this way, voluntarism prioritised the achievement of union security over other industrial relations goals because it was believed that collective bargaining would lead to the orderly resolution of industrial conflict and thereby bring about industrial peace.

The industrial parties also supported securing industrial peace via voluntarism. Unions preferred to sort out conflict with employers through industrial tactics during the bargaining process rather than through the common law courts. According to Flanders, the British trade union movement's staunch support for voluntarism was based upon not distrust of labour legislation but rather of the courts.[8] He observed that when legislation has the object of bringing employers and unions before courts of law it is met with almost universal disapproval by the parties, as they are sceptical of the courts' ability to make an impartial decision.[9] Flanders quotes both Lord Justice Scutton and former British prime minister Winston Churchill in their acknowledgement of the actual and perceived class bias of the courts, with the latter observing that 'it is not good for trade unions to be brought in contact with the courts' because 'where class issues are involved, it is impossible to pretend that courts command the same degree of general confidence'.[10] Wedderburn also identifies a strong sentiment of suspicion of the courts

5 Charles Barrow, *Industrial Relations Law* (Taylor & Francis, London 2000) 138.
6 Whitley Committee, 'Interim Report on Joint Standing Industrial Councils' (Cd 8606, 1917) [5].
7 Henry Clay, *The Problem of Industrial Relations* (Macmillan & Co, London 1929) 154.
8 Allan Flanders, 'The Tradition of Voluntarism' (1974) 12 BJIR 352.
9 Ibid 354.
10 Winston Churchill, 1911, quoted in Flanders, ibid.

by British trade unions and a correspondingly strong sentiment of support for voluntarism in industrial relations. He attributes this to the fact that judicial legal intervention in the nineteenth century was inimical to the unions, as 'it was the judges who repeatedly declared trade unions and their activities criminal during the first half of that century'.[11] It was not just the trade union movement that was committed to voluntarism but also employers. The Contracts of Employment Act 1963, often seen as the first deliberate inroad by the government to abandon voluntarism in industrial relations, was passed against the wishes of both the Confederation of British Industry and the Trades Union Congress.[12]

Both the peak employer and union bodies were initially opposed to statutory unfair dismissal reform and favoured the extension of voluntary procedures.[13] Even though there was recognition that voluntarism did not effectively protect individual employees' job security or unfair dismissal rights, the primary sentiment of unions and employers up until the late 1960s was aversion to use the courts to resolve unfair dismissal disputes. While it is perhaps less surprising that employers did not lobby governments to confer statutory unfair dismissal protection upon employees, as this would have eroded their managerial prerogative, it is interesting that the unions too exhibited a strong preference for the extension of voluntary procedures rather than legal intervention. The core agenda of British unions was not to secure unfair dismissal rights for individuals but to secure favourable terms and conditions for the collective and to ensure that unions were able to bargain and strike as part of a system of free collective bargaining. In this way, British unions perceived that the achievement of trade union security trumped the achievement of job security. Their support for the British tradition of voluntarism in industrial relations hinged upon their belief that voluntarism strengthened their position in collective bargaining, as it limited the involvement of the law, in particular the courts. They were suspicious that adjudicating unfair dismissal disputes in the courts would erode the position of unions as the exclusive spokespeople for British workers and that the courts would ultimately side with the employer in unfair dismissal decisions. Successive governments were also complicit in supporting the development of a particular British culture of voluntarism in industrial relations. While labour legislation was enacted prior to 1971, this legislation tended to favour the promotion of collective bargaining and the maintenance of the autonomy of the industrial parties. This was not a policy of legal non-intervention but rather a state commitment to provide the conditions necessary to enable employers and unions to resolve industrial relations disputes via collective bargaining.

This chapter assesses how the British tradition of voluntarism impacted upon the evolution of unfair dismissal law. The first section explores how the voluntarist tradition initially acted as a constraint upon the development of statutory unfair dismissal protection, as the industrial parties preferred to rely on voluntary

11 Wedderburn (n 4) 18.

12 Ibid 355.

13 Ministry of Labour, 'Dismissal Procedures' (Report of a Committee of the National Joint Advisory Council, 1967) [11]–[13].

methods to resolve unfair dismissal disputes so as to achieve industrial peace. The strong commitment to promoting collective bargaining by successive British governments meant that legislation to protect individual employment rights was introduced only where there was perceived to be a pressing case for legislative intervention because persistent industrial conflict was seen as damaging the United Kingdom's economic performance. In this way, a trade-off was made between union security and job security, as under the voluntarist tradition it was believed that the most effective method of remedying the disadvantaged contractual position of individual employees was to compensate for this through collective organisation. The second section of this chapter explores the emergence of challenges to the British tradition of voluntarism, in particular the perceived failure of unions and employers to act in the national interest and the growing willingness to chip away at voluntarism in industrial relations through legislation, exhibited in the modernisation statutes of the 1960s.

Nonetheless, despite the growing perception that greater legislative intervention in industrial relations could be warranted in order to achieve the national interest, the building of momentum to confer greater unfair dismissal protection on employees was conceived as part of a voluntary industrial relations system aimed at extending collective bargaining. This is the focus of the third section, which looks at the recommendations for unfair dismissal reform contained in the final reports of both the National Joint Advisory Council and the Donovan Commission. While the latter advocated statutory protection of unfair dismissal rights, this recommendation was not intended to provide a break with the United Kingdom's cultural heritage of voluntarism in industrial relations. The fourth section of this chapter looks at the introduction of unfair dismissal law and the dismantling of the voluntarist tradition. I argue that this tradition was replaced by a new concern with the achievement of industrial justice and that this can be identified in the policy platforms of both Labour and the Conservatives, and in the reliance upon industrial tribunals staffed by lay members. This concept of industrial justice is not just a post-hoc rationale of the unfair dismissal system by theorists but was actively adopted by both political parties and the members of the tribunal system as the basis for the United Kingdom's unfair dismissal system.

Unfair dismissal under the voluntarist tradition

The voluntarist tradition initially acted as a constraint upon the development of statutory unfair dismissal protection as the industrial parties preferred to rely on voluntary methods to achieve industrial peace. Unions were highly suspicious of any attempt to involve the courts in British industrial relations and preferred to resolve disputes according to the relative strength of the parties. Accordingly, unions were reluctant to lobby governments to provide statutory protection of unfair dismissal rights and instead preferred to rely on traditional industrial tactics to secure reinstatement for an unfairly dismissed employee. Employers also did not advocate for reform in this area, although their commitment to voluntarism in this respect was perhaps motivated by other concerns, namely, their desire to avoid litigation around dismissal disputes and their preference for relying upon unions to pursue industrial action only for disputes which were of merit. In this way, both unions and employers placed little pressure on the British government to provide statutory protection of unfair dismissal rights.

Industrial autonomy

Successive British governments committed to preserving the autonomy of the parties in collective bargaining. Kahn-Freund's collective laissez-faire theory suggested that this principle of 'industrial autonomy' meant that employers and employees 'formulated their own codes of conduct and devised their own machinery for enforcing them'.[14] This resulted in the rights, obligations and duties of employers and employees being determined and enforced according to industrial tactics rather than via the parties resorting to legal measures. Nonetheless, while the parties were mainly able to avoid the law in resolving their disagreements, the principle of industrial autonomy was preserved by the presence of auxiliary legislation that conferred upon unions a basic framework for engaging in collective bargaining with employers. By 1871 the right of trade unionists to associate was enshrined by the UK Parliament, which decreed that the common law doctrine of 'restraint of trade' should no longer apply to trade unions. Also pivotal to the development of a strong labour movement was the Trade Union Disputes Act 1906, which protected the capacity of British unions to take industrial action. The right to take industrial action was increasingly being eroded by the development of corporate tortious liability for unions after the *Taff Vale Case*.[15] The cumulative effect of these two Acts in excluding the common law doctrines constraining union activity provided a framework for collective bargaining but could not be characterised as overly interventionist, as 'the legislators of 1906 did not go on, as they might have done, to erect their own statutory structure of restrictions on the contract of employment of social sanctions in trade disputes'.[16]

In practice, the principle of industrial autonomy meant that unions and employers set the industrial relations agenda, with the former primarily concerned with achieving strength in collective bargaining negotiations and favourable outcomes in terms of wages and working conditions. Less pressing to the union agenda was securing the fairness of an employee's dismissal through exerting industrial pressure on the employer to develop formal procedures for determining dismissal decisions or by lobbying Parliament to impose statutory duties upon employers during dismissal. In 1961 the Trades Union

14 Otto Kahn-Freund, 'Legal Framework' in Allan Flanders and Hugh Clegg (eds), *The System of Industrial Relations in Great Britain* (Blackwell, Oxford 1954) 44.
15 *Taff Vale Railway v Amalgamated Society of Railway Servants* [1901] AC 426 (HL).
16 Paul Davies and Mark Freedland, *Labour Legislation and Public Policy* (Clarendon Press, Oxford 1993) 22.

Congress questioned officials of its affiliated unions on their attitude towards the introduction of legislation providing protection against unfair dismissal. The majority of respondents, from forty-four out of fifty-seven unions, said they preferred the matter to be dealt with through collective bargaining.[17] This view was of course in keeping with the voluntarist tradition whereby it is thought that workers could best achieve their goals by relying on their own organisation. The traditional strategy employed by unions to protect individual employees facing a dismissal which they deemed to be unreasonable was to threaten the employer with industrial action in order to secure the individual's reinstatement. From the union's perspective, this situation was mainly satisfactory, as they could use their industrial leverage to enable an unfairly dismissed employee to get his job back. This was an industrial tactic unions were not afraid to use. Unofficial dismissal-related strikes were a well-known phenomenon of British collective laissez-faire; for example, between 1964 and 1966 there were 276 strikes resulting from dismissals.[18] Furthermore, it was not high on the unions' agenda to secure statutory unfair dismissal protection for workers in non-unionised industries, as it was perceived that the first priority was to achieve unionisation of these workers. It was believed that this would then result in greater all-round protection for these workers, including protecting their right to job security by using industrial tactics rather than legal measures. The unions' position is aptly summed up by the following submission from a union representative to the Donovan Commission:

> I do not think there is any one on the TUC side who would argue against the rights of the worker to be protected equally with the rights of the employer, but we are facing the law as it stands and what we are saying is, do we want the court to protect it or do we want the ordinary industrial machinery to protect it? *The evidence of the TUC has been in favour of the strengthening of the industrial machine.* . . . [I]t is not an argument as to whether we think the worker is entitled to the protection, but the method by which the protection is given [emphasis added].[19]

A key reason behind the union position favouring the extension of voluntary methods for resolving unfair dismissal disputes was the strong suspicion held by the British trade union movement towards legal intervention. In the 1950s and 1960s, while other European countries were well under way in the process of developing dismissal protections for employees,[20] and there was increasing

17 'Protecting Against Unjustified Dismissal' *The Times* (London 15 March 1965).

18 Report of the Royal Commission on Trade Unions and Employers' Associations (Cmnd 3888, 1969) [528] ('Donovan').

19 Royal Commission on Trade Unions and Employers' Associations, Minutes of Evidence of 29 November 1966 and 31 January 1967 (Her Majesty's Stationery Office, 1967) [10402] (Frank Cousins).

20 For example, see the discussion of international developments in France, Germany, Italy and the US in Wedderburn (n 4) 89–94.

international pressure for unfair dismissal rights to be recognised, British unions perceived the individual's claim to job security as being secondary to the collective's claim for favourable terms and conditions of employment, and secondary to the union's claim for the right to bargain freely and engage in industrial action. Unions favoured a non-legal solution to the perceived problem that many employees were left unprotected from unfair dismissal and were against involving the courts. During its oral evidence before the Donovan Commission, the General Secretary of the TUC voiced the unions' opposition to the use of labour courts and lawyers to resolve unfair dismissal disputes: 'we say no to the outside labour court with the judicial approach and the judicial function. It has got to be within the setting of the industry and we say that the machinery should be established for that purpose'.[21]

The unions were also sceptical of the ability of labour courts to understand industrial relations realities. They argued that a legal solution to an individual's unfair dismissal disputes would not prevent the escalation of these disputes into a collective issue because if the other union members were unsatisfied with the legal solution, then they would strike in solidarity with the individual. There was a strong sense that 'legislation begets legislation'[22] and that the introduction of statutory protection of unfair dismissal rights would lead to increased legal intervention in industrial relations generally, thus undermining the role and position of unions over the long term.

It was not just unions who were reluctant to lobby for the introduction of statutory unfair dismissal protection, but employers too. The principle of industrial autonomy meant it was unlikely that employers would press for any limit on their contractual right to dismiss employees. While the high incidence of dismissal-related strikes was an issue of potential concern to employers, the prevailing attitude amongst employer groups was that a statutory scheme protecting an individual from unfair dismissal would lead to a greater number of contested dismissals as unions acted as a filtering mechanism, weeding out weak complaints, as they only resorted to industrial action for dismissals they genuinely disagreed with.[23] When employer groups raised this concern about a statutory scheme with the Donovan Commission, Professor Kahn-Freund of the commission responded by suggesting that the Confederation of British Industry (CBI) consider the American model, where the union decides whether or not to take the unfair dismissal case to the arbitrator as a mechanism for preventing vexatious litigation. However, one CBI official, Mr Taylor, rejected this approach, arguing that under collective laissez-faire the union recognises that to take on an unfair dismissal claim it may ultimately have to call upon industrial action, whereas a union is

21 Royal Commission on Trade Unions and Employers' Associations (n 19) [10383]–[10384] (Victor Feather).

22 Ibid [10392] (Sir Harry Douglass).

23 Royal Commission on Trade Unions and Employers' Associations, Minutes of Evidence of 23 November 1965 and 7 December 1965 (Her Majesty's Stationery Office, 1966) [1529] (Mr Taylor).

more likely to support a claim if the union is only responsible for pursuing a case before a tribunal instead of organising a strike.[24]

The role of legislation

The strong commitment of successive British governments to collective bargaining meant that legislation to protect individual employment rights was only considered when it was believed to be urgently needed in the national interest. Under the United Kingdom's voluntarist industrial relations tradition it was believed that the most effective method of remedying the disadvantaged contractual position of individual employees was to supplement this through collective organisation. For Kahn-Freund the theory of collective laissez-faire did not demand the complete absence of government intervention; rather, he identified a distinctive British mode of positive intervention via a method of indirect inducements to encourage and facilitate collective bargaining and, where this failed, the provision of substitute standards enforceable by law.[25] The objective of this 'organised persuasion' by the government was the entrenchment of collective bargaining and the achievement of orderly industrial relations through providing a framework for employers and unions to interact. In Kahn-Freund's words:

> The collective bargaining process itself and the observance of concluded agreements are supported by a series of legislative measures, of institutions and of administrative practices. The gist of these is that they provide a statutory framework for organised persuasion. . . . Persuasion and indirect sanction, that is, promise of benefits and threat of disadvantages, are the ways by which in this country the law traditionally exercises its functions as auxiliary to collective bargaining.[26]

This principle of organised persuasion achieved via a method of indirect inducements meant that the dominant role for legislation introduced by the British government was to promote collective bargaining.[27]

Despite this, British governments did legislate to protect certain rights of individual employees because of the perceived inadequacy of collective bargaining to achieve protection in some areas, ultimately paving the way for the introduction of a statutory unfair dismissal scheme once it was recognised that the collective bargaining system could not speedily be adapted to provide more comprehensive protection of individual employees during dismissal disputes. Kahn-Freund's

24 Ibid.
25 Davies and Freedland (n 16) 27.
26 Otto Kahn-Freund, 'Retrospect and Prospect' (1969) 7 BJIR 301, 304.
27 For a comprehensive exploration of the types of legislative devices used by British governments to promote collective bargaining such as wage boards and Order 1376, see: Simon Deakin and Gillian Morris, *Labour Law* (5th edn Hart, London 2009) 15–16, 21–22. See also: Davies and Freedland (n 16) 26–34.

theory of collective laissez-faire did conceive of a role for regulatory legislation as a supplement to collective bargaining in order to fill the gaps left by the latter.[28] Over time, British governments developed health and safety standards, working hours regulations and laws protecting women and juveniles from exploitative working conditions because these areas required 'gap filling' by the law, as they were ineffectively addressed by collective bargaining.[29] The achievement of full employment in the postwar period until the 1960s meant that the unfair dismissal rights of individual employees was not seen as an important enough issue to warrant regulatory legislation. Moreover, this legislation would directly interfere with voluntary methods of ensuring fair dismissal which were already being developed through collective bargaining and enforced through the threat of industrial action by unions. However, Davies and Freedland observe that once this concept of the need for regulatory legislation to fill the gaps left by collective bargaining became linked with the fact that 'even in the flourishing British system of collective bargaining, a substantial proportion of the workforce was not covered by collective agreements, the way would be open for a considerable extension of regulatory legislation'.[30] Nonetheless, in the period prior to the mid-1960s, the durability of the voluntary tradition, underpinned by the principle of industrial autonomy, the presence of auxiliary legislation to promote collective bargaining and a perceived marginal, 'gap-filling' role for regulatory legislation were pivotal to restraining the momentum of the argument that statutory unfair dismissal protection should be introduced. It was only when it became clear that economic conditions had worsened significantly, unions could not be relied upon to moderate their wage claims and collective bargaining was not achieving as widespread coverage as had been hoped was the path cleared for alternatives to voluntarism in industrial relations to be considered.

The emergence of challenges to voluntarism

In the 1960s, when cracks began to emerge in the ability of voluntary collective bargaining to achieve stable and efficient industrial relations, successive governments displayed a willingness to chip away at the edifice of the United Kingdom's traditional industrial relations system. Pressure began to mount for reform of industrial relations either through winding back the voluntarist tradition, long considered characteristic of industrial relations, or through developing an alternative system. Initially, these challenges were prompted by the United Kingdom's declining economic position relative to its trading partners and the emerging problem of rising unemployment and inflation. This led to renewed pressure to improve the productivity of workplaces and the efficiency of the economy overall. Strikes were now seen as clearly undermining the national interest even if they were in unions' sectional interests. The cumulative effect

28 Otto Kahn-Freund, *Selected Writings* (Stevens & Sons, London 1978) 25.
29 Davies and Freedland (n 16) 36.
30 Ibid.

of these factors was an increasing willingness to depart from two foundational aspects of the United Kingdom's voluntary industrial relations tradition. First, there was a growing awareness that the principle of industrial autonomy did not result in the achievement of the national interest, as it legitimised the rights of unions and employers to pursue their own agendas. Attempts to build a national partnership between the government, employers and unions to moderate wage claims and to improve national productivity during the 1960s were not entirely successful. Second, there was a growing willingness by successive governments during this period to legislate for industrial relations because the voluntary system was seen as too slow to innovate in delivering much-needed reform of industrial relations. The consensus emerging in the 1960s was that modernisation of the industrial relations system was needed in order to improve labour mobility and efficiency, and this led to an increased preparedness on the part of governments to legislate for industrial relations directly. Dissatisfaction with the United Kingdom's tradition of voluntary industrial relations led to Kahn-Freund's reflection that the end of the 1960s was marked by a mounting conviction that 'collective bargaining machinery has stalled and legislation has to take its place'.[31]

The failure of industrial autonomy to achieve the national interest

Some of the pressure to introduce unfair dismissal law came from a growing recognition by the political parties that wide-reaching labour law reform was needed to address the failure of unions and employer associations to act in the national interest. Despite its long industrial relations pedigree, there was an increasing perception that voluntarism did not safeguard the national interest when it came to responding to the economic challenges facing the United Kingdom. Collective bargaining between unions and employers seemed unable to guarantee the necessary preconditions for improving the United Kingdom's performance in the world economy. In the postwar period, the United Kingdom was outperformed by all its major trading partners with the exception of the USA. The primary challenge was spiralling inflation, as retail prices were increasing at a faster rate than economic productivity and the increase in money wages was on average 6 per cent, which comfortably exceeded the growth of output per capita.[32] In this context, wage restraint was vital to reducing inflation, but under the voluntarist tradition industrial relations outcomes were contingent upon collective bargaining. This required unions to place the national interest of reducing inflation above that of their own sectional interest of achieving the highest possible wage increase that their industrial muscle allowed them to achieve. Because of this inherent tension, there was a growing realisation that collective bargaining

31 Otto Kahn-Freund, *Labour Law: Old Traditions and New Developments* (Clarke, Irwin and Co, Toronto 1968) 40–41.

32 Davies and Freedland (n 16) 109.

did not always serve the United Kingdom's economic interests, as evinced by the following statement in the government's White Paper:

> But the satisfactory operation of this whole system depends upon everyone involved being fully aware of the issues at stake, and upon their acceptance of the full duties of citizenship which this realisation places upon them. If they always place sectional interest before the nation's welfare, economic stability will be endangered and the possibilities of future expansion impaired, possibly to the extent of jeopardising those very sectional interests which they seek to protect.[33]

This inherent tension was also identified by the Ministry of Labour in its covering note which introduced its written evidence to the Donovan Commission:

> It is obvious that trade unions have a cardinal role in promoting the interests of their members. It is not self-evident that they have an obligation to play a part in accelerating the social and economic advance of the nation, and there is certainly scope for an argument about the priorities between the two and the way in which possible conflict between the roles can be reconciled.[34]

The significance of this recognition that the industrial autonomy principle was unable to secure the United Kingdom's best interests led to an increasing willingness on the part of the government to intervene in the national economy and to canvass industrial relations reforms that went beyond the scope of traditional collective bargaining. This paved the way for both Labour and the Conservatives to conceive of a statutory unfair dismissal system that would resolve disputes without resorting to traditional industrial relations machinery and to propose legislative intervention according to a rationale of industrial justice.[35] Successive governments exhibited a willingness to adopt a more interventionist economic policy for the sake of the national economy. In 1962 the Conservative government set up the National Economic Development Council, which set a growth objective of 4 per cent per annum for the years between 1961 and 1964. Upon their election in 1964, the Labour government strengthened the state's commitment to economic planning with the establishment of the Department of Economic Affairs (DEA), which developed a National Plan with a growth target of 25 per cent between 1964 and 1970. The purpose of the DEA was to promote economic growth through coordinating the economic decisions of the government, unions and employers by developing and implementing a productivity, prices and incomes policy.[36] This policy saw the establishment of a National

33 Treasury, 'The Economic Implications of Full Employment' (Cmd 9725, 1956).

34 Royal Commission on Trade Unions and Employers' Associations (n 19) 246.

35 This is the focus of the following two sections of this chapter.

36 For a gripping account of the events and political machinations leading to the establishment of the DEA, see Peter Jenkins, *The Battle of Downing Street* (Charles Knight & Co, London 1970) 3–4.

Board for Prices and Incomes charged with scrutinising the justifications for wage and price movements and advising the DEA on ways to increase productivity. Despite the government's intention that the prices and incomes policy would take a long-term view of what was needed in order to promote economic growth, as the economic crisis became more severe it became increasingly used to prevent wage rises. After July 1966 a total freeze was imposed and backed with state powers to delay wage and price increases. As Jenkins writes, 'at each sterling crisis the clamps were tightened. An originally voluntary experiment became an exercise in state compulsion.'[37]

Support for the voluntarist tradition was also undermined by the perception that it was unable to guarantee industrial stability. Once this perception took root it paved the way for the introduction of a statutory system for dealing with dismissal disputes, as it was argued that under voluntarism individual disputes often escalated into collective disputes because of the involvement of unions to resolve them. There was increasing concern that the productivity of the economy was being diminished by the loss of too many working days to industrial action. This prompted a growing willingness on behalf of Labour and the Conservatives to intervene in industrial relations without union consent on the grounds that the national interest was at stake. In 1958 the Inns of Court Conservative and Unionist Society published a document, 'A Giant's Strength', which identified some union officials as 'overmighty subjects' who used their industrial muscle to achieve their own ends. Davies and Freedland observe that this document 'set down a marker for the future' because it represented an emerging conservative opinion that some unions were prepared to risk national economic interests.[38]

There was also an increasing belief that there were too many dismissal-related strikes, which were unnecessarily disrupting productivity, as a result of the collectivisation of an individual's desire to challenge the legitimacy of his or her dismissal. The Ministry of Labour, in its evidence to the Donovan Commission, emphasised that 'the employment and discharge of workers' was the second major cause of disputes after wage disputes, accounting in the period between 1960 and 1964 for between 10 and 11 per cent of both numbers of stoppages and days lost.[39] Labour, too, was increasingly willing to canvass economic solutions without union support. It released its White Paper on industrial relations reform, 'In Place of Strife', without consulting the unions and with proposals that allowed the secretary of state to ban strikes breaching the statutory procedure and to allow a conciliation pause of twenty-eight days to help the parties to reach agreement. According to Jenkins, these proposals were the proverbial last straw for the union movement because whilst 'the trade unions for some while had stomached the Government's income policy powers', 'a restriction on the *proceeds* of collective bargaining, necessarily temporary, was one thing, while

37 Ibid 4.
38 Davies and Freedland (n 16) 129.
39 Royal Commission on Trade Unions and Employers' Associations (n 19) [10402].

a permanent restriction on the *process* of collective bargaining was another'.[40] Describing this tumultuous period, Davies and Freedland observe that 'by the end of the 1960s relations between the government and the TUC had reached a very low point as the unions were reasserting in militant fashion the illegitimacy of governmental "interference" in wage setting'.[41]

The growing willingness to chip away at voluntarism through legislation

Perhaps the biggest challenge to the voluntarist tradition was the push to modernise the economy via a series of legislative measures aimed at improving the efficiency of the United Kingdom's industrial relations. This initial phase of modernisation in the 1960s was characterised by a significant amount of bipartisan support as both political parties conceived of a more active role for the state in order to increase economic efficiency and growth. The first of the modernisation statutes was the Contracts of Employment Act 1963, which conferred a statutory right to a minimum period of notice for employees who were dismissed for reasons other than misconduct and a new requirement that written particulars should be supplied by employers for those on oral employment contracts. This Act achieved bipartisan support because of the cross-party belief that it would aid the regularisation of British industrial relations and reduce industrial disputes by enabling the parties to have a better grasp of the basic conditions of their employment contract. The Industrial Training Act of 1964 was aimed at improving the overall productivity of the British economy by imposing a levy upon employers to finance the establishment and operation of Industrial Training Boards administered by the government. The Redundancy Payments Act 1965 established minimum entitlements to redundancy payments on the basis that it would increase labour mobility, as the monetary payment upon redundancy would increase an employee's willingness to move into another job. The National Insurance Act of 1966 introduced the principle of relating unemployment benefits to previous earnings in exchange for a linking of the contributions in the same way.

A striking feature of each of these Acts was the government's willingness to seize the initiative in order to achieve industrial relations reform. The National Joint Advisory Council, comprising employers and unions, was not consulted about the 1963 Act and during the parliamentary debates in this period both parties exhibited a preparedness to eschew the voluntary system of collective bargaining because of a belief that it was too slow to innovate. Both sides of Parliament recognised the limits of the traditional system, with the Conservative government's minister for labour stating in 1963: 'voluntary methods are fine but they are fine only if they are effective. Some progress has been made on a voluntary basis in recent years but not nearly enough.'[42] A similar attitude was

40 Jenkins (n 36) 50.
41 Davies and Freedland (n 16) 177.
42 Hansard HC vol 671 col 1505 (14 February 1963).

shared by the Opposition, with Mr Gunter, the future minister for labour, stating that under Labour 'there will be greater intervention by the State in industry. . . . [W]e and the party opposite will have to accept State intervention if the national needs are to be met'.[43] The Contracts of Employment Act 1963 and the Redundancy Payments Act 1965 indicate that both Labour and the Conservatives were prepared to support legislative efforts to confer statutory rights upon individuals. This was justified by the economic argument that by giving employees legal entitlements to money payments upon dismissal or redundancy, they would be less likely to resist the loss of their jobs and more willing to undertake the risks involved in looking for alternative employment. Davies and Freedland draw a distinction between these two Acts and the unfair dismissal legislation introduced in 1971, as the 'latter was designed to make dismissal less likely; the former to make it easier for management to secure termination'.[44] However governmental motives are construed in this period, what is certain is that the commitment to voluntarism was eroded over time and could be trumped in specific cases by the argument that government intervention was necessary on economic grounds.

Proposals for unfair dismissal reform from within a voluntarist paradigm

Despite the growing perception that greater legislative intervention in industrial relations could be warranted in order to achieve the national interest, the building momentum to confer greater unfair dismissal protection on employees was conceived as being part of a voluntary industrial relations system aimed at extending collective bargaining. The movement to confer unfair dismissal rights upon individual employees was aided by the United Kingdom government's acceptance of International Labour Organization (ILO) Recommendation 119 concerning Termination of Employment at the Initiative of the Employer (1963). This acceptance meant that the government was indicating its willingness to consider the proposals of the recommendation, although it noted at the time that it had 'certain reservations . . . in light of [industrial relations] practice in this country'.[45] In this White Paper the government did acknowledge that it considered that the application of the principles embodied in the recommendation could play a useful part in promoting a sense of security at work, which was in the interests of both employees and the national economy.[46] Following on from the White Paper, the government asked the National Joint Advisory Committee (NJAC), made up of employer and union representatives, to consider the present extent of unfair dismissal protection in the United Kingdom in light of the recommendation and to canvass potential avenues for reform.

43 Hansard HC vol 684 col 1017 (20 November 1963).
44 Davies and Freedland (n 16) 158.
45 Ministry of Labour, 'White Paper on the International Labour Conference' (Cmnd 2548, 1964) 255.
46 Ibid.

The NJAC's final report indicates a substantial degree of unwillingness by employers and unions to depart from the voluntary tradition in the resolution of dismissal disputes. Despite establishing that existing procedures do not cover the whole of industry, particularly in the private sector, and that in other countries statutory unfair dismissal schemes seem to work fairly well, the committee resisted the argument that the United Kingdom should introduce a statutory scheme. The committee advanced the assumption that some formal procedure is better than none when dealing with dismissal disputes and made two recommendations: that voluntary agreements on dismissal procedure, both internal and external, were to be encouraged and that the Ministry of Labour should 'keep under review' the possible need for statutory machinery to supplement these voluntary agreements. This position indicated the strong attachment of unions and employers to the voluntary system and their support for the autonomy that it afforded them in dispute resolution. The parties viewed a statutory scheme for unfair dismissal as a disincentive to cultural change within workplaces that would inhibit the internal development of fair dismissal processes.[47] The NJAC believed that voluntary procedures would be more effective in obtaining reinstatement, and employers and unions would be more likely to set up adequate internal procedures if they could avoid outside interference.[48] The NJAC was also of the view that a statutory scheme might import a legalistic element into industrial relations, leading to employers increasingly recording workers' misdeeds or shortcomings to manage the risk of an unfair dismissal claim.[49] The NJAC believed that such legalism would fracture the ongoing relationship between workers and employers and impede the development of fair dismissal procedures beyond the legal minimum.[50]

The reasons underlying the reluctance of the parties to support the development of a statutory unfair dismissal scheme were made even clearer in their submissions to the Donovan Commission. A strong supporter of the NJAC final report and the most vocal industrial relations player opposing a statutory unfair dismissal scheme was the CBI. In both oral and written evidence submitted to the Royal Commission on Trade Unions and Employers' Associations, the CBI expressed its belief in the traditional system of voluntary collective bargaining as the best method of securing unfair dismissal protection for employees and ensuring industrial stability.[51] The only area where the status quo could be improved that the CBI was prepared to concede was that, where necessary, unions and employers should be encouraged to establish joint rules to scrutinise the fairness of an employer's decision to dismiss. In addressing one of the primary perceived inadequacies of the voluntarist tradition in according unfair dismissal protection

47 Ministry of Labour (n 13) [170].
48 Ibid [171]–[174].
49 Ibid [171].
50 Ibid.
51 Royal Commission on Trade Unions and Employers' Association, Minutes of Evidence of 12 December 1967 (Her Majesty's Stationery Officer, 1968) [11362].

to all employees, including the non-unionised, the CBI argued that this situation would ameliorate over time as 'the balance of advantage lies in developing procedures so that we can gradually reduce the numbers of unprotected workers'.[52] While the CBI acknowledged that the lack of statutory machinery left workers in non-unionised sectors of employment without unfair dismissal protection, it argued that 'legislating [for a statutory scheme] would provide a poor second best' and that the NJAC had obtained 'no evidence that in these sectors there were large numbers of unjustified dismissals or of workers with grievances over dismissals'.[53] The CBI also argued that the statutory scheme would favour compensation over reinstatement and that the advantage of encouraging voluntary procedures is that they allow for reinstatement, which 'goes to the heart of what an unjustly dismissed worker wants'(ibid).[54]

Another employer group strongly advocating the traditional system was the Engineering Employers' Federation (EEF), which believed that its procedure, which graduated from informal to formal mechanisms for dealing with unfair dismissal, was more flexible and responsive to employee needs than a statutory scheme.[55] In providing evidence before the Donovan Commission, the EEF was extremely critical of a statutory scheme, as it thought it unlikely that reinstatement would be awarded, unlike under its own scheme where reinstatement was regularly achieved.[56] In response to the criticism of Professor Kahn-Freund that it would be more just and forward thinking to develop a statutory scheme, the EEF's view was that its system predicated upon the collective laissez-faire notion of industrial autonomy afforded more justice to the worker. One EEF official, Mr Brown, stated:

> [W]e believe that the unions and the employee is [*sic*] much more concerned with getting his job back than with monetary compensation. Our figures show in a surprising number of cases he does in fact get his old job back which shows that we do not favour the employer in dealing with these cases.[57]

Unions, too, were strong advocates of the traditional model and believed the expansion of collective bargaining would lead to greater unfair dismissal protection for employees over time. The Trades Union Congress (TUC) also spoke out in favour of extending voluntary procedures, believing that disputes about dismissal should not be individualised and it should not be incumbent upon individual employees to present their case before tribunals. In its evidence before the

52 Ibid.
53 Ibid [11357].
54 Ibid.
55 Royal Commission on Trade Unions and Employers' Associations, Minutes of Evidence of 1 February 1966 (Her Majesty's Stationery Office, 1967) [3069].
56 Donovan (n 18) [3958].
57 Ibid [3072].

Donovan Commission, the TUC argued for the strengthening of the industrial machinery and widening access to unions.[58] In responding to Professor Kahn-Freund's questioning of whether a statutory system would reduce the number of strikes resulting from dismissals, the TUC's Mr Douglass stated that 'if a man is sacked on the job and his mates make up their mind he should not have been sacked, you can put up all the courts you like, they are not just going to tolerate it'.[59] Mr Lowthian of the TUC gave evidence that a statutory unfair dismissal scheme would not address the primary problem associated with unfair dismissals, which, in his view, was the management belief that it had a blanket power to hire and fire.[60] Mr Lowthian also argued that there needed to be scrutiny of the decision to dismiss before it was made, as afterwards was too late. Given these fundamental objections to the introduction of a statutory unfair dismissal scheme, the TUC was only prepared to articulate support for a scheme that allowed the worker to be suspended on full pay while making an unfair dismissal claim in a system that processed claims speedily through a non-court body such as a tribunal.[61] This position reflected significant TUC suspicion of the unfair dismissal system becoming legalistic and its preference for the maintenance of the principle of industrial autonomy. In their view, this allowed unions and employers to negotiate without the shadow of the courts.

Despite the reluctance of employers and unions to back statutory protection of unfair dismissal rights, the Donovan Commission supported the introduction of independent machinery to adjudicate the fairness of dismissals from within a collective laissez-faire paradigm. The Commission's view was that this expansion of individual rights should not replace, but merely supplement, collective bargaining. The Donovan report argued that 'properly constituted, collective bargaining is the most effective means of giving workers the right to representation in decisions affecting their working lives, a right which is or should be the prerogative of every worker in a democratic society'.[62]

While the Donovan Commission was divided in its final report, the majority was of the view that the current system was unsatisfactory in protecting job security for a number of reasons. First, the majority noted that there were 276 unofficial strikes between 1964 and 1966 resulting from dismissal disputes and believed that a statutory unfair dismissal scheme would aid industrial peace.[63] Second, the majority was of the view that the introduction of a statutory scheme would lead to an immediate raising of standards to a more satisfactory level, as employers would seek to comply with the legislative framework governing dismissal procedures.[64] Third, a statutory scheme would protect workers in

58 Royal Commission on Trade Unions and Employers' Associations (n 19) [10402].
59 Ibid [10360].
60 Ibid [10370].
61 Ibid [10373]–[10375].
62 Ibid [212].
63 Ibid [528].
64 Ibid [540].

non-unionised industries and would provide greater protection for workers in unionised industries, as even in the latter, 'employer procedures tend to leave the final decision on dismissal in the hands of management and this cannot be accepted as sufficient to ensure that an employee both has fair treatment and is seen to have it'.[65] The cumulative weight of these arguments led the majority to advocate the establishment of statutory machinery to adjudicate unfair dismissals.

Nonetheless, the Donovan Commission's support for a statutory scheme was predicated on their belief that the scheme should operate from within a collective bargaining paradigm and should facilitate the extension of voluntary methods to remedy unfair dismissals. They believed that the existence of a statutory unfair dismissal scheme would prompt employers and unions to develop joint procedures within workplaces for dealing with dismissal disputes, resulting in procedural reform of firms' internal management:

> If employers know that employees have the right to challenge dismissal in a statutory tribunal, then there is a clear incentive for them to see that dismissals are carried out under a proper and orderly procedure, so as to ensure that as many cases as possible are settled satisfactorily without recourse to an outside appeal and that in those cases where appeal is made it can be shown that the dismissal was fair and justified.[66]

Their belief that the statutory system could simultaneously operate as both a safety net and a floor of rights drew upon the ideas of Kahn-Freund, who argued that 'regulatory legislation' such as that concerning dismissal, which lays down rules of employment, provides a safety net for those with no access to collective bargaining but also exists as a floor 'on which we can all stand . . . a ground floor for an edifice of collective bargaining'.[67] It was believed that in addition to stimulating collective bargaining, the statutory unfair dismissal system would aid the activities of unions. Professor Wedderburn, an important witness to the Donovan Commission, provided his support for a statutory unfair dismissal system on the proviso that it would foster trade unionism and be underpinned by strong unions:

> The employment rights should as far as possible involve collective machinery. It would seem not unreasonable to say specific grounds for summary dismissal ought to be negotiated with the trade union. They are not necessarily things which concern management alone, and they ought not to be open to the dictation of management alone at the place of work.[68]

65 Ibid [542].
66 Ibid [533].
67 Otto Kahn-Freund, 'Comparative Law as an Academic Subject' (1966) 82 LQR 40, 43.
68 Royal Commission on Trade Unions and Employers' Associations, Minutes of Evidence of 22 March 1966 (Her Majesty's Stationery Office, 1966) [4760].

Professor Wedderburn did not support the wholesale introduction of labour law to regulate industrial relations but favoured 'the introduction of new laws which can be grafted on to the present, essentially voluntary, system'.[69] In his influential text, *The Worker and the Law*, Wedderburn sets out his argument that a statutory unfair dismissal scheme should contain an official place for the individual employee's trade union because of his belief that 'far too much English procedure brings on to the stage the individual contestants, employer and employees, but leaves their backers in the shadows in the wings'.[70]

The Donovan Commission's final report provides another example of the prevailing belief in the late 1960s that a statutory unfair dismissal scheme would coexist with a strong union movement and encourage the growth of collectivism in industrial relations. While advocating independent machinery to adjudicate unfair dismissal claims, the majority supported the extension of voluntary procedures and proposed an exemption scheme, whereby the secretary of state could exempt certain industries or undertakings from the statutory scheme if an agreed voluntary procedure was of a satisfactory standard.[71] The majority intended this provision to facilitate the development of voluntary schemes. Even when this was not achieved, the majority believed that the existence of a statutory unfair dismissal scheme would improve the position of unions, arguing that '[s]tatutory machinery can afford increased protection for the exercise of freedom of association . . . and will therefore assist the growth of collective bargaining on sound lines. Without such growth, the circumstance in which effective voluntary dismissal procedures can be developed will in some areas of employment not exist.'[72]

Finally, another indication that the Donovan Commission's support for a statutory unfair dismissal system was closely connected with their desire to facilitate more efficient collective bargaining is their choice of industrial tribunals, rather than the courts, to adjudicate dismissal disputes. As Dickens et al note, 'the voluntary principle in British industrial relations has never denied legislation a role but has displayed a pragmatic approach'.[73] In advocating a legal remedy for unfair dismissal, the Donovan Commission recognised the need for statutory intervention to combat the deficiencies of the common law and the inadequacy of collective bargaining to achieve comprehensive unfair dismissal protection. However, this was not a rejection of the voluntary tradition because there was still a clear desire to introduce a system of dispute resolution that was speedy, accessible and non-legalistic, and therefore unlike the procedures associated with the common law courts. As Flanders noted:

> It is when legislation has the effect, or appears to have the effect, of bringing unions and their members into courts that it meets with almost universal

69 Ibid [4760].
70 Wedderburn (n 4) 98.
71 Donovan (n 18) [540].
72 Ibid.
73 Linda Dickens, Michael Jones, Brian Weekes and Moira Hart, *Dismissed: A Study of the Unfair Dismissal and the Industrial Tribunal System* (Blackwell, Oxford 1985) 253.

> disapproval and the [collective laissez-faire] tradition asserts its full force. This is exactly what one would expect given the unions' history and their accumulated lessons of experience.[74]

Therefore, the Donovan Commission's belief that a statutory unfair dismissal scheme would stimulate the growth of voluntary procedures, supplement collective bargaining and be free from the legalism of the common law courts indicates their attachment to collective bargaining and their support for the traditional voluntary model as the ideal framework for industrial relations. By the end of the 1960s the prevailing belief of the industrial parties, academics and the Donovan Commission was that a legislative scheme to protect job security should 'build in the collective reality from the start rather than leave the new storey perched uneasily on the summit of the old individualist legal structure'.[75]

The introduction of unfair dismissal law and the dismantling of voluntarism

The late 1960s were characterised by heated debate over the future of British industrial relations, with a growing belief that 'collective bargaining machinery has stalled and legislation has to take its place'.[76] The context to this debate was spiralling inflation and unemployment from the mid-1960s coupled with increasing industrial disputation which the Wilson Labour government seemed unable to stem. Davies and Freedland make the following observation illustrating the breakdown of relations between the Labour government and the union movement during this time:

> This was a period in which a public perception intensified of an industrial relations problem consisting of the inability of trade unions to control or channel into constructive form the shop-floor militancy which was causing more and more unofficial wild-cat strikes, and hence delay in delivery of orders which was fundamentally weakening the manufacturing economy and destroying foreign confidence in British exports.[77]

Newspaper headlines from April 1969, the month when relations between the government and unions were perhaps at their most fraught, indicate a situation of impalpable tension: 'Unofficial Strike Halts London Freightliners',[78] 'Strike Hits Welsh Steel Plant's Output',[79] 'Strike by 1,500 Dockers',[80] 'Walk Out by 1,500

74 Flanders (n 8) 354.
75 Wedderburn (n 4) 98.
76 Kahn-Freund (n 31) 40–41.
77 Davies and Freedland (n 16) 241.
78 'Unofficial Strike Halts London Freightliners', *The Financial Times* (London 11 April 1969).
79 'Strike Hits Welsh Steel Plant's Output', *The Financial Times* (London 11 April 1969).
80 Geoffrey Whiteley, 'Strike by 1,500 Dockers', *The Guardian* (London 12 April 1969).

at Ipswich Factory',[81] 'Car Men to Strike if DEP Rejects £2 Rise',[82] 'Electricians' Strikes Holds Up Magazine Production',[83] 'Nurses May Strike Over Meal Row',[84] 'Warning of Destruction by Unofficial Strikes',[85] and 'Textile Unions' Militant "No" to Pay Offer: Steel Row Continues'.[86] Strikes were threatened or taking place in a number of different industries, so much so that Prime Minister Wilson described the situation as 'industrial relations anarchy' in a meeting with the TUC.[87] He acknowledged that the government would prefer to resolve the problem of unofficial strikes without reliance on legislation but that relying upon collective bargaining would not be an immediate enough solution for the public.[88] Indicating the pressure confronting the government to act on industrial relations, Prime Minister Wilson stated, 'we can be destroyed economically and politically if we have no answer to unofficial strikes. We cannot just fold our arms and say that because the TUC do not like it we will not do anything about it.'[89] Davies and Freedland characterise this period as one of 'constitutional crisis' because the union movement was challenging the primacy and legitimacy of the government to regulate industrial relations.[90] Thus, it was in this context that both the Conservatives and Labour advocated the introduction of a statutory unfair dismissal scheme. Given the evidence that many of the unofficial strikes were about dismissals, there was a prevailing belief that providing a statutory remedy to determine the fairness of a worker's dismissal would help tame shop-floor power without interfering with free collective bargaining. As Collins notes, 'the law of unfair dismissal was conceived in order to manage a crisis in industrial relations'.[91]

Despite the prevailing belief in academic circles that unfair dismissal law was the fruit of a bipartisan political consensus that ensured the longevity of the unfair dismissal provisions, this consensus between Labour and the Conservatives was precarious and arose at a time of fierce contestation over labour law between the political parties. Given the growing divergence between Labour and the Conservatives during the 1970s over the substantive operation of the unfair dismissal system, to what extent can a political consensus around the principles for introducing the system be identified? Two main principles which achieved bipartisan

81 'Walk Out by 1,500 at Ipswich Factory', *The Financial Times* (London 11 April 1969).

82 'Car Men to Strike if DEP Rejects £2 Rise', *The Guardian* (London 12 April 1969) 11.

83 'Electricians' Strikes Holds Up Magazine Production', *The Guardian* (London 12 April 1969) 11.

84 'Nurses May Strike Over Meal Row', *The Times* (London 12 April 1969).

85 'Warning of Destruction by Unofficial Strikes', *The Times* (London 12 April 1969) 9.

86 'Textile Unions' Militant "No" to Pay Offer: Steel Row Continues', *The Times* (London 12 April 1969) 13.

87 Prime Minister Wilson cited in John Torode, 'Wilson Brushes off TUC Plea against Reform', *The Guardian* (London 12 April 1969).

88 Ibid.

89 Ibid.

90 Davies and Freedland (n 16) 242–43.

91 Hugh Collins, 'Capitalist Discipline and Corporatist Law – Part I' (1982) 11 ILJ 78, 87.

support, albeit to varying degrees, can be identified. First, both Labour and the Conservatives were united in their desire to reduce the incidence of dismissal-related strikes and to achieve greater industrial stability. Second, there was an increasing willingness to support the introduction of safeguards protecting the rights of individual employees during dismissal on the basis of an argument for industrial justice. This was not a new argument but it was distinct from the traditional argument under the voluntarist system that justice for individual employees was best achieved through collective bargaining facilitated by unions. This new strand of the industrial justice argument emerging in the 1970s was much more concerned with facilitating the achievement of industrial justice for individual employees regardless of whether they had union representation according to individual employees' rights that accrue to them by virtue of their employment. While there was a certain amount of consensus about the principle that statutory unfair dismissal protection should exist in order to aid the achievement of industrial justice for individual employees, this consensus did not extend to political agreement over the substantive achievement of industrial justice. In the 1970s the key concern was not whether a return to the voluntarist tradition should be canvassed but rather how to reform the legislative model of resolving dismissal disputes so as to achieve industrial justice in practice.

The fragile political consensus over the principle of industrial justice

Despite the heavily contested labour law debates occurring during this period, there existed a fragile consensus between Labour and the Conservatives that a statutory scheme for unfair dismissal should be introduced according to a rationale of industrial justice. The Conservatives' support for general reform of British industrial relations beyond unfair dismissal law was predicated on their desire for a new era of responsible trade unionism closely regulated by the state. Its policy platform, *Fair Deal at Work*, contained a prescription for how this could be achieved, namely through the comprehensive regulation of British industrial relations with a state-supervised system of trade union registration enabling the state to regulate collective bargaining in a procedural sense. The aim was to stop the proliferation of industrial conflict and to achieve stability in industrial relations. To this end, the Conservatives' proposal for a statutory unfair dismissal scheme was contained in the section on industrial disputes and justified on the basis that the introduction of a legal right not to be unfairly dismissed would remove the cause of dismissal and discipline-related strikes.[92] Therefore, the Conservatives' primary motivation for proposing a statutory unfair dismissal scheme was the achievement of industrial peace by removing one of the primary causes of industrial action. This fit in with their reform agenda overall, which sought to achieve state-regulated collective bargaining aimed at securing industrial stability.

92 Conservative Political Centre, *Fair Deal at Work* (Conservative Political Centre, London 1968) 41–42.

Writing in a national newspaper prior to the national election, the Opposition Spokesperson on Employment and Productivity, Mr Robert Carr, wrote:

> We do not claim that the system proposed in Fair Deal at Work would bring about any magic cure overnight. What we do claim is that it would alter the balance of power significantly in favour of those employers and trade union leaders who wish to act responsibly and tilt the balance against the irresponsible minority. This is an indispensable condition for the success of the voluntary action within industry, on which the solution must ultimately depend.[93]

It is also possible to identify an alternative motivation for the Conservatives in introducing unfair dismissal protection: a desire to achieve industrial justice for individual employees by drawing upon the idea of a common ground between unions and employers as to what constitutes good industrial relations practice in the treatment of individual workers. In *Fair Deal at Work*, this notion was said to necessitate the introduction of a statutory unfair dismissal system 'on principle' by providing important new safeguards for individual employees.[94] Conservative support for this developing notion of industrial justice as a basis for statutory unfair dismissal protection was also evinced in the government's justification for the new system contained in the second reading debates for the Industrial Relations Bill 1970. As articulated by Mr Robert Carr, the Secretary of State for Employment and Productivity:

> I believe that we have in this Bill the most comprehensive and enlightened code of workers' rights in the history of our country. . . . As the Royal Commission pointed out, we are almost the only industrialized country that does not have some kind of statutory protections against unfair dismissal. We agree that it is high time that this is put right.[95]

Nonetheless, the Conservative government's time in office was short-lived because, despite the fragile consensus over the necessity of their unfair dismissal reform, the other aspects of their industrial relations agenda were heavily contested. Despite winning the 1970 election by successfully branding itself as a party willing to pass industrial relations reform despite union protestation, the Heath Conservative government period from 1970 until 1974 was typified by intense conflict between the government and the unions. The latter's campaign of deregistration successfully undermined the operation of the Industrial Relations Act 1971.

Labour's agenda post-1971 was not one of responsible unionism but the pursuit of collective and individual rights as an alternative to both the chaos

93 Robert Carr, 'Britain's Urgent Need of a Code for Industrial Relations' *The Times* (London 30 July 1968) 9.

94 Conservative Political Centre (n 92) 42.

95 HC Deb vol 808 cols 961–1076 (14 December 1970).

of the voluntarism of the 1960s and the juridification during the Heath years. Labour justified strengthening the unfair dismissal protection afforded to individual employees on the basis that this was necessary to achieve industrial justice. However, the adoption of a rights-based approach to industrial relations had not always been the Labour agenda. Prior to the 1971 election the Labour Government had outlined proposals in its White Paper 'In Place of Strife' to accord coercive powers to the government to regulate industrial disputes. This was vehemently rejected by the union movement, and was never statutorily enacted. The Labour Government's Industrial Relations Bill 1970 contained no mention of these coercive powers and thus 'the impetus behind the White Paper "In Place of Strife" [was] altogether deflected'.[96] In winning the 1974 election, Labour had rerouted its industrial relations agenda, believing that if it could provide the unions with a floor of statutory rights, including the right to a legal remedy for unfair dismissal, this would minimise industrial action and halt the instability of the Heath government years. Labour's idea was not the wholesale juridification of labour law but support for the voluntary system through a series of legal measures aimed at improving the starting position of unions and individual employees. This included maintaining the unfair dismissal system enacted in 1971 by the Heath government but strengthening the protection afforded under it by mandating re-employment as the primary remedy under the Act,[97] by unequivocally placing the burden of proof in dismissal cases on employers[98] and the introducing a compensatory award for unfair dismissal to supplement the existing basic award.[99] Cumulatively, these provisions were aimed at building an industrial relations system in the United Kingdom upon the foundation of industrial justice, thus minimising the need for industrial action and the so-called 'British disease' of destructive industrial relations. As Mr Janner, a Labour member of the House of Commons, stated during the debates about whether the protection afforded by the unfair dismissal system should be strengthened:

> This is what the law is for – to set up minimum standards with which people should comply and with which, unfortunately too many do not comply. Therefore, I suggest that these laws should not be regarded as a burden on industry but should be welcomed by industry as providing the best environment in which to produce better treatment and conditions for and relations with their own work forces.[100]

In strengthening the protection afforded under the unfair dismissal system, Labour further developed the notion of industrial justice as an important justification for statutory intervention.

96 Davies and Freedland (n 16) 273.
97 Employment Protection Act 1975 s 72.
98 Employment Protection Consolidation Act 1978 s 57(3).
99 Employment Protection Act 1975 s 71(1).
100 HC Deb vol 923 cols 42–114 (20 December 1976).

While during the years when the Conservatives were in government between 1971 and 1974 the articulation of industrial justice was limited to recognising that such a system should be introduced 'on principle' and to the desire to achieve more stable industrial relations, during their years in opposition the Conservatives began to reconceptualise the notion of justice in employment to address the disadvantage faced by employers as well as individual employees. In developing the employer, particularly the small business employer, as a legitimate subject of legislation aimed at the achievement of industrial justice, the Conservatives argued that employers should be protected from the excess militancy of unions or vexatious litigation by individual employees. The Conservative Opposition increasingly articulated an argument that industrial justice not only included the achievement of fair dismissal processes for employees but also included justice for the employer based on a need to achieve a fair balance of rights and responsibilities between the parties in the employment relationship. This was first signalled by the Conservative amendment during the Second Reading of the Employment Protection Bill 1975:

> That this House, while recognizing that parts of the EPA give legislative effect to good industrial practice, declines to give a Second Reading to a Bill which makes no attempt to establish a fair balance between the rights of management and unions, adds a heavy burden of cost without proper consideration of how it should be shared by employer, employee and State, and takes no account for particular problems of small business.[101]

While this amendment was defeated because of Labour's slim majority in the House of Commons, Conservative pressure to reform the unfair dismissal system to be more responsive to the needs of business continued to mount after 1975. The Conservative argument was not just predicated on the grounds of unfair dismissal regulation but also on a whole raft of government policies impacting upon business. In 1976 Mr Ian Stewart of the Conservatives moved a motion urging the government to alleviate the growing legislative burden on business.[102] Mr Finsburg commented in this same debate about the Employment Protection Act: 'This Act has cost jobs, because companies are not taking on people because of the burdens placed on them by the Act. These are companies with first class records of employment.'[103]

The unfair dismissal system was increasingly represented by the Conservatives as undermining the achievement of industrial justice because it impacted unfairly upon the viability of small business. In a 1977 debate on the topic of job creation, Mr James Prior stated: 'I do know that every small business man in the country believes the Employment Protection Act is now an Act stopping him from taking on additional labour because he does not know what the future holds.'[104] Even a debate on the topic of 'the family' in the House of Lords during 1978 included

101 HC Deb vol 891 cols 47–48 (28 April 1975).
102 HC Deb vol 923 cols 42–114 (20 December 1976).
103 Ibid.
104 HC Deb vol 938 cols 689–814 (9 November 1977).

a reference to the adverse impact of the Employment Protection Act on small business, indicating the increasing perception that the unfair dismissal legislation was hindering job creation and business efficacy:

> There exists a large number of small firms and if each of them took on one unemployed person it would make a very great difference to the figure of those who are unemployed. From talking to a number of people in that position I am led to believe that one of the things which prevents them from taking on any additional person is the effect of the EPA. I think this needs to be taken very seriously by the Government. The situation is made very difficult because after six months, no matter what the circumstances of the person or the firm, almost any dismissal is deemed to be unfair dismissal. The effect of this situation, whatever may have been intended by the Government, is that everybody is very reluctant indeed to employ one extra person. I believe that this is having a very real effect on unemployment.[105]

Labour resisted Conservative attempts to reduce the qualifying period or create an exemption for small business according to a different perception of industrial justice, that is, their belief that a small business exemption was unjust as it would create a two-tier labour market. In response to the Conservative attempt to introduce the Employment Opportunities (Small Business) Bill in 1979, Labour's Mr Cryer stated:

> If this Bill were enacted it would create two classes of citizen. That is not fair on small businesses. There are some small business organisations that take the view that because they face difficulties, various steps should be taken. They always take that view and their wants vary enormously. Different small business organisations put forward different points of view about the effect of a Government policy, but the fact is that if this Bill were enacted there would be one set of values for people working in businesses employing fewer than 200 and another set of values for businesses employing more than 200 people. That is unfair.[106]

From Labour's perspective, the principle of industrial justice mandated that access to unfair dismissal protection should not be constrained because of the size of an individual's employer. However, the Conservative Opposition consistently maintained the position that Labour's employment protection legislation was over-burdensome upon employers and this was fundamentally unjust to 'good' employers who did not need this legislative intervention in order to ensure their employees were fairly treated. As Mr Knight of the Conservatives stated:

> Good employers frequently are dragged in front of the industrial tribunals when they have done nothing wrong. Even when the tribunal absolves them, the cost that they have to bear is immense. The Secretary of State said that

105 HL Deb vol 391 cols 15–122 (2 May 1978).
106 HC Deb vol 962 cols 1441–1539 (16 February 1979).

> he had no evidence that the legislation acts unfairly. I beg him to read the reports from the CBI conference last week. Ample evidence that it does act unfairly was given at that conference. The cost to industry of industrial tribunals in the way in which they deal with unfair dismissals is enormous. The cost to the taxpayer is disgraceful and the cost in terms of job opportunities is serious. One of the heaviest of all the burdens that small businesses have to carry is the industrial tribunals.[107]

Industrial justice and the tribunals

The decision to confer protection against unfair dismissal as an individual legal right, calling for the interpretation and application of rules to a particular factual scenario, established judicial adjudication as the most suitable form of decision making for unfair dismissal disputes. The 1971 Act conferred this decision making upon industrial tribunals rather than the ordinary courts, although the former were set up as quasi-courts with legal chairpersons leading proceedings. This choice of industrial tribunals as the arbiter in unfair dismissal disputes represents a replacement of the voluntarist tradition in industrial relations. Keeping out the courts was a cornerstone of traditional industrial relations in the United Kingdom. As Flanders noted in 1974, 'it is when legislation has the effect, or appears to have the effect, of bringing unions and their members into the courts that it meets with almost universal disapproval and the tradition asserts itself in full force'.[108] Instead, the unfair dismissal system introduced in 1971 instituted industrial tribunals at the apex, and while these bodies were not intended to operate as courts, their tripartite composition and the distinctive way they conducted their business led them to be described as a 'specialist, modern form of court'.[109]

The replacement of the voluntary method for resolving dismissal disputes with industrial adjudication was predicated upon a conception of industrial justice administered by lay members. Lay members were accorded equal status with the legal chair of the tribunal and were appointed on the basis of their industrial experience and practical knowledge.[110] The rationale for choosing one lay representative from an employer perspective and another from a union background was to achieve just decision making not based on legal principles but upon custom and practice in British industrial relations. This also aided the perception that the unfair dismissal system was centred upon the achievement of justice as fairness. Fairness was seen to exist because the tribunal comprised lay members drawn from each side of industry. As one chairperson stated during the tribunals' early days of dealing with unfair dismissal disputes:

> Lay members, experienced in industrial relations, know what an employer should or should not put up with, equally they know what an employee can

107 HC Deb vol 939 cols 1113–1171 (21 November 1977).
108 Flanders (n 8) 354.
109 Brian Abel-Smith and Robert Stevens, *In Search of Justice* (Penguin, London 1968) 228.
110 Industrial Tribunals (Rules of Procedure) Regulations 1980 SI 1980/884.

> expect. They know the unwritten custom and practice which form such an important part of industrial relations. *Thus they have a most valuable part to play in reaching a just decision* [emphasis added].[111]

The choice of industrial tribunals to resolve unfair dismissal disputes was based upon a desire to establish a mechanism for administering justice that was 'easily accessible, speedy, informal and inexpensive'.[112] This oft-quoted prescription of how industrial tribunals should operate illustrates that the Donovan Commission's conception of industrial justice was one of tribunal adjudication of dismissal disputes that was both efficient and fair in resolving differences between the parties. Accordingly, the primary duty of the tribunal was to bring about an amicable settlement between the employer and employee as the achievement of industrial peace was seen as a fundamental component of administering justice.[113] Another aspect of the type of justice being facilitated by industrial tribunals was reflected in the desire to create a non-court-like setting where individual employees would feel comfortable to bring their disputes. This notion of informal justice was identified by the one-time president of Industrial Tribunals, Sir Diarmaid Conroy, who stated that 'the tribunals are meant to provide simple informal justice in an atmosphere in which the ordinary man feels he is at home'.[114]

Conclusion

The introduction of unfair dismissal law was characterised by a replacement of the view that the voluntary tradition was adequate for resolving dismissal disputes with a new idea that industrial justice should be the cornerstone of the unfair dismissal system. Industrial justice was not just a post-hoc rationale on the part of theorists but was actively adopted by both political parties and the members of the tribunal system as providing the justification for the unfair dismissal system. While industrial justice was not strongly articulated by either the Conservatives or Labour in their policy documents in the late 1960s, it became strongly embedded in the industrial relations discourse embodied within the parliamentary debates between the two parties throughout the 1970s; it is contained within the ethos of the tribunals and became strongly associated with the idea of those tribunals having lay members who give effect to this notion of industrial justice.

111 M Jukes, 'Reply: Tribunals – Justice for All?' (1968) 60 Indust Soc 1, 5–6.
112 Donovan (n 18) 156.
113 Ibid 159.
114 Diarmaid Conroy, 'Do Applicants Need Advice or Representation?' (Conference on the Future of Administrative Tribunals, edited transcript of proceedings of a conference held at Institute of Judicial Administration, University of Birmingham, April 1971) 4–5.

3 United Kingdom – Part II

The evolution and erosion of unfair dismissal law

Introduction

In this chapter I examine the basis for reform to the United Kingdom's statutory unfair dismissal scheme after 1971. Although frequently amended after its introduction, the United Kingdom's statutory unfair dismissal scheme has never been dismantled, proving to be a fairly durable addition to the corpus of British labour law. The introduction of a statutory unfair dismissal scheme in 1971 as the result of rigorous debate in the previous decade over how to address the perceived inadequacies of the common law of wrongful dismissal meant that both sides of politics largely accepted the scheme's merits at its inception.[1] While there was political agreement over the need to introduce unfair dismissal protection for workers, this arose at a time of labour law crisis more generally, and there was significant disagreement over the future of the United Kingdom's industrial relations system.[2] The convergence over the rationale for statutory unfair dismissal protection began to unravel towards the tail end of the 1970s, and the differences between Labour and the Conservatives became more acute with the development of an argument of principle against unfair dismissal law by the Conservative government in the 1980s. Davies and Freedland coined this term to describe government acceptance of 'an argument of principle against unfair dismissal legislation, namely that it discouraged employers from taking on labour and so contributed to unemployment'.[3] The Conservative government advocated a return to the common law of wrongful dismissal because of its belief in the right of employers to dismiss staff without independent scrutiny. Unlike its manifestation during the Conservative government's duration in office, under subsequent governments this argument of principle was not used to argue against unfair dismissal law but rather to justify mechanisms for reducing access to the system and the substantive protection it offered.

1 Conservative Political Centre, *Fair Deal at Work* (Conservative Political Centre, London 1968) [103].

2 For an explanation of the fiercely contested nature of labour law during this period, see Paul Davies and Mark Freedland, *Labour Legislation and Public Policy* (Clarendon Press, Oxford 1993) 241–43.

3 Ibid 200.

While Davies and Freedland suggest that this 'argument of principle' was against unfair dismissal legislation, I propose here that the decades subsequent to the 1980s reveal the need to refine this position somewhat. I suggest that there is an argument of principle against the resolution of unfair dismissal complaints through the employment tribunal system. Although the Conservative government (1979–97) may have had aspirations to dismantle the unfair dismissal system in its entirety, this was not the government's main objective, which was to break the power of the trade unions. However, no subsequent government has had the aim of abolition. There was not an argument of principle against unfair dismissal legislation more generally. If there were, it would not adequately explain the fact that although frequently reformed, no attempt has been made to dismantle the unfair dismissal system in its entirety. However, it is possible to identify an argument of principle about the processing of dismissal disputes via the employment tribunal system, as each government, regardless of its political persuasion, sought to limit access or reduce the amount of compensation awarded.

This chapter explores how this argument of principle against the perceived inefficiencies of tribunal resolution of unfair dismissal complaints developed over time. I first trace the debates during the first decade of the unfair dismissal system and chart the growing divergence between the political parties over how job security should be protected. The next section explores the emergence and formulation of the argument of principle against the unfair dismissal system during the initial years of the Conservative government. This section is followed by an analysis of how the argument of principle was subsequently developed by the Conservative government in the early 1990s. While it is arguable that initially there existed an outright argument of principle against the unfair dismissal system, by the early 1990s it is possible to identify an argument of principle against the tribunal system in terms of the perceived problem of vexatious litigation and burdensome regulation. The Conservative government was successful in reframing the parameters of the debate around the unfair dismissal system to be about protecting business from these perceived problems rather than protecting employees from the threat of unfair dismissal. This resulted in a new effort to facilitate the resolution of unfair dismissal disputes within businesses and by reference to the contract of employment.

Instead of articulating a renewal of the Donovan Commission ideals of protecting job security and guaranteeing justice in dismissal, New Labour after its election in 2007 built upon the pro-business rhetoric and policies of the previous Conservative government and by 2008 were beating the same drum. While the first term of the New Labour government saw some moderation of this argument of principle with attempts to improve the protective quality of the unfair dismissal system by indexing the compensation cap to inflation and reducing the qualifying period, New Labour's second and third terms in government ushered in new ways to constrain access to employment tribunals and to limit the quality of protection these tribunals could afford to unfairly dismissed employees. While New Labour presented its 2002 and 2008 reforms under the guise of achieving a marriage of economic efficiency and social justice, these reforms represented a continuation of the argument of principle against tribunal resolution of unfair dismissal and a willingness to be persuaded by employer dissatisfaction with tribunal resolution of unfair dismissal complaints. These reforms sought to facilitate localised dispute resolution by relying upon the mechanisms for resolving conflict under the contract of employment.

The most recent evolution of unfair dismissal law has occurred under the Cameron Conservative-Liberal Democratic coalition government after its election in 2010 and the election of the Cameron Conservative government in 2015. In part, the Cameron government's reforms have continued the argument of principle against tribunal resolution of unfair dismissal disputes through seeking to deter tribunal claims and limit access to tribunals. However, some of its reforms have also gone beyond this and ushered in a new impulse towards employment at will for certain employees. This can be seen through the no-fault dismissal proposal and the reforms introducing employee-shareholder status, extending settlement agreements, introducing fees for making and pursuing claims, and doubling the qualifying period to two years. As this chapter will explain, the Cameron government's argument of principle against statutory unfair dismissal law has been cautiously made, but at its core is a deregulatory desire focused upon reducing the regulatory burden on business and pursuing economic efficiency.

The growing political divergence over unfair dismissal law

Despite the divergence that would ensue, the first decade of the unfair dismissal system was characterised by bipartisan political support for the existence of the system. The primary concern of both Labour and the Conservatives was how the system could substantively deliver industrial justice for unfairly dismissed workers. The parliamentary debates about the unfair dismissal system were concerned with the remedies which could be awarded by the tribunal, the length of the qualifying period and who should bear the burden of proof. In none of these debates was there a desire to dismantle the system altogether, as in this decade the debate between Labour and the Conservatives was about practicalities. In one light, it could be argued that these disagreements were nothing more than a necessary sifting through the teething problems associated with a new system in order to make it more efficient. However, an alternative analysis could be that both Labour and the Conservatives sought to reform the unfair dismissal system during the 1970s based upon their different conceptions of industrial justice. For Labour, prioritising the remedy of reinstatement, reducing the qualifying period and placing the burden of proof squarely upon the employer were all necessary components of achieving industrial justice. In Labour's view, achieving justice in dismissal was not limited to awarding compensation for unfair treatment suffered, which was the main aim of the Conservatives. Labour saw that while industrial justice was concerned with preserving the dignity and autonomy of individual employees against unchecked management power during dismissal, this could not be separated from the broader trade union concern with the control of jobs by management. Accordingly, Labour sought to have reinstatement as a viable remedy for unfair dismissal, to increase access to the tribunal system by reducing the qualifying period and to ensure that employers bore the burden of proof for disproving a charge of unfair dismissal. As the 1970s progressed, Labour's position increasingly diverged from that of the Conservatives, who sought to develop the idea of industrial justice as encompassing justice for employers too. Thus, despite the unfair dismissal system originating from a political consensus that such legislation was necessary, by the end of 1979 the political consensus on unfair dismissal had unravelled.

The debate between Labour and the Conservatives over remedies during the 1970s reflected their different conceptions of industrial justice. For Labour, the unfair dismissal system needed to provide for the possibility of reinstatement, as justice for unfairly dismissed employees included the opportunity to return to their jobs. In this way, Labour was influenced by Meyers' theory of job ownership and Hepple's theory of a right to work, both of which encompassed recognition of the right of an unfairly dismissed employee to be reinstated.[4] The Labour government's lapsed Industrial Relations Bill provided for reinstatement to be the primary remedy. Tribunals were required to order reinstatement where the employee wished to be reinstated and the tribunal thought it an appropriate case for reinstatement. If the reinstatement order was not complied with, the tribunal could award additional compensation of up to six month's pay.[5] While the Conservatives claimed that their Industrial Relations Act 1971 retained reinstatement as the primary remedy, the provisions in Labour's Bill were effectively weakened by the downgrading of the tribunal's ability to make an order of reinstatement to a recommendation and by the Act's failure to regard reinstatement as a remedy of priority over compensation.[6] The parliamentary debates over this point indicate that there was never any political consensus with regard to remedies. The Conservative government's solicitor general argued that Labour's Bill could not secure reinstatement, as under both Bills 'an employer could buy off someone who is unfairly dismissed'.[7] Labour's industrial relations spokesperson, Mrs Barbara Castles, responded by asserting:

> What I provided in my Bill was that the tribunal must have some freedom at the end to decide in a particular situation whether reinstatement would be unworkable. *That is very different from saying that the employer shall decide whether it is unworkable. Our purpose was to safeguard the right to reinstatement without which this is meaningless* [emphasis added].[8]

Upon winning the 1974 general election, Labour introduced provisions into the Trade Union and Labour Relations Act 1974 specifying reinstatement as a

4 For explanations of these perspectives, see Chapter 1.
5 Bill 164, Session 1969/70 cls 37–9, 52.
6 Industrial Relations Act 1971 s 106.
7 HC Deb vol 813 col 1285 (16 March 1971).
8 HC Deb vol 813 col 1286 (16 March 1971).

separate remedy to re-engagement.[9] These provisions regarding reinstatement and re-engagement were strengthened the following year when more weight was given to both remedies under the Employment Protection Act 1975, which empowered tribunals to order, and not merely recommend, re-employment. The sanction for non-compliance is the payment of compensation between thirteen and twenty-six weeks' pay, or double this if the dismissal was found to be based on discrimination.[10] Although tribunals must consider whether re-employment is 'practicable',[11] the fact that the employer has taken on a permanent replacement is not an automatic indication of impracticability.[12] Nonetheless, Labour was unsuccessful in its desire to make reinstatement the primary remedy, as the new provisions did not alter the fact that only a tiny proportion of successful unfair dismissal complainants were reinstated or re-engaged. In 1973, 4.2 per cent of those whose cases were settled through conciliation were given back their jobs and by 1979 this had fallen to 1.8 per cent.[13] Of those who went to a tribunal hearing, 2.3 per cent secured a recommendation that they be given their jobs back in 1973 but by 1979 only 0.8 per cent received reinstatement orders.[14] Davies and Freedland note that Labour's commitment to reinstatement was limited at best: 'the crucial point, however, is that the 1970 Bill, 1971 Act and 1975 reforms all protected the freedom of the employer to buy its way out of an award of reinstatement upon payment of a relatively modest additional lump sum.'[15]

Unlike the issue of remedies, which was contentious from the start, there was an initial political consensus prior to 1979 on reducing the qualifying period for unfair dismissal claims. The introduction of the statutory scheme for unfair dismissal in 1971 was accompanied by concern from both Conservative and Labour governments that lower qualifying periods would provide too many people with access to the tribunal system, which would buckle under the increased demand. At this stage, both parties believed there should be a two-year qualifying period before an employee could access unfair dismissal protection. In the House of Lords debates about the 1971 Act there was recognition that this two-year period was too long and only a temporary measure that would ultimately come down once the tribunal system could cope with the expansion of its jurisdiction into unfair dismissal. As Earl Jellicoe stated in the House of Lords debate, 'it is our intention as soon as may be to lower the ceiling of this exclusion clause, to make it clear that there is absolutely nothing between noble Lords opposite and myself on this issue'.[16] He added on another occasion:

9 Trade Union and Labour Relations Act 1974 sch 1, pt 3, para 17(2).
10 Employment Protection Act 1975 s 72(2)(b).
11 Ibid s 69 (5)(b) and (6)(b).
12 Ibid s 70(1).
13 Bob Hepple, 'A Right to Work?' (1981) 10 ILJ 65.
14 Ibid.
15 Davies and Freedland (n 2) 210.
16 HL Deb vol 317 cols 4–192 (5 April 1971).

> I too should like to see 104 become 52. I do not believe that there is anything sacrosanct about 52. I think it could well come down. . . . I am quite certain that my right honourable friend will use his powers [under the Act] to reduce that ceiling as rapidly as possible.[17]

In Labour's Trade Union and Labour Relations Act 1974 the qualifying period was halved to one year, despite amendments at the committee stage for the qualifying period to be reduced to twelve weeks. Again, the concern of the government, this time a Labour government, was to protect the tribunal system from breaking down, but the long-term goal was still to broaden access to this jurisdiction. In fact, as Michael Foot, the Minister of Labour, stated:

> We are faced with the difficulty that the tribunals are not fully manned to carry out the procedure, and that is the only reason we are not able to agree to the amendment proposed and carried by my honourable friends in Committee being made in one step. We are, however, proposing to do it in two or three steps.[18]

Evidence of this commitment was that the qualifying period was reduced to six months in 1975 according to schedule 1, para 10 of the Trade Union and Labour Relations Act 1974.

The political consensus supporting the ongoing reduction of the qualifying period unravelled in the late 1970s as the Conservatives began to question the impact of the unfair dismissal system on business, and in particular small business. Again, this growing political divergence over qualifying periods reflected the broader philosophical divergence between Labour and the Conservatives over how to achieve industrial justice in dismissal disputes. Labour conceived of industrial justice as a universal entitlement and sought to provide every person with a right to industrial justice in dismissal which could not be diluted or affected by a worker's length of service. In contrast, the Conservatives, while initially committed to reducing the length of the qualifying period, came to develop the notion of industrial justice as encompassing justice for the employer too. In this way, the Conservatives argued that industrial justice includes an employer's right to a legitimate period of probation or qualification as employers should have the time to see whether the decision they made to recruit certain workers is supported by their performance on the job. While the Conservatives did not articulate this concern about an employer's right to a period of qualification at the start of the 1970s, by the end of this decade they were increasingly influenced by complaints from business owners and the fear, and perception, that the unfair dismissal system allowed vexatious litigation. After Labour's 1974 amendment halving the qualifying period to twenty-six weeks, over the next five years Conservative MPs repeatedly asked the minister for labour about the possibility of reducing the qualifying

17 HL Deb vol 321 col 777 (5 July 1971).
18 HC Deb vol 876 cols 1721–23 (11 July 1974).

period.[19] In a 1979 debate the Conservative Party's Mr James Prior stated, 'I believe that the six months rule relating to unfair dismissal ought to be changed to 52 weeks. All experience since then has suggested that 6 months is too short a time and that it ought to be changed to 52 weeks.'[20] However, Labour appeared firmly wedded to the twenty-six-week qualifying period throughout its time in government. The secretary of state for employment, Mr Harold Walker, stated:

> I am satisfied that the 26 weeks qualifying period is right. The honourable Member will know that the qualifying period has been progressively reduced since 1972. We consider, however, that the qualifying period of 26 weeks is necessary to give an employee time to establish himself in his job. It is also sufficient time generally for an employer to assess an employee's suitability and capability for the job.[21]

After winning the 1979 general election, the Conservative government made it one of its first tasks to double the qualifying period, indicating a clear point of demarcation between the unfair dismissal systems envisaged by Labour and the Conservatives by the end of the 1970s.

The final area emerging as a point of division between the political parties prior to 1979 was the question of who should bear the burden of proof in unfair dismissal claims. The original burden of proof provisions in the Conservative government's Industrial Relations Bill 1971 appeared to impose no clear burden of proof upon the employer in relation to unfairness of dismissal. This was indicative of the Conservatives' conception of industrial justice as encompassing justice for both parties to the employment relationship. In contrast, Labour believed that the burden of proof in unfair dismissal cases should rest squarely upon the employer. For Labour, industrial justice was about providing protection from arbitrary dismissal for the employee because their belief in the inherent power imbalance under the contract of employment mandated statutory protection. Labour was very critical of the Conservatives' lack of clarity in their 1971 legislation with regard to the burden of proof:

> The whole question is who has to prove. That is what matters in these cases, and that is what the ILO Convention says. Therefore we say that we have proof that these Clauses on unfair dismissal are so weak as to be practically meaningless in the view of many independent legal observers.[22]

Lord Bernstein made a similar observation: 'moreover, as I read the Bill, as soon as the employer shows a "good reason", which need not be a "fair" reason, the

19 For example: HC Deb vol 876 cols 1692–737 (11 July 1974); HC Deb vol 904 col 581W (4 February 1976) (Mr Kimball); HC Deb cols 655–7W (6 March 1979) (Mr Dodsworth).
20 HC Deb vol 963 col 1547 (8 March 1979).
21 HC Deb cols 655–7W (6 March 1979).
22 HC Deb vol 813 cols 1281–84 (16 March 1971).

burden of proof shifts to the employee. What chance has an employee against a mighty, powerful employer?'[23] These concerns led to an amendment introduced by the government at the report stage in the House of Lords, which led to the enactment of section 24 of the Industrial Relations Act 1971. This section introduced a two-stage process for determining the unfairness of a dismissal, with different rules about the burden of proof operating at each stage. Section 24(1)(a) requires the employer to establish the reason for dismissal and subsection (b) requires a consideration of whether in the circumstances of the claim the employer acted fairly in treating his reason as a sufficient reason for dismissing the employee. Labour accepted this amendment, with Lord Delacourt-Smith expressing Labour's position as follows:

> My Lords, this amendment is not an easy one for those of us who are not deeply experienced in legal matters to appreciate, but I am fortified by the assurance of the noble and learned Lord, which naturally I accept, that its intention and effect is to place beyond any doubt at all the proposition that the onus of proof is on the employer to establish that the dismissal was a fair one.[24]

In practice, however, the burden of proof was only partially placed upon the employer under section 24 of the Conservatives' 1971 legislation, as the employer had to prove the reason for the dismissal but not necessarily that the dismissal was a fair one.[25] Under section 24(1)(b) the employee had to bear the evidentiary burden of making out a prima facie case of unreasonableness. This situation was clarified by Labour via section 57(3) of the Employment Protection Consolidation Act 1978, which unequivocally placed the burden on the employer to satisfy the tribunal that the employer acted reasonably in treating the reason for dismissal as sufficient. In a subsequent debate on the Employment Protection Acts, the Conservative Opposition criticised this, saying that it required 're-examination',[26] but Labour defended it on the basis that 'only the employer can know the reasons why he has dismissed a worker. For that reason alone it would be sufficient and proper to place the burden of proof on the employer'.[27] However, only a short while later in 1980, the onus of proof was amended once again, with the Conservative government placing the burden of proving the reasonableness of dismissal equally between employer and employee.[28]

By 1979 it was clear that the unfair dismissal system had become a point of division between Labour and the Conservatives, with the former advocating a system premised on protecting employees' job security and the latter advocating

23 HL Deb vol 318 cols 1380–519 (13 May 1971).
24 HL Deb vol 321 col 744.
25 Mark Freedland, 'The Burden of Proof in Claims of Unfair Dismissal' [1972] ILJ 20.
26 HC Deb vol 963 col 1547 (8 March 1979).
27 HC Deb vol 963 col 1614 (8 March 1979).
28 Employment Act 1980 s 6.

a system responsive to the needs of business and of facilitating job creation. Crucially, neither party called for the abandonment of statutory unfair dismissal, as both maintained that the system was useful in achieving industrial justice. However, while there was political agreement over the notion of industrial justice as the basis of the United Kingdom's unfair dismissal system, the emerging divisions as to how to achieve this in substance, present in the parliamentary debates between 1974 and 1979, indicated the growing willingness by the Conservatives to enlarge the notion of industrial justice in dismissal to include a new concern with how to remedy the disadvantage faced by employers, not just employees.

The emergence of an argument of principle against unfair dismissal law

Davies and Freedland observe that an argument of principle against unfair dismissal legislation emerged with the election of the Thatcher Conservative government in 1979.[29] They mark the origins of this argument in a 1979 Conservative working paper which revealed a new agenda of amending laws 'where they damage small businesses – and larger too – and actually prevent the creation of jobs'.[30] The argument of principle against employment legislation protecting against unfair dismissal represents a departure from the broad consensus which existed for most of the 1970s supporting the enactment of unfair dismissal legislation. According to Davies and Freedland, in mounting the argument of principle against unfair dismissal, 'the substantive formulation of the right was left largely untouched, but the conditions of access to that right became more stringent'.[31]

While not left untouched, the statutory unfair dismissal system avoided a full-frontal attack to its legitimacy during the years of the Conservative government (1979–97). Prime Minister Margaret Thatcher's famous statement about social security, 'there is no society', could perhaps have been uttered about job security, 'there is no unfair dismissal'. However, the Conservative government did not go through with its intention of abolishing the jurisdiction altogether,[32] as scaling back the unfair dismissal system was only a sideline concern of the Conservative government's labour law agenda. The driving force behind the Conservative government's industrial relations reforms was economic policy and a desire that the labour market operate free of the perceived obstacles created by trade unions. The government's strategy for achieving this was articulated in the 1985 White Paper 'Employment: The Challenge for the Nation', which provided a platform for the government to justify its existing policies and future program of reform for the deregulation of the labour market.[33] This White Paper sought to reorient

29 Davies and Freedland (n 2) 200.

30 Department of Employment, 'Proposed Amendments to the Employment Protection Legislation' (1979) Working Paper [1], set out in IRLIB 146 (10 October 1979) 3.

31 Davies and Freedland (n 2) 200.

32 Department of Employment, 'Building Businesses . . . Not Barriers' (Cmnd 9794, 1986).

33 Department of Employment, 'Employment: The Challenge for the Nation' (White Paper, Cmnd 9474, 1985).

labour law so that its central concern was fostering employment through the formula of a free market economy. As stated in the White Paper's Introduction, 'the key contribution of Government in a free society is to do all it can to create a climate in which enterprise can flourish, above all by removing obstacles to the working of markets, especially the labour market'.[34] The stated impetus for this White Paper was the high unemployment facing the economy, which the Thatcher government believed was caused by the failure of the jobs market. Following this White Paper, reforms were implemented that restricted the right to strike, constrained the ability of trade unions to organise members and to bargain effectively, and eliminated closed shops.[35] Thus, the Conservative government's industrial relations reforms were primarily concerned with damaging the power of collective labour, and so the unfair dismissal system, albeit weakened, was not subject to a concerted attempt to eliminate it altogether.

Despite not being the main target of the reform agenda, the Conservative government did mount an argument of principle against the unfair dismissal system. This case rested upon acknowledging the need for protection for unfairly dismissed workers whilst simultaneously arguing that such protection should not stymie managerial prerogative or job creation. Despite a brief recognition of the need for 'proper protection for workers', the overarching emphasis of the White Paper was on limiting 'over-burdensome regulation', as 'too much regulation can make employing people not only expensive but also time-consuming and complicated, and a company may then hesitate before taking on more workers'.[36] According to the government, 'the most significant worry'[37] in terms of employment protection regulation was unfair dismissal claims leading to industrial tribunal proceedings, which provided the basis for the government's efforts to reduce access to, and the quality of, remedies for unfair dismissal in the United Kingdom during their years in elected office.

Both prior and subsequent to the 1985 White Paper, there was significant reform to the unfair dismissal laws, although the Conservative government did not go through with its original intention of abolishing the jurisdiction altogether.[38] The government raised the qualifying period from its historic low of six months in 1979 back up to two years, at first for small employers and then from 1985 on a general basis. This was justified on the basis that 'this change will give a fair balance between the genuine concern of employers about becoming too easily embroiled in claims, and maintaining full protection for all employees with any significant length of service'.[39] This focus on increasing the qualifying period so that an employee had to be employed for two years before an application could

34 Ibid 1.
35 For a detailed look at the labour market policies of the Thatcher and Major governments between 1979 and 1997, see: Simon Deakin and Gillian Morris, *Labour Law* (4th edn Hart, Oxford 2006) 30–42.
36 Department of Employment (n 33) 14.
37 Ibid 21.
38 Department of Employment (n 32).
39 Ibid 21.

be brought was a clear attempt to restrict access to the unfair dismissal system, as it extended the period in which an employer could terminate a worker's employment without legal ramifications. Such an extended period is unnecessary if the rationale of a period of a qualification is to ensure that the employer's positive impression of a person during the recruitment process is validated by the person's performance on the job. Arguably, two years is not needed in order to assess a person's suitability. The government's enactment of a two-year qualifying period demonstrates that they prioritised business needs above protecting workers' job security.

The Conservative government not only constrained access to the unfair dismissal jurisdiction but also reduced the size of the award that could be given by a tribunal. In 1980 the two weeks' pay minimum for the basic award was abolished and tribunals were instructed to reduce compensation according to the conduct of an employee prior to dismissal. The failure to index the compensation limit meant that by 1994 the maximum possible remedy was only £11,000, when it should have been almost £28,000.[40] Significant procedural hurdles were introduced as a disincentive to bringing an unfair dismissal application, including the possibility of being made to pay a pre-hearing deposit as a contribution to the employer's costs.[41] The justification for this was the desire to 'deter ill-founded claims': this was the first time arguments of vexatious litigation were seriously mounted in the debate over unfair dismissal legislation.[42] In 1980 a 'pre-hearing assessment' stage was introduced to weed out the weakest cases, which the Advisory, Conciliation and Arbitration Service (ACAS) reported was unhelpful in its work of conciliation.[43] Ironically, whilst these measures were instituted to deal with the perceived problem of vexatious litigation, their very existence sought to embed this perception further and legitimise the fear of it in the minds of British employers. This galvanising of employers and in particular the small business lobby was highly effective in cementing the emergence of an argument of principle against unfair dismissal and, according to Davies and Freedland, 'commanded the active sympathy and support of 1980s governments'.[44] Writing in the mid-1980s, Wedderburn was extremely sceptical about whether this fear of vexatious litigation in the unfair dismissal jurisdiction was legitimate, citing research to suggest that it did not act as a deterrent to recruitment and arguing that a mere perception that the unfair dismissal system unfairly favours employees and prevents legitimate dismissals 'is a poor basis for legal policy'.[45]

40 Linda Dickens, 'Individual Statutory Employment Rights Since 1997: Constrained Expansion' (2001) 24 ER 619, 622.
41 Employment Act 1989 (UK).
42 Department of Employment (n 30) 23.
43 ACAS (1984), cited in KW Wedderburn, *The Worker and the Law* (3rd edn Penguin, Harmondsworth 1986) 259.
44 Davies and Freedland (n 2) 556.
45 Wedderburn (n 43) 260.

The Conservative government (1979–97) was also influential at an international level in developing an argument of principle against unfair dismissal legislation. Despite the impact of the International Labour Organization's Termination of Employment Recommendation 1963 (No 119) on the Donovan Commission in formulating its conception of unfair dismissal and on the subsequent introduction of a right to unfair dismissal in British individual employment law, during the negotiations for the updating Convention (No 158) and Recommendation (No 166) on Termination of Employment at the Initiative of the Employer, the government sought to reduce the protective quality of international unfair dismissal law.[46] In particular, the United Kingdom's government mounted strong resistance to the proposal that standards previously contained in the form of a recommendation should be replaced by a convention, as the latter is conceived to directly influence national legislation while the former acts more as a guideline influencing national policy over time.[47] The government also tried, albeit unsuccessfully, to convince the ILO that the new provisions on burden of proof would be more appropriate in the recommendation than the convention in an attempt to dilute the influence these provisions would have on British unfair dismissal law. Consistent with their resistance during negotiations, the government rejected the final convention and recommendation when they were adopted by the ILO in 1982.

The Conservative government's regulatory approach to unfair dismissal law between 1979 and 1990 cast a long shadow and its effects are still being felt today – a subject to which I will turn in the last section of this chapter. Whilst its central reform was to double the qualifying period, the mounting of an argument of principle against the unfair dismissal system during the 1980s was significant, as it ended the bipartisan political consensus that unfair dismissal protection was desirable. As Davies and Freedland write of the 1980s, 'labour law began to move out of the zone of "social law" and worker protection and became part of a larger and rather different vision of labour market regulation in the interests of a free market economy'.[48] At this time, new concerns with reducing the regulatory burden on business, deterring vexatious claims and protecting small business were used to prompt reform to unfair dismissal law. This was worlds apart from its original anchorage as a statutory scheme to protect employees' job security.

46 Brian Napier, 'Dismissals: The New ILO Standards' (1983) 12 ILJ 17.

47 For details of the comments received by the Committee of Experts, see: Committee of Experts, 'Termination at the Initiative of the Employer' (International Labour Conference, 68th Session, 1982). The comments made by the government of the United Kingdom are contained in a letter (6/OS 319/81) sent from the Department of Employment in December 1981.

48 Paul Davies and Mark Freedland, *Towards A Flexible Labour Market: Labour Legislation and Regulation since the 1990s* (OUP, Oxford 2007) 5.

The emergence of an argument of principle against tribunal resolution of unfair dismissals disputes

Whilst the Conservative government of 1979–90 advocated stronger deregulation of unfair dismissal law, under the Conservative government of 1990–97 led by Prime Minister John Major, the Conservative position became one of supporting the efficient dispute resolution of unfair dismissal disputes. The focus was not upon eliminating state intervention in the employment relationship but ensuring that where regulation existed it was administered efficiently. This view recognised that some government intervention was necessary to achieve justice but that this intervention should require as little interference with managerial prerogative as possible and should not operate as a burden on employers. This position meant that whilst the Conservative government of 1990–97 recognised the possibility that employees could be unfairly dismissed, this was tempered by a desire to ensure that tribunals achieved efficient resolution of unfair dismissal disputes with minimum cost to the taxpayer and disruption to business. The government's 1994 Green Paper 'Resolving Employment Rights Disputes: Options for Reform' was highly significant in augmenting the argument of principle against the unfair dismissal system to an argument against tribunal resolution of unfair dismissal complaints and identifying the key agenda items for the ensuing decade.[49] This Green Paper highlighted four key ideas, which subsequent New Labour governments largely adopted. First, there was a preoccupation with achieving efficient dispute resolution and marginalising the traditional worker-protective goals of the unfair dismissal system. This focus on efficient dispute resolution became part of the 'Third Way' agenda trumpeted by New Labour. The second idea focused on encouraging in-house dispute resolution as a mechanism for avoiding tribunal cases. This idea was central to the Conservative government of 1990–97 promoting a more efficient operation of the contract of employment to resolve disputes between employers and employees. The third idea was clear preference for conciliation and other non-tribunal alternatives for resolution of disputes, and the fourth was the official recognition of the perceived problem of vexatious litigation undermining the efficiency of the tribunal system. All four themes were identified in the 1994 Green Paper but continued to influence reform of the unfair dismissal jurisdiction by New Labour after 1997. With regard to unfair dismissal law, there was a high level of continuity between Majorism and Blairism. This section discusses these trends in some depth and explores the normative assumptions behind them.

The Conservative government's argument of principle against the unfair dismissal system led to reconsideration of the tribunal system's viability and purpose. By the early 1990s the government saw the tribunal system as costly and inefficient. In its 1994 Green Paper the government sought to 'review the operation of the industrial tribunals with a view to identifying any changes which

49 Department of Employment, 'Resolving Employment Rights Disputes: Options for Reform' (Consultation Paper, Cmnd 2707, 1994).

would help them to cope with an increasing volume and complexity of cases with reduced delays, while containing demands on public expenditure'.[50] The terms of this review were explicitly oriented to reducing the costs of the tribunal system and increasing the efficiency of its operation. The government chose to focus on improving the standard of service provision by reducing delays as the objective of the review. In so doing, what the government chose *not* to focus on is noteworthy. The review did not seek to achieve greater fairness in tribunal outcomes, or a better review of dismissal decisions, or a balance to managerial prerogative given the increasing absence of a collective presence in the workforce.

Nor was there recognition that the Green Paper's terms of reference represented a shift from the original anchorage of the tribunal system in a primary concern with workers' claims to job security.[51] In fact, this was masked by the government's open acknowledgement and support for the continuing relevance of the Donovan Commission's prescription of tribunals as being 'easily accessible, informal, speedy and inexpensive'.[52] However, perhaps this oft-quoted phrase of the original prescription of tribunals was somewhat misleading about their intended operation in 1968. This prescription of the tribunal system, which has survived since 1968 and is still relied on in the present debates over the unfair dismissal system, focused solely on the need for efficient dispute resolution. Yet this phrase, and the government's decision to rely upon it in 1994, makes no mention of *why* tribunals were established in the first place, or the perceived need in 1968 for an equitable means of providing dispute resolution. As I mentioned in the preceding chapter, the Donovan Commission recognised that for many workers 'dismissal is a disaster'[53] and that a tripartite tribunal system was necessary given the negative consequences for dismissed employees and the concern that collective bargaining outcomes were unequal, leaving many employees unprotected from unfair dismissal because of the lack of collective bargaining arrangements overall.[54] The Donovan Commission's recognition of the need for the tribunal system to provide remedies in the case of unfair dismissal was obscured by the discourse on efficient dispute resolution favoured by the government in its 1994 Green Paper.

Given the framing of the review of the tribunal system in chapter 1 of the Green Paper, the Major Conservative government's findings in the remainder of the paper are unsurprising. In chapter 3, the government reviewed expenditure trends and influences in the tribunal system, finding that the percentage of cases coming to hearing within twenty-six weeks was well below the efficiency target of 80 per cent and that the cost of daily tribunal hearings was around £966. Chapter 4 outlined the government's preference for resolving unfair dismissal complaints in-house as 'any reductions in the caseloads of the tribunals

50 Ibid 4.
51 Report of the Royal Commission on Trade Unions and Employers' Associations (Cmnd 3888, 1969) 162.
52 Ibid 5.
53 Ibid [526].
54 Labour Party, 'In Place of Strife' (Cmnd 3888, 1969) [103].

and ACAS which might result from such measures would assist towards reducing delays and improving the quality of service provided to the public'.[55] There was a key normative assumption in the government's argument that caseload reduction prima facie leads to improved service provision. Whilst this may be true in terms of dealing with cases expediently, which no doubt saves the public purse and assists applicants and employers in resolving their dispute sooner, *other* measures of quality service provision, such as dealing with cases fairly, informally and consistently, are conspicuously absent from this assumption.

Another assumption that deserves critique was the view expressed in the 1994 Green Paper that conciliation of unfair dismissal disputes was preferable to tribunal resolution. In chapter 5 the government acknowledged that 'a major theme of the review has been the desirability of increasing the number and proportion of complaints resolved without recourse to a tribunal hearing'.[56] After cataloguing the benefits of conciliation, at no point did the Green Paper attempt to discuss the drawbacks of this method. In stating the advantages of conciliation it did not break down the advantages and disadvantages in terms of employers and employees as it assumed a mutuality of interests: 'conciliation offers the potential for the dispute to be settled relatively quickly, informally and without publicity. No charges are made. ACAS is independent and its services are impartial and confidential. Conciliation is voluntary and can be declined by either party.'[57] The Green Paper did not take into account how the conciliation settlement was reached, what pressure was placed on the parties to settle or even whether settlement was a fair outcome in situations where one party was wholly in the wrong. Collins has criticised the British conciliation process because there is no duty for the conciliation officer to ensure that the settlement is fair to the employee, as his central duty is to prevent applications proceeding to trial.[58] Relying on Dickens' study of the system, Collins has argued that 'in most cases the officer assists a bargaining process and advises the employer to accept the employee's first offer'.[59] The Green Paper did not attempt to grapple with these critiques and instead recommended an expansion of conciliation and the development of voluntary arbitration as an alternative to tribunals.

While it is difficult retrospectively to pinpoint when a particular concern became central to the mainstream agenda, the 1994 Green Paper was significant in that it contained strong rhetoric about the perceived problem of vexatious litigation. This paper extended the mentioning of this issue of vexatious litigation in the 1985 White Paper and explicitly lent it credibility and prominence in an official government policy document. In chapter 6 on tribunal procedure the Green Paper referred to anecdotal evidence from chairs of the tribunal seeking

55 Department of Employment (n 49) 20.
56 Ibid 27.
57 Ibid.
58 Hugh Collins, *Justice in Dismissal: The Law of Termination of Employment* (Clarendon Press, Oxford 1992) 138.
59 Ibid.

the power to dismiss cases out of hand. The paper commented favourably on the introduction of the concept of 'reasonable prospects of success' to the unfair dismissal jurisdiction the previous year, and there was consideration of a proposal requiring the applicant to place a bond with the court to discourage frivolous claims and encourage pre-tribunal settlement.[60] This paper marked the origins at an official governmental level of significant pressure, continuing to the present day, for governments to reform the unfair dismissal system based on the perception that it is failing to process unfair dismissal applications efficaciously.

In perceiving a problem with vexatious litigation, the Conservative government focused on the need to inoculate business owners from unfair dismissal law, animated by a desire to protect business owners, in particular small employers, from vexatious litigation and over-burdensome regulation. This agenda was revealed both in the government's attempts at unfair dismissal law reform and beyond. For example, Part One of the Deregulation and Contracting Out Act 1994 specifically refers to 'reducing burdens on business' and 'cutting red tape'. Also in the Disability Discrimination Act 1995 the government included a number of caveats to the protection afforded in the Act, including barring those working for small businesses employing fewer than twenty employees. As Davies and Freedland note, 'this exclusion, highly controversial at the time, was justified by spokesmen for the government partly by the general rhetoric of minimising burdens upon businesses, especially small ones'.[61]

In conclusion, the Major Conservative government's 1994 Green Paper was highly significant in its articulation of an argument of principle against tribunal adjudication of unfair dismissal. The government chose to reduce the number of unfair dismissal disputes reaching tribunals. Although the government was rejected at the subsequent general election, its approach to unfair dismissal and its preoccupation with achieving efficient dispute resolution within businesses and the efficient operation of the tribunal system strongly resonated and were largely continued by the unfair dismissal policies of New Labour, and have been renewed in earnest by the Cameron government since 2010. In the ensuing section, I argue that New Labour's election did not bring about a return to the traditional formulation of labour law, with its original concerns of worker protection and industrial harmony. Instead, the argument of principle against unfair dismissal was initially moderated, and then continued, by New Labour.

The evolution of the argument of principle against tribunal resolution of unfair dismissal disputes

This section explores the ideas underpinning New Labour's reform of unfair dismissal law during its three terms in office. I argue that it is possible to discern in New Labour's reforms the development of an argument of principle against tribunal

60 Department of Employment (n 49) 23.
61 Davies and Freedland (n 48) 33.

resolution of unfair dismissal disputes which formed the basis for its promotion of both alternative dispute resolution and localised resolution of unfair dismissal disputes. Instead of articulating a renewal of the Donovan Commission ideals of protecting job security and guaranteeing justice in dismissal, New Labour consistently showed its willingness to be persuaded by employer dissatisfaction with tribunal resolution of unfair dismissal complaints and implemented reforms limiting access to the tribunal system and the quality of the remedy that could be awarded. New Labour's catchcry was 'better regulation', which encompassed two principal ideas for how state intervention in the labour market should operate. The efficient administration of justice was an idea which emerged under the previous government through the recognition that employees' right to challenge their dismissal should be tempered by the public policy goal of ensuring that tribunals achieved efficient resolution of unfair dismissal disputes with minimal cost to the taxpayer. The second notion inherent in New Labour's 'better regulation' position was a desire to reduce the adverse impact of regulation upon business. 'Better regulation' was distinct from Labour's concern in the 1970s with the achievement of industrial justice as New Labour's objective was to ensure that the competitiveness of business was not hampered by the rights of individuals to pursue a claim against employers. In New Labour's view, employee rights existed but disputes arising from the existence of these rights should be resolved expediently and with as little disruption to the employer as possible. At its essence, 'better regulation' was about the pursuit of labour market regulation in the interests of a free and competitive market economy.

Whilst Labour of the 1990s had a different industrial relations agenda to traditional Labour of the 1970s, the self-proclaimed title of 'New' Labour belied the significant degree of continuity between the Blair government and its Conservative predecessor. As this section will show, both the previous Conservative government and the New Labour governments were primarily concerned with achieving resolution of unfair dismissal disputes within businesses. They each sought to address the perceived legalism, costs and delays associated with the tribunal system. New Labour's two 'new' ideas for managing the perceived inefficiencies of the unfair dismissal system, namely arbitration and a mandatory three-step process for resolving disputes, were both first canvassed in the 1994 Green Paper commissioned by the previous government.[62] New Labour, like its Conservative predecessor, took the view that business could be relied upon to be the arbiter of substantive fairness. This was an idea that would have been antithetical to the Labour Party of the 1970s, which believed in the inherent conflict between the agenda of employers and employees necessitating trade union protection of employees, or at the very least state intervention to safeguard individual rights. As Mr Janner, a Labour member of the House of Commons, stated during the debates about whether the protection afforded by the unfair dismissal system should be strengthened:

> This is what the law is for – to set up minimum standards with which people should comply and with which, unfortunately too many do not comply.

62 Department of Employment (n 49).

> Therefore, I suggest that these laws should not be regarded as a burden on industry but should be welcomed by industry as providing the best environment in which to produce better treatment and conditions for and relations with their own work forces.[63]

New Labour, like its Conservative predecessor, was susceptible to arguments that the unfair dismissal system was burdensome upon business and sought to reform the system to minimise this burden. In each term that it was in government, particularly in its second and third terms, New Labour continued the argument of principle and did not seek to carve a new trajectory for the tribunal system beyond the ideas conceived by the preceding government. The industrial justice paradigm in which the unfair dismissal system was born evolved by the 1990s into a new paradigm where the primary concern was the pursuit of labour market regulation in the interests of a free and competitive market economy. This resulted in New Labour seeking to deregulate unfair dismissal law in favour of promoting alternative dispute resolution and localised dispute resolution of unfair dismissal disputes.

The establishment of 'partnership' between employers and employees as a central plank of New Labour's industrial relations platform was built upon its belief in the employment contract as a bargain between equals. In the Prime Minister's Foreword to New Labour's 1998 White Paper 'Fairness at Work' Mr Blair stated, 'this White Paper is part of the government's program to replace the notion of conflict between employers and employees with the promotion of partnership'.[64] The foreword reflected a New Labour agenda of economic success driving social prosperity as it conceived that the achievement of a modern enterprise economy would lead to social gains across the board. Accordingly, the three pillars of New Labour's industry policy, as articulated in 1998, were the pursuit of strong markets, modern companies and the creation of an enterprise economy. Conspicuously absent was any explicit concern with workers' rights or protection of workers in this perceived need to create a modern, free market British economy. In 'Fairness at Work' the government stated that 'individual contracts of employment are not always agreements between equal partners', implying that the contract of employment *was* a bargain between equals in the majority of cases.[65]

The promotion of the metaphor of partnership to represent the employment relationship revealed the government's belief that the contract of employment was negotiated individually between the employer and the employee. In its view, the employee was not in need of special assistance or support, as the contract of employment would then be tailored to meet the individual circumstance of the parties: 'Employers and workers in the UK generally determine the detailed terms and conditions of employment at a local or individual level . . . [which] subject to minimum standards – leads to greater diversity of employment patterns because

63 HC Deb vol 923 cols 42–114 (20 December 1976).

64 Department of Trade and Industry, 'Fairness at Work' (White Paper, Cmnd 3968, 1998) 3.

65 Ibid 21.

the outcome is dependent on millions of individual decisions by individual workers and employers'.[66]

In this way, New Labour's concept of partnership was used to represent the idea that in a modern company the employee is no more disadvantaged than the employer, as the imperative on the latter to make the business competitive and profitable is akin to the investment of time, energy and resources that the individual employee makes in his or her job. According to New Labour, both the employer and the employee are partners in making the business a success, and the contract of employment reflects the equitable nature of this partnership. Collins has argued that the election of the Blair government represented the emergence of a new theme of 'regulating the employment relation for competitiveness' with the dominant objective being 'to improve the competitiveness of businesses so that they may survive and prosper in an increasingly global economic system'.[67] He characterised New Labour's quest for competitiveness as 'facilitating changes in the organisation of the workplace that entails a transformation in the nature of the employment relation'.[68] As such, whilst 'traditional' Labour sought to protect workers from their perceived disadvantaged position under the contract of employment, 'New' Labour believed regulating the employment relationship for competitiveness would create a partnership between employers and employees that would reduce the need for statutory protection. New Labour conceived the contract of employment as a symbiotic contract in which 'the basic framework of incentives is designed as two simultaneous principal and agent relations' and although 'the interests of management and workers conflict . . . in order to maximise their self-interest they have to engage in extensive cooperation with each other'.[69] New Labour viewed employees as the ultimate beneficiaries of the Third Way agenda of creating a partnership model at work based on fostering competitiveness because this agenda would provide employees with greater access to employment opportunities and protection through a minimal safety net.

So what was the impact of New Labour's idea of partnership on unfair dismissal law? First and foremost, New Labour's belief in the ability of employers and employees to work together as partners led to the deregulation of unfair dismissal law through the resolution of unfair dismissal disputes within businesses and without recourse to tribunals. New Labour experimented with a variety of reforms during its three terms in office, each with the primary objective of diverting unfair dismissal applicants away from the tribunal system in favour of localised dispute resolution. This deregulation was intended to encourage employers and employees to rely upon the contract of employment to resolve unfair dismissal

66 Treasury, 'Full and Fulfilling Employment: Creating the Labour Market for the Future' (2002) 42–43.

67 Hugh Collins, 'Regulating the Employment Relation for Competitiveness' (2001) 30 ILJ 17, 18.

68 Ibid 34.

69 Hugh Collins, 'Is There a Third Way in Labour Law?' in Joanne Conaghan, Richard Fischi and Karl Klare (eds), *Labour Law in an Era of Globalization* (OUP, Oxford 2002) 459–60.

disputes within the workplace. New Labour's reforms with this objective were: the establishment of a right to a support person, the introduction of an arbitration scheme for resolving dismissal disputes, the experiment with a mandatory three-step dismissal procedure, the introduction of pre-claim conciliation and the simplification and revision of the ACAS Code. In each of these reforms, discussed below in chronological order of implementation, it is possible to discern a New Labour argument of principle against tribunal resolution of unfair dismissal disputes and a desire to resolve these disputes locally within the workplace and without recourse to tribunals.

Arbitration

The first attempt to dissuade unfair dismissal applicants from proceeding to the tribunal system was in 1998 with the establishment of a voluntary arbitration route that precluded users from making a subsequent tribunal claim. The government supported the Employment Rights (Dispute Resolution) Act 1998 introduced by Lord Archer of Sandwell, which created a new voluntary arbitration scheme developed by ACAS to settle unfair dismissal claims. The government intended that arbitration would 'create a change of culture so that individuals who have been dismissed unfairly are more likely to get their jobs back'.[70] Under the Act, ACAS was asked to devise a scheme for providing a voluntary, alternative route for parties to eschew the traditional tribunal route and rely upon ACAS to adjudicate their unfair dismissal claim. The arbitral option came into effect in May 2001 and was aimed to provide parties with the opportunity to resolve their dispute via binding arbitration.[71] Nonetheless, this scheme failed in its purpose to create cultural reform of the unfair dismissal system by diverting applications away from tribunals, as less than fifty applications were dealt with during its first four years in operation.[72] Many reasons have been suggested for the unpopularity of the scheme, such as over-formalisation, the restriction of the scheme to two jurisdictions when the vast proportion of tribunal cases are multi-jurisdictional and the fact that ACAS arbitration is voluntary and both parties must agree to this route.[73]

The right to accompaniment

Another attempt by New Labour to resolve unfair dismissal disputes within businesses and without recourse to tribunals was the establishment of a right to accompaniment within the disciplinary process. This right to accompaniment, established

70 Department of Trade and Industry (n 64) 15.

71 Jill Earnshaw and Stephen Hardy, 'Assessing an Arbitral Route for Unfair Dismissal' (2001) 30 ILJ 289.

72 ACAS, 'Making More of Alternative Dispute Resolution' (2005) Policy Discussion Paper No 1.

73 Department of Employment (n 49).

in sections 10 to 14 of the Employment Act 1999, was for meetings that could result in a disciplinary sanction and for meetings at which an employer was examining an employee complaint about either a statutory or common law duty owed by them to a worker. The right to support in the disciplinary process was not intended to be a right to legal representation. The government expressly stated in 2003 that it wished to maintain the distinction between the right to a companion and the right to a representative, with only the former being allowed to attend meetings under the law.[74] The government rejected calls to widen the role of the 'companion' into that of a 'representative' and clarified that a companion was only there to 'provide support and not to substitute for the worker'.[75] Thus, the companion could only be one of two people: either a fellow worker or a trade union official.

The constraint against representation and the limitation on whom the employee could bring as a support person reflected New Labour's belief that the contract of employment was a bargain between equals. They argued that whilst the employee may be in need of support from a co-worker or unionist, there was no need for representation or legal advice because the employee was not in a disadvantaged position when responding to the employer's questioning. Nonetheless, low levels of unionisation mean that not all employees have the option of bringing a union official as their companion, whilst asking a fellow employee to attend the meeting as a support person widens the number of those involved in the dispute and could perhaps place the fellow employee in a difficult position. In some situations, it may be difficult for the employee to find a fellow employee who could act as a support, especially where the employee has been a victim of widespread bullying or harassment in the workplace. Two cases expanded this right to accompaniment into a right of representation for the purpose of workplace disciplinary proceedings.[76] In both cases the employee was accused of sexual misconduct, but the employer refused the employee's attempt to bring a legal representative to the disciplinary meeting. However, the court held that a right to representation does arise where the employee's right to practise his or her profession is in jeopardy. Furthermore, if the employer's own disciplinary policy allows the employee to bring a legal representative and the employee's contract of employment incorporates the employer's policies into the contract, then the court will deem this as providing the employee with a right to representation.[77]

The three-step dismissal procedure

The clearest indication of New Labour's desire to promote localised dispute resolution was its intention to legislate to imply a mandatory three-step dismissal

74 Department of Trade and Industry, 'Review of the ERA 1999: Government Response to the Public Consultation' (DTI, 2003) [3.43].

75 Ibid.

76 *Kulkarni v Milton Keynes NHS Trust* [2009] IRLR 829; *R (on the application of G) v Governors of X School* [2010] IRLR 222.

77 *Kulkarni v Milton Keynes NHS Trust* [2009] IRLR 829.

procedure into all contracts of employment. This proposed reform was aimed to aid the efficient internal resolution of unfair dismissal disputes and reflected the government's desire to safeguard job security through facilitating workplace cultural reform. In the government's view, the fact that there existed an estimated 6 million out of 25 million employees who had no access to internal dispute resolution procedures needed to be addressed. Of particular concern to them was the situation within small businesses, which tended to be less formalised in their approach to dismissal. In response to this state of affairs, the government proposed, via clause 30 of the Employment Bill 2002, that a three-step statutory procedure to govern the dismissal of employees be implied into all contracts of employment. Lord Wedderburn recognised that the implication of statutory dismissal procedures into the employment contract was a 'novel legal innovation' because a process for resolving unfair dismissal disputes would become an inherent part of the employment relationship based on the contract.[78] According to Lord Falconer from the government, this contractualisation of unfair dismissal law would equalise the balance of power between employers and employees under the contract of employment by providing that both parties would have to follow a set procedure in resolving disputes: 'Clause 30 ensures that the statutory procedures will be incorporated into contracts as an implied term where employers do not already operate more elaborate procedures. This means that all employers and all employees will henceforward have disciplinary and grievance procedures.'[79]

Despite New Labour's fanfare in unveiling clause 30 to the Parliament, it was never enacted. Rather predictably, New Labour responded to the concern of employers that clause 30 would lead to the qualifying period being circumvented, as applicants could pursue a breach of contract claim in the common law courts, and that this would lead to an increase in litigation. In its response to the government's consultation on the dispute resolution regulations in 2004 the Confederation of British Industry (CBI) argued that clause 30 would represent a 'huge bureaucratic burden' for business and would lead to an increase in tribunal cases.[80] The Trades Union Congress (TUC) made a contrasting submission to the government's consultation process as the unions supported the statutory procedures being implied into employment contracts on the basis that this would universalise systems for resolving disputes within the workplace before they escalated. The TUC argued that abandoning clause 30 represented a squandered opportunity, as 'what is being proposed now is a fast-track, sacking procedure that is so confusing it will probably lead to an increase in tribunal cases rather than the desired decrease'.[81] In choosing to defer the introduction of clause 30, New Labour indicated, once again, how susceptible it was to reforming labour

78 HL Deb vol 632 col 263 (21 March 2002).
79 Ibid.
80 HL Deb vol 658 col 93 (23 February 2004).
81 Trades Union Congress, 'Government Squandered Reform of Work Dispute System' (media release, 16 December 2003).

law according to employer arguments about business efficiency and controlling regulatory burdens.

Despite the abandonment of clause 30, New Labour soon revived its plan to impose statutory dismissal procedures on employers, continuing a New Labour agenda of achieving efficient internal dispute resolution so as to minimise the number of employees accessing the tribunal system. The rules, which all employers had to follow in dismissal, were established in the Employment Act 2002 (Dispute Resolution) Regulations 2004. This required the employer to inform the employee of their intention to dismiss via a letter, to set up a meeting with the employee and to allow the employee to appeal this decision. Failure to follow this three-step procedure rendered the dismissal 'automatically unfair', and as a result the employer risked the compensation awarded after a tribunal finding of unfair dismissal being increased by between 10 and 50 per cent. In the case of gross misconduct of which the employer possessed incontrovertible evidence, an employer could dismiss an employee by using a modified version of this procedure which involved writing to the employee about his dismissal and giving him the right to an appeal.

This statutory dismissal procedure affected all businesses regardless of their size but was particularly conceived with small business in mind, given the attempt to streamline and simplify the requirements upon employers carrying out a dismissal. According to the minister responsible for implementing the new system, Ms Patricia Hewitt, the three-step dismissal procedure would 'provide further incentives for business to raise productivity and to follow best practice'.[82] However, the procedure introduced in the 2004 regulations represented a minimalist approach to dispute resolution and was not indicative of best practice in this area. The paucity of the requirements reflected a New Labour government unwilling to place too heavy a burden upon employers but instead seeking to foster a consistent and coherent approach to dismissal across businesses of varied shapes and sizes. Despite many proposed amendments during the Grand Committee stage to introduce more obligations upon employers seeking to dismiss staff,[83] the government was committed to a streamlined three-step dismissal procedure, arguing that 'the purpose of the statutory procedures is simply to require suitable minimum procedures to be followed when employees are dismissed'.[84] As a result, there was no requirement that multiple warnings be given or that an employee be given a chance to improve performance, or any obligations upon employers to provide training and development. Instead, the three-step procedure was remarkable for its brevity. During the Grand Committee debates Lord McCarthy characterised the primary purpose of the statutory dismissal procedures as being to reinstate the power of managers to dismiss staff:

> Behind all this . . . is nothing less than the philosophy of the treatment of workers. It is not an accident that the idea of a statutory procedure – the

82 HC Deb vol 375 col 869 (27 November 2001).
83 HL Deb vol 632 cc 263–320 (21 March 2002).
84 HL Deb vol 632 col 225 (20 March 2002).

> essential elements of the statutory procedure – comes from the employers. Discipline is seen as something that can be done by anybody. Discipline does not have to be consistent; it does not have to be based on your past record; and it does not have to be placed on anything else but an exercise of managerial prerogatives. That is the philosophy. The alternative is that discipline could be consistent, that it should fit itself to the individual and that as far as possible it should be remedial and constructive. This is the philosophy of personnel management, not the philosophy of managerial prerogatives.[85]

Thus, it could be argued that the significance of New Labour's commitment to the achievement of localised dispute resolution through the statutory dismissal procedures was that it represented a movement towards allowing internal regulation of unfair dismissal disputes. Flanders argues that internal rules are set by 'managements seeking to bring the work behaviour of employees under greater control'.[86] This is consistent with the traditional doctrine of managerial prerogative which provides that it is an employer's right to organise their work arrangements in such a way as to ensure the most efficient operation of the business.

Whilst New Labour's statutory dismissal procedures were imposed by the government upon business, the paucity of the requirements under these procedures gives credence to the argument that the real effect of this reform was to increase managerial prerogative during the dismissal process and to deter applications away from the tribunal process. The United Kingdom government believed that the three-step procedure would lead to a significant reduction of 23 to 31 per cent in the caseload of employment tribunals.[87] The statutory grievance procedure was clearly aimed at reducing the number of employment tribunal claims by forcing employers and, most importantly, employees to exhaust internal procedures before resorting to an employment tribunal claim.[88] As such, failure to comply with the procedure and exhaust internal mechanisms for resolving unfair dismissal disputes prevented an employee from accessing the tribunal system. Despite New Labour's legislation to limit the number of claims through the use of statutory codes, case law from 2004 to 2008 reveals a willingness by tribunals to assess whether compliance with the code was genuinely achieved, which, in fact, led to increased litigation after the introduction of the statutory grievance procedure.[89]

85 HL Deb vol 632 col 270 (21 March 2003).
86 Allan Flanders, *Industrial Relations: What Is Wrong with the System?* (Faber & Faber, London 1965) 15–18.
87 Employment Bill, Explanatory Note, paras 179, 197; Standing Committee F (12.2.02) col 93 (Minister of State for Employment and the Regions, Alan Johnson).
88 Department of Trade and Industry, 'Routes to Resolution' (DTI, 2001).
89 Michael Gibbons, 'Better Dispute Resolution: A Review of Employment Dispute Resolution in Great Britain' (Department of Trade and Industry, 2007).5. In fact, Gibbons found the so-called 'red tape' and administrative burden associated with the statutory grievance procedure to be particularly onerous on small businesses, which typically have less sophisticated human resource management techniques. He found that 'small businesses tend to have a more informal culture and the requirement to express problems in writing could act as a trigger for greater conflict' ([2.11]).

The introduction of statutory dismissal procedures was accompanied by another reform, in section 98A of the Employment Act 2002, which provided that the failure by the employer to follow a 'procedure' other than the three-step procedure in relation to the dismissal of an employee shall not by itself make the employer's action unfair if the employer shows that the dismissal would have occurred if the procedure had been followed. By reinstating the so-called 'no difference rule', employers were no longer required to comply with their own internal procedures governing dismissal or even the government's more expansive ACAS Code of Practice.[90]

Within two years the statutory dismissal procedure was reviewed and decreed a failure, prompting its repeal. In 2006 the government commissioned a review of the dispute resolution system by Michael Gibbons, aimed at assessing the extent to which the 2002 reforms of the unfair dismissal system had met their objectives. The Gibbons Review found a number of problems with the new statutory dismissal procedure. Firstly, the number of unfair dismissal cases proceeding to tribunals had not fallen and there was even anecdotal evidence to suggest that the new statutory grievance procedures had created 30 per cent more cases.[91] Secondly, employers consulted during the Gibbons Review frequently referred to problems with formalisation as employers feared that if anything was left informal they would be open to claims, while employees wanted to ensure that a grievance was registered so that it could be used in a tribunal claim if need be. Gibbons found this so-called 'red tape' and administrative burden to be particularly onerous on small business with less sophisticated human resource management techniques. He found that 'small businesses tend to have a more informal culture and the requirement to express problems in writing could act as a trigger for greater conflict'.[92] Thirdly, the Gibbons Review found that the statutory grievance procedure was too complex and tended to 'drive users to seek legal advice earlier', resulting in further complication and escalation of the dispute.[93] As a result of this critique, the Gibbons Review recommended the repeal of the three-step statutory grievance procedure, which the government subsequently carried out through its Employment Act 2008. This repeal of the statutory dispute resolution procedures was on the basis that these procedures amplified the administrative responsibilities of employers and had unintended consequences which outweighed their benefits.[94]

90 *Kelly-Madden v Manor Surgery* (2006) UK EAT 0105/06/1910. See further, Astrid Saunders, 'Expanding the "No Difference" Rule in the Law of Unfair Dismissal' (2007) 36(3) ILJ 355.

91 Gibbons (n 89) 5.

92 Ibid [2.11].

93 Ibid [2.7]–[2.19].

94 For more on this repeal process and the debates over the Employment Bill 2008, see: Astrid Saunders, 'Part One of the Employment Act 2008: "Better" Dispute Resolution?' (2009) 38 ILJ 30.

Reforms to conciliation

Another effort to resolve disputes without tribunals was New Labour's encouragement of conciliation. In an attempt to resolve more disputes at the conciliation stage, the Blair government introduced fixed conciliation periods. The Employment Act 2002 (Dispute Resolution) Regulations 2004 introduced provisions which in most cases restricted the ACAS duty to conciliate to a fixed period of seven or thirteen weeks. After that period was over, ACAS could still exercise a statutory power to conciliate, but ACAS used that power sparingly because it viewed the clear intention of Parliament to be that conciliation outside the prescribed periods should be made available in only exceptional circumstances. This experiment with fixed conciliation periods was short-lived, with the review conducted by Michael Gibbons in 2006 finding that limiting when conciliation was available to the parties had not led to more or earlier resolution of disputes about individual employment rights. ACAS's own research suggested that opportunities for resolving cases were frequently lost because parties were unable to access the conciliation service after the fixed period had expired.[95] The feedback of ACAS conciliators was that fixed periods led to a damaging focus by the parties on the minutiae of process, including timescales which hampered the flow of the conciliation dialogue and the critical exploration of the substantive issues in the dispute.[96]

The decision to repeal fixed conciliation periods in 2008 was accompanied by a new experiment with pre-claim conciliation, also with the aim of resolving employment disputes at an earlier stage and prior to tribunal. ACAS considers that this reform has been far more successful in resolving disputes by encouraging conciliation. Pre-claim conciliation is initiated when one of the parties calls the ACAS helpline to discuss a problem in the workplace or a complaint that this party is considering making before the tribunal. The ACAS phone operator then gives the caller advice on how to proceed and with the party's acquiescence calls the other party in order to arrange a conciliation meeting. This entire process hinges upon the willingness of both parties to participate, but there are unwritten incentives: earlier resolution of the dispute, the offer of free conciliation, a low-cost alternative to bringing a claim before the tribunal and the opportunity to keep the employment relationship going instead of it breaking down completely. By the end of December 2010 almost 20,000 potential employment tribunal claims had been referred for pre-claim conciliation since the service was launched in April 2009, with demand for the service continuing to rise.[97] ACAS has estimated that resolving a claim through its early conciliation service saves a

95 ACAS, 'Response to the Government Consultation: Resolving Disputes in the Workplace' (ACAS, 2007) 22.

96 Ibid.

97 ACAS Research and Evaluation Section, 'Evaluation of the First Year of ACAS' Pre-Claim Conciliation Service' (Research Paper by ORC International, 2011).

business on average £5,200 when staff time and legal costs are factored in.[98] In a survey of users carried out for ACAS by an independent research organisation, businesses said they found disputes resolved through pre-claim conciliation typically occupied less than a day of management time, whereas cases settled after an employment tribunal claim has been made take up on average five days of management time.[99] This increased to nine days for those that reached a tribunal hearing. Similar time savings were evident for employees.[100] Seventy-five per cent of calls were converted into pre-claim conciliations, with 80 per cent of these avoiding recourse to the tribunal system; 88 per cent of users of the helpline said that they would use the service again.[101] Thus, the ability of the pre-claim conciliation process to resolve disputes earlier and divert employers and employees away from the tribunal system has been largely successful in achieving New Labour's objective of facilitating partnership in the workplace by preventing the escalation of conflict so as to reduce the need for tribunal adjudication.

The simplification of the ACAS code

Another attempt by New Labour to facilitate localised dispute resolution was a revised ACAS Code of Practice identifying the key procedures employers should follow in dismissing an employee. The ACAS Code of Practice has existed as part of the United Kingdom's unfair dismissal system since 1977 but in 2008 the government revised this code to provide incentives for better dispute resolution practices. Prior to 2008, whilst the code was never legally binding, it could be taken into account by industrial tribunals in determining what was to be expected of a reasonable employer. However, under section 3 of the Employment Act 2008, tribunals were given discretionary powers to increase or decrease awards by 25 per cent if parties failed to comply with the revised ACAS code. The question before the tribunal was whether the employer or employee acted unreasonably in failing to comply with the code. Birrell has criticised the equality of arms envisaged by the unfair dismissal system post-2008, as he suggests the placement of behavioural obligations upon both employers and employees assumes a false parity:

> Whilst for many employees this brush with their employer's disciplinary or grievance procedures is likely to be their first, for the employer it is merely the latest episode of a familiar continuum. The stakes too are very different: for an employer it is about eliminating undesirable conduct or behaviour, for an employee it represents a threat to their livelihood.[102]

98 Ibid.
99 Ibid.
100 Ibid.
101 Ibid.
102 Ian Birrell, 'The Employment Act 2008' (Institute of Employment Rights, 2009) 7.

The revised ACAS Code of Practice was considerably shorter than its predecessor code and diluted the right to unfair dismissal as it existed in British labour law prior to 2004. In contrast to previous versions, the 2008 code gave no guidance to tribunals as to the behaviour of a 'reasonable' employer and came close to replicating the minimalist standard set by the three-step statutory dismissal procedure introduced in 2004. The revised 2008 code did not require proportionality in deciding on the appropriate action,[103] and paragraph 17 of the new code did not compel the employer to take account of the employee's record or length of service. The detailed guidance provided by the new Guide to Discipline and Grievances at Work[104] had no legal standing, as tribunals were not required to take the non-binding guidance into account when determining the fairness of a dismissal.

The extension of the argument of principle against tribunal resolution of unfair dismissal disputes and a new inclination towards employment at will

The election of the Conservative-Liberal Democrat coalition government in 2010 and the Conservative government in 2015 led to an extension of the unfair dismissal reforms of New Labour and a reorientation in a new direction towards employment at will for certain employees. Consistent with previous Conservative governments, the emphasis has been on reducing the regulatory burden of unfair dismissal law, which is perceived as stymieing job creation and business efficiency.[105] At the outset of its first term in office, the Cameron government announced an 'Employment Law Review' to last for the length of the Parliament and a 'Red Tape Challenge', both of which sought to rebalance employment law in favour of employers.[106] This resulted in the Cameron government extending the argument of principle against tribunal resolution, through reforms to tribunal composition, a renewed emphasis on conciliation, a reduction of the cap for compensatory awards and reforms to filing fees and costs orders. These initiatives, as I will explain, have rendered the tribunal system less effective in protecting job security.

However, the Cameron government has gone beyond merely limiting the operation of tribunals in adjudicating unfair dismissal disputes. New reforms have been canvassed, some of which have been implemented, which prevent external review

103 ACAS Code of Practice on Discipline and Grievance (2004) [17].
104 Ibid.
105 Davies and Freedland (n 2) 200.
106 For an overview, see: Department for Business, Innovation and Skills, 'Flexible, Effective, Fair: Promoting Economic Growth Through a Strong and Efficient Labour Market' (BIS, 2011). On the issue of balance, see 'Employers' Charter' (27 January 2011, updated 15 March 2012) [12]; Department for Business, Innovation and Skills, 'Employment Law Review: Annual Update 2012' (BIS, 15 March 2012): 'the UK has one of the most lightly-regulated labour markets amongst developed countries. . . . But we are not complacent' [1.16].

of dismissal decisions, thereby neutering the unfair dismissal jurisdiction altogether. The doubling of the qualifying period leaves employees in an employment-at-will situation for the first two years of employment. The introduction of settlement agreements and employee-owner status are two reforms which may not be widely taken up but are symbolic of a new inclination towards employment at will, as they induce employees to sign away their rights to use the unfair dismissal system. Finally, the no-fault dismissal proposal, although ultimately scuttled, was indicative of a desire to prevent external review of an employer's dismissal decision in return for a predetermined monetary payment. This combined attack had for a long time been considered impossible: 'the right not to be unfairly dismissed seems to have been thought to be too well entrenched to invite a frontal assault'.[107] Yet, increasingly, arguments about economic efficiency and business burdens seem to be eroding – and in some cases eradicating altogether – the ability of the United Kingdom's unfair dismissal law to protect job security.[108]

Reforms to tribunals' resolution of unfair dismissal disputes

Through a series of reforms, the Cameron government has both continued and extended the argument of principle against tribunal resolution of unfair dismissal disputes. These have been mainly oriented towards imposing barriers to access for prospective claimants and seeking to deter claims being made in the first place.

A key driver for the Cameron government has been its concern with vexatious litigants taking advantage of an unfair dismissal system that allows tribunal claims to be lodged fairly easily and simply. In the government's view, 'the risk is that the fear of being faced with tribunal claims impedes growth because businesses become too cautious to hire people or to address capability issues in the workforce'.[109] The perceived ease in launching a claim and the associated costs founds the government's concern over costs.[110] It argues that in order to manage the risk of an unfair dismissal claim, employers need to reserve money because, when a claim is lodged, employers face an average of £3,700 worth of time and legal representation costs.[111] This is despite the fact that only 5 out of every 100 of those who claim succeed, and the median compensation award has

107 Davies and Freedland (n 48) 200.

108 The UK's Institute of Employment Rights has described these reforms as 'the biggest change to employment law since the introduction of the right to claim unfair dismissal forty years ago': D Renton and A Macey, *Justice Deferred: A Critical Guide to the Coalition's Employment Tribunal Reforms* (IER, Liverpool 2013) 50.

109 Department for Business, Innovation and Skills, 'Employment Law 2013: Progress on Reform' (BIS, 2013) 24.

110 E Jordan, AP Thomas, JW Kitching and RA Blackburn, 'Part A: Employer Perceptions and the Impact of Employment Regulation' (Employment Relations Research Series 123, BIS, 2013) 18.

111 Department for Business, Innovation and Skills, 'Facilitating Settlement Agreements: Impact Assessment' (BIS, 2012) 9–10.

been around £4,000–£5,000 for the last six years.[112] From an employer perspective, despite the fact that few unfair dismissal claims succeed, risk management requires resources to be shelved in case of an unfair dismissal claim, and when one does arise, even if it is fairly baseless or even if it succeeds and results in a modest payment of compensation, a substantial amount of resources are needed to respond to the claim in the first place. One survey shows that even though employers are four times more likely to win an unfair dismissal claim, 26 per cent still settle even when told they can win.[113] These statistics reinforce concerns over wasted expenditure when it comes to employment claims. In response, the government has introduced filing fees, hearing fees and fees for appeals.[114] The rationale behind the introduction of fees for launching claims is that those who use government services should pay for them[115] and that they may lead to a reduction in overall tribunal claims as individuals will consider more carefully whether an unfair dismissal claim is meritorious and likely to succeed.

A central component of the argument of principle against tribunal resolution of unfair dismissal disputes is that claims should be resolved earlier and without recourse to tribunals. Motivating the Cameron government in favour of early dispute resolution is a concern with the costs for businesses of defending a tribunal claim. A new reform is that prior to submitting a tribunal claim, prospective claimants must report their claims details to ACAS.[116] During the period of conciliation, an ACAS officer must endeavour to promote settlement of the dispute; however, conciliation is not mandatory, as either party can refuse to participate.[117] The government believes that fostering greater reliance on conciliation can reduce the number of tribunal claims by 12,000 and remedy the present situation where only one third of claimants attempt conciliation before proceeding to the tribunal.[118] The government's decision to encourage ACAS involvement in resolving unfair dismissal claims addresses business concerns insofar as employers have not had to put out any money at this point and the claims may potentially be averted. However, the emphasis on ACAS's role in the 'settlement' of disputes is of concern, as it places pressure on the ACAS conciliator to achieve a certain outcome irrespective of the merits of the case and of whether such an outcome is fair or just to the parties. Consistent with my argument is Hepple's analysis: 'The

112 Department for Business, Innovation and Skills, 'Unfair Dismissal Compensatory Awards: Impact Assessment' (BIS, 2012) 7.
113 CBI/Harvey Nash, 'Facing the Future: CBI/Harvey Nash Employment Trends Survey 2012' (2012) 25–6.
114 Employment Tribunals and the Employment Appeal Tribunal Fees Order 2013 SI 2013/1893.
115 Department for Business, Innovation and Skills, 'Resolving Workplace Disputes: A Consultation' (BIS, 2011) 49.
116 Enterprise and Regulatory Reform Act 2013 s 7, adding section 18A to the Employment Tribunals Act 1996.
117 Department for Business, Innovation and Skills, 'Ending the Employment Relationship: Government Response to Consultation' (BIS, 2013) 108.
118 Department for Business, Innovation and Skills (n 117) 21–2.

motivation for . . . early conciliation is the avoidance of tribunals, rather than improving employment practices in the workplace. The perverse impact is that employers have an incentive to become less compliant with legal requirements because they can buy off those who may make complaints.'[119]

Furthermore, given that the legislative framework still enables either party to opt out of conciliation, it is unlikely that the numbers of claimants seeking conciliation will increase to any substantial degree.

Another reform aimed to deter unfair dismissal claims is the reduction in the cap for compensation awards.[120] Although opposed by the trade unions which responded to the government consultation, this reform was supported by 89 per cent of the employer respondents on the basis that it would lead to more realistic expectations for claimants and reduce the potential risk for employers by guaranteeing that awards cannot exceed an employee's annual earnings.[121] The government justified the new cap on the basis of the 'unhelpful perceptions' of employers and the 'unrealistic expectations' of employees.[122] The real motivation for the cap seems to have been to send a signal to employees that they should not bring claims or should settle prior to a tribunal hearing because tribunal awards are low.[123]

The rationale for tripartite tribunal composition was outlined in the previous chapter, but this has now been disregarded for unfair dismissal disputes, as the industrial (non-legal) members are no longer required, unless the employment judge decides otherwise.[124] This change was made despite the views of the majority of employment judges that the industrial members add value in unfair dismissal cases.[125] This reform has rendered tribunals more like ordinary civil courts,[126] as the industrial members were key to ensuring that the tribunals took into account industrial realities and understood the power imbalance in the employment relationship. Scholars like Kahn-Freund[127] and Wedderburn[128] have

119 Bob Hepple, 'Back to the Future: Employment Law under the Coalition Government' (2013) 42 ILJ 203, 218. See also: Jordan et al. (n 110) 32.
120 Enterprise and Regulatory Reform Act 2013 s 15.
121 Department for Business, Innovation and Skills (n 117) 7.
122 Ibid.
123 Department for Business, Innovation and Skills, 'Findings from the Survey of Employment Tribunal Applications 2008' (Employment Relations Research Series No 107, 2010) 26; see Department for Business, Innovation and Skills (n 112) 12, Table 4, which shows that 99 per cent of unfair dismissal claimants and 95 per cent of all employees earn less than £72,300 annually.
124 Employment Tribunals Act 1996 (Tribunal Composition) Order 2012 SI 2012/988.
125 Susan Corby and Paul L Latreille, 'Tripartite Adjudication – An Endangered Species' (2012) 43 IRJ 94.
126 Corby and Latreille have explained this as 'institutional isomorphism': Susan Corby and Paul L Latreille, 'Employment Tribunals and the Civil Courts: Isomorphism Exemplified' (2012) 41 ILJ 387.
127 Sir Otto Kahn-Freund was the author of ch 15 of the Report of the Royal Commission on Trade Unions and Employers' Associations (n 51), which set out a scheme for British labour courts.
128 KW Wedderburn, 'Labour Law: From Here to Autonomy' (1987) 16 ILJ 1.

argued that tripartite tribunal composition was essential in securing the autonomy of labour law from the general law and to entrust adjudication of disputes to specialist labour courts with judges who grasped industrial relations.

Reforms to neuter unfair dismissal law altogether

The proposal for a no-fault dismissal scheme to replace unfair dismissal law was the first initiative of the Coalition government which revealed an intention of peeling back the statutory superstructure protecting job security in favour of an employment-at-will situation. Although ultimately abandoned by the government, the no-fault dismissal proposal can be characterised as a particularly aggressive mode of what Davies and Freedland have characterised as '*deep* deregulation', 'in the particular sense of abolition or scaling down of an existing worker-protective measure or regime'.[129] This is because the substantive effect of the no-fault dismissal proposal would have been to replace an employee's right to external review of an employer's dismissal decision with a statutorily determined monetary amount of compensation.

In October 2011, a report commissioned by the Coalition government was leaked to a national newspaper, revealing proposals for the abolition of employees' rights to claim unfair dismissal in certain circumstances.[130] As an alternative, the report proposed introducing a 'no fault' scheme, whereby employers could dismiss employees without giving them a reason and by making only basic redundancy and notice payments.[131] The no-fault dismissal recommendation contained in the Beecroft Report hinged on the notion that the current protection enjoyed by workers was stifling British enterprise, allowing employees to 'coast along' and preventing employers from hiring new staff in case they proved to be 'unknown quantities' that proved impossible to sack.[132] Adam Beecroft, a venture capitalist and the report's author, wrote of the 'terrible impact of the current unfair dismissal rules on the efficiency and hence competitiveness of our businesses, and on the effectiveness and cost of our public services'.[133] His solution was to abolish unfair dismissal law and instead offer workers a pay-off, a system that operated in some parts of Europe such as Belgium. The compensation, or 'compensated no fault dismissal', was designed to soften the blow of losing one's job but did not provide an individual with the right to external scrutiny and review of an employer's dismissal decision.

Significant public concern led to pressure on the Coalition government to reject the Beecroft Report's proposal of no-fault dismissal. Following the leaking of the Beecroft Report, media stories suggested that the Liberal Democrats were

129 Davies and Freedland (n 48) 242–43.
130 'Give Firms Freedom to Sack Unproductive Workers, Leaked Downing Street Report Advises' *Daily Telegraph* (London 25 October 2011); Elizabeth Rigby, 'Workplace Proposals are a Step too Far', *The Financial Times* (London 26 October 2011).
131 Ibid.
132 Adam Beecroft, 'Report on Employment Law' (2011) 4–5.
133 Ibid.

opposed to introducing no-fault dismissal and the Coalition government distanced itself from the no-fault dismissal proposal. The impact assessment for the consultation on workplace disputes stated that 'a complete end to enabling employees to bring a case for unfair dismissal on any grounds, as some business commentators have suggested, was not considered as it could have had a significant impact on employee protection'.[134] Instead the Coalition government decided to consider the compensated no-fault dismissal proposal for micro firms with ten employees or less,[135] launching a call for evidence about the proposal[136] and releasing a research paper on the topic.[137] In September 2012 the government announced its rejection of the no-fault dismissal idea for micro firms because of significant opposition to the proposal,[138] with only lukewarm support from the business lobby.[139] Many submissions questioned the evidential basis of alleged economic benefits of the no-fault dismissal proposal, arguing that it might stymie growth because micro businesses may be less inclined to grow above the threshold, as this would disqualify them from access to no-fault dismissal as a dismissal mechanism.[140]

Although the no-fault dismissal idea was abandoned, the Coalition government moved on to other proposals to reduce the regulatory burden of unfair dismissal law through shifting certain types of employees into an employment-at-will situation. One mechanism which achieves this, although its limited take-up by business suggests its impact is more symbolic than real, is the legislative provision for a new employee-shareholder status. Consultation on this proposal[141] followed a surprise announcement by the chancellor of the exchequer that a new employment status was to be considered by the government, that of 'employee-owner', justified according to a triple win formulation:[142]

> Today we set out proposals for a radical change to employment law. It's a voluntary three-way deal. You the company: give your employees shares in the business. You the employee: replace your old rights of unfair dismissal

134 Department for Business, Innovation and Skills and Tribunals Service, 'Resolving Workplace Disputes: A Consultation – Impact Assessment' (BIS, 2011) 147.

135 HC Deb col 26WS (23 November 2011).

136 Department for Business, Innovation and Skills, 'Latest Developments' (2012).

137 Department for Business, Innovation and Skills, 'Dealing with Dismissal and "Compensated No Fault Dismissal" for Micro Businesses' (BIS, 2012).

138 Department for Business Innovation and Skills, 'Dealing with Dismissal and "Compensated No Fault Dismissal' for Micro Businesses, Government Response' (BIS, 2012).

139 The British Chamber of Commerce (BCC) reported, 'The views we received from our membership on the specific proposal under consultation were mixed, with many saying that it would be of only minimal benefit to most firms' (BCC response, p 7). The Confederation of British Industry noted that increased hiring by small firms was not a guaranteed fruit of compensated no fault dismissal and stated that 'substantial research on this area is required' (CBI response, p 6).

140 Ibid 9.

141 Department for Business, Innovation and Skills, 'Consultation on Implementing Employee-Owner Status' (BIS, 2012).

142 The 'employee-owner' status was rebadged as 'employee-shareholder' during legislative enactment.

> and redundancy with new rights of ownership. And what will the government do? We'll charge no capital gains tax at all on the profit you make on your shares. Get shares and become owners of the company you work for. Owners, workers, and the taxman, all in it together.[143]

Despite trade union opposition,[144] the distinct lack of enthusiasm from business,[145] and the fraught parliamentary process,[146] a new section 205 was inserted into the Employment Rights Act 1996, providing that 'employee-shareholders' forgo unfair dismissal rights in return for shares in the business.[147] This 'employee-shareholder' model is a form of no-fault dismissal, in one sense, as it permits arbitrary dismissal in return for an employer gaining shares in the business.[148] It seems doubtful that this is an adequate substitute for job security rights, as under the proposal shares do not confer any real voting or voice rights. As with no-fault dismissal, the employee-owner proposal allows the employer to dictate dismissal outcomes. This removal of the external adjudicative mechanism providing review of an employer's dismissal decision represents a serious erosion of job security, leaving an employee entirely vulnerable to an employer's prerogative to dismiss without cause.

Another reform that seeks to replace unfair dismissal law for certain employees is the amendment to settlement offers to provide an incentive for the early resolution of disputes.[149] The government inserted a new section 111A to the Employment Rights Act 1996 in order to make settlement negotiations inadmissible in an unfair dismissal proceeding except where there has been improper conduct.[150] This followed concern by business that employers feel unable to start discussions with employees about ending their employment by means of a settlement agreement without a formal dispute. The crucial difference between this reform and the no-fault dismissal proposal is that in the former, an employee consents to leave the business at a designated price, whereas no-fault dismissal enables an employer to force the employee to leave at a price stipulated by the legislation.[151]

143 George Osborne, 'Party Speech 2012' (Conservative Party Conference, Birmingham, 8 October 2012).
144 Trades Union Congress, 'Trading Rights for Shares' (TUC, 2012).
145 Department for Business, Innovation and Skills, 'Implementing Employee Owner Status: Government Response to Consultation' (BIS, 2012) 34.
146 Despite support during the early legislative stages from both Coalition parties, the proposal encountered opposition in the House of Lords and then later in the House of Commons. See: HC Deb col 186 (16 April 2013); HL Deb col 1278 (22 April 2013).
147 Growth and Infrastructure Act 2013 s 31.
148 For more, see Jeremias Prassl, 'Employee Shareholder "Status"? Dismantling the Contract of Employment' (2013) 42 ILJ 307.
149 Settlement agreements are consensual, legally binding documents which can be used to end an employment relationship. Typically, an employee will receive a severance payment, and perhaps a reference, in return for waiving the right to take a case to an employment tribunal on any grounds covered by the settlement agreement. See: Department for Business Innovation and Skills (n 117) 37.
150 Enterprise and Regulatory Reform Act 2013 s 14.
151 Department for Business Innovation and Skills, 'Ending the Employment Relationship: Consultation' (BIS, 2012).

However, the Coalition government's promotion of settlement agreements does open the door for unscrupulous employers to put undue pressure on vulnerable employees to give up their job security rights.

Although the two aforementioned proposals are concerning because they reveal the Coalition government's willingness to replace statutory unfair dismissal protection with a seemingly consensual employment-at-will situation for certain employees, the limited take-up of these reforms means their actual impact has been fairly negligible. This cannot be said of the doubling of the qualifying period, which has placed all employees in an employment-at-will situation for the first two years of their employment.[152] This has effectively removed an estimated 2.7 million workers (many of them young workers, migrants and women who work part-time) from unfair dismissal protection.[153] Addressing the argument for extension of the qualification period, Adrian Beecroft wrote of the difficulty employers had in making such an important determination within one year of employing an individual.[154] Similarly, both the Chambers of Commerce[155] and Federation of Small Businesses[156] have claimed that unfair dismissal law is one of the principal 'regulatory burdens' on business because it is weighted too far in favour of the employee. Despite the alleged economic efficiency and job creation justifications for the doubling of the qualifying period, scholars have been critical of the insufficient evidential basis for the reform. Hepple has argued that 'no evidence had been produced that increasing the qualifying period does lead to more jobs; indeed between 1999 and 2011, when the qualifying period was one year, 1.75 million new jobs were added',[157] and Ewing and Hendy have developed a powerful critique of the extended period.[158]

Conclusion

This chapter has shown how the trajectory of the United Kingdom's unfair dismissal law post-1971 has been to peel back the statutory superstructure regulating unfair dismissal. The 1970s did not see major reform to the unfair dismissal system but the parliamentary debates from this period reveal growing differences between Labour and the Conservatives about the length of the qualifying period, who should bear the burden of proof and the remedy of reinstatement. The election of the Conservative government in 1979 saw the emergence of an argument of principle against statutory protection of unfair dismissal. Whilst the government

152 Employment Rights Act 1996 s 108, as amended by the Unfair Dismissal and Statement of Reasons for Dismissal (Variation of Qualifying Period) Order 2012.
153 Hepple (n 119) 215.
154 Beecroft (n 132) 4.
155 British Chambers of Commerce, 'Employment Regulation: Up to the Job' (BCC, 2010) (available on British Chambers of Commerce website www.britishchambers.org.uk accessed 24 July 2013).
156 Federation of Small Businesses, 'Regulatory Reform: Where Next?' (FSB, 2012) (available on Federation of Small Businesses website www.fsb.org.uk accessed 24 July 2013).
157 Hepple (n 119) 215.
158 K Ewing and J Hendy, 'Unfair Dismissal Law Changes – Unfair?' (2012) 41 ILJ 115.

was unsuccessful in achieving its original intention of abolishing unfair dismissal law, it did reduce access to the tribunal system by substantially increasing the qualifying period and limiting the quality of the award that could be given by failing to index the compensation cap to inflation. For the subsequent Major and New Labour governments, the agenda became one of encouraging, or in some cases mandating, that employers and employees resolve disputes about dismissal themselves. This produced the deregulation of unfair dismissal law based on an argument of principle against tribunal resolution of unfair dismissal disputes. This deregulation of the unfair dismissal system overall has also led to new types of regulation seeking to prevent disputes about dismissal from escalating. Reforms such as pre-claim conciliation, arbitration, a right to accompaniment, a revised ACAS code and a three-step dismissal procedure were adopted on the basis that they would facilitate the settlement of disputes within businesses and prevent them from requiring tribunal resolution. The philosophy underpinning this preference for localised dispute resolution was one that conceived of the contract of employment as an equal bargain between the parties. According to this view, the traditional notion of the disadvantaged employee under the contract of employment is counterbalanced by the contemporary understanding of employer disadvantage because of the pressures facing business owners to remain competitive. These ideas have led to the peeling back of the statutory unfair dismissal superstructure established in 1971 because of renewed questioning of the place and legitimacy of statutory unfair dismissal protection for employees. This deregulation of unfair dismissal law has been continued and extended since the election of the Cameron government in 2010 and 2015. Further reforms have been made which seek to deter the making of claims and erect barriers to accessing the tribunal system.[159] This has been accompanied by a shift towards employment at will for certain employees through settlement agreements, employee-shareholder status and the introduction of a two-year qualifying period. These reforms have greatly undermined job security in pursuit of economic efficiency through reducing the perceived regulatory burden of unfair dismissal law upon employers.

As I will describe in the coming chapters, a similar questioning of the foundations of unfair dismissal law in protecting job security has occurred in Australia. We will return to these themes in the final part of this book, which seeks to understand the contestation of normative ideas behind the convergent evolutionary dynamic of the United Kingdom and Australia's unfair dismissal laws despite their origins in divergent labour law traditions, and why there is an increasing convergence towards a US-style employment-at-will situation.

159 These reforms seem to have achieved their objective of deterring claims. The statistics for April to June 2014 show a 71 per cent drop in claims as against the same period in 2013: Tribunal Statistics Quarterly, April–June 2014, 11 September 2014. Nonetheless, recent empirical research suggests that it is not only unmeritorious or vexatious claims which have been weeded out, finding that 'pursuing a tribunal claim was an enormous struggle before fees were introduced. Now, many people are priced-out, as well as being put off by the real as well as imagined difficulties they will face': Eleanor Kirk, Morag McDermont and Nicole Busby, 'Employment Tribunal Claims: Debunking the Myths' (Policy Report 1, PolicyBristol Hub, Bristol 2015).

4 Australia – Part I

The journey to unfair dismissal law

Introduction

Australia's traditional labour laws were built upon the ideal of industrial peace. This idea was strongly associated with the work of Justice Henry Bourne Higgins, who as president of the Conciliation and Arbitration Court and through his highly influential writings sought to respond to Australian industrial relations questions through the lens of industrial peace. Industrial peace was developed as the overriding justification for the creation and continuing existence of the conciliation and arbitration mechanism. According to this perspective, the key to accessing employment protection was not issues concerning individuals but rather the collective economic and social vulnerability of employees.

Australia's commitment to industrial peace, achieved through prioritising collective industrial relations, was sustained until 1992. We can discover the reasons for the comparatively late arrival of unfair dismissal law in Australia through a closer examination of the commitment by the Australian industrial relations system to industrial peace. In turning our focus to why the conciliation and arbitration mechanism was so enduring over a period of ninety years, we can perhaps explain why unfair dismissal law was off the mainstream agenda for so long, and why, when it was introduced in the federal system in 1993, it relied upon a pre-existing collective mechanism to resolve unfair dismissal disputes.

Despite reliance upon the traditional conciliation and arbitration system to adjudicate federal unfair dismissal disputes, the underlying policy orientation of the federal unfair dismissal system introduced in 1993 was industrial justice and industrial fair play and not the traditional notion of industrial peace. Prior to 1993, the industrial peace tradition had, for the most part, attempted to achieve justice for individual employees through relying on unions and the collective mechanism of conciliation and arbitration, although from the 1970s on some Australian states introduced legislation to accord individual employees with unfair dismissal rights. With the unravelling of conciliation and arbitration more generally and with the introduction of a federal system premised on enterprise bargaining in 1993, there was a clear shift away from industrial peace as the normative basis of Australia's labour laws. This provided an opportunity to develop safeguards for individual rights even if violation of these rights was not especially threatening to industrial stability overall. Accordingly, the notion of industrial justice for individuals, which had its origins in the state unfair dismissal systems, began to emerge as the justification for Australia's federal unfair dismissal system after 1993. This concept encompassed recognition of universal access to the system regardless of union affiliation and was closely interwoven with the uniquely Australian phenomenon of industrial fair play.

This chapter is structured in three parts: first, there is an analysis of the writings of Justice Henry Higgins in establishing industrial peace as the normative foundation of labour law in Australia; second, a discussion of how industrial peace became embedded in Australia's institutional framework; and third, an examination of how the dominance of industrial peace in Australia's labour laws influenced the development of unfair dismissal law both at a state and federal level.

As I will explain in this chapter, the Australian momentum for the development of unfair dismissal law in the federal system was delayed by the foundation of the traditional system in industrial peace. The federal conciliation and arbitration system was seen as the primary way to settle disputes and achieve industrial peace. Under this system, a federal unfair dismissal law was conceived as mostly unnecessary or even inappropriate. It was only when the federal labour law system was reformed after 1993 and the normative dominance of the industrial peace tradition whittled away that statutory unfair dismissal protection was introduced at a federal level in Australia.

Justice Higgins and industrial peace

Writing extrajudicially, in a series of three papers published in the *Harvard Law Review*,[1] Higgins outlined his belief that industrial peace provided the best explanatory basis for Australian labour law.[2] For Higgins, industrial peace was not a utopian endpoint but a realistic appraisal of the emergence of Australian labour laws relating to conciliation and arbitration, and the development of minimum wages and conditions. The title of his three papers, 'A New Province for Law and Order', was significant: it conveyed his belief that the new realm to be rescued from anarchy was that of industrial matters. Higgins believed that labour law could be used to achieve orderly industrial relations. This was not support for the juridification of labour law but rather a desire for the law to create the conditions for the parties to resolve their differences without undue legalism and recourse to the common law courts. He supported the continuing existence of a

1 These papers were subsequently published as part of a compilation of Higgins' writings: Henry Bourne Higgins, *A New Province for Law and Order* (Constable & Co, London 1922).

2 For an account of Higgins' life and work, see John Rickard, *HB Higgins: The Rebel as Judge* (Allen & Unwin, Sydney 1984).

conciliation and arbitration system that was inexpensive to maintain and did not rely on lawyers to present the cases of the parties.[3]

As president of the Conciliation and Arbitration Court (CAC), it is unsurprising that Higgins saw conciliation and arbitration as the optimal framework for guaranteeing industrial peace.[4] In an oft-quoted passage reflecting on the first ten years of conciliation and arbitration, Higgins observes that 'the process of conciliation, with arbitration in the background, is substituted for the rude and barbarous processes of strike and lock-out. Reason is to displace force; the might of the State is to enforce peace between industrial combatants.'[5]

For Higgins, industrial peace could not be achieved through traditional industrial weapons.[6] In his view, these were too contingent upon the relative strength of the parties, and as such, fair outcomes could not be guaranteed. More importantly, the process of ascertaining the stronger party necessitated industrial action, often of a protracted nature. Instead, his view was that the parties should be compelled to discuss their differences, in the first instance with a conciliator and, if this failed, with an arbitrator who would assess the relative merits of their positions.[7] Higgins argued that the commitment to achieving industrial peace trumped managerial prerogative. In listing the many aspects of the employment relationship that the employer is free to regulate, such as choosing employees, using technology, developing new methods, organising their finances and so on, Higgins stated that 'the Court leaves every employer free to carry on the business of his own system so long as he does not perpetuate industrial trouble or endanger industrial peace'.[8] In this way, Higgins viewed industrial peace as a normative ideal that should trump both managerial and union decisions and judicial outcomes.

Key to the notion of industrial peace is recognition of the inherent inequality of the employment relationship. Failure of the industrial relations system to recognise this power imbalance and compensate for it was believed to result in industrial conflict. Higgins was of the view that an individual employee was relatively powerless to assert his or her desire for more favourable wages and conditions or to make complaints to the employer, as the latter could arbitrarily end the relationship. He was sceptical of the notion of freedom of contract, as he believed that an employer was in a strategically stronger position during the negotiation of employment contracts. In another oft-quoted passage, he stated this in no uncertain terms: 'the power of the employer to withhold bread is a much more

3 For example, Higgins supported legal provisions which allowed either party to refuse consent for the other to use a lawyer as he believed that union officials and employers should be responsible for articulating their positions before the Conciliation and Arbitration Court: Henry Bourne Higgins, 'A New Province for Law and Order' [1915] Harv L Rev 13.
4 The first president of the CAC was a member of the High Court, Justice O'Connor. The second president was HB Higgins, who was also appointed from the High Court.
5 Higgins (n 3) 14.
6 Ibid.
7 Ibid 91.
8 Ibid 21.

effective weapon than the power of the employee to refuse to labour. Low wages are bad in the worker's eyes, but unemployment, with starvation in the background, is worse.'[9]

In tandem with this notion of the disadvantage of the individual employee was Higgins' belief that it could be remedied by collective organisation. Accordingly, Higgins supported a state system which legitimised the presence of unions in the employment relationship so as to achieve industrial peace.[10] He felt this would minimise disruption because of individual complaints, as employers would develop a more consistent and equitable approach to managing their staff.[11] Higgins believed that 'complaints should be presented collectively by some responsible union' and that the best venue for this to occur was the Conciliation and Arbitration Court.[12] In his view, the primary purpose of the Court was to resolve disputes and that the Court's ability to determine wages and conditions was incidental to the central 'object of the Court' which was 'to preserve or restore industrial peace'.[13]

If recognition of unions was important to curing the defect of an unequal employment relationship, Higgins' methodology for ensuring unions would preference dialogue over strikes was the pursuit of industrial fairness as the means to achieving industrial peace. Said differently, according to this view, the aim of the Australian system was to achieve industrial peace via a method of industrial fairness. This is because if each party were accorded what is rightly theirs, they would have far less reason to engage in industrial action. In the most pivotal decision of the early Court to determine the minimum wage, Higgins adopted a standard based on 'the normal needs of the average employee, regarded as a human being living in a civilized community'.[14] To determine 'normal needs', Higgins instigated a process where the Court looked at real life household budgets to determine the cost of living in each of the Australian states. The Court decided to adopt a 'living wage' rather than a minimum wage – the former takes into account not just the skill level of the work being performed but the costs associated with the worker's ordinary existence.[15] In justifying the development of a 'living wage' culture whereby 'fairness' and 'reasonableness' in remuneration was determined according to human need, Higgins stated:

> Industrial peace cannot be secured without recognition of the principle which the Court has adopted, that each worker must have, at the least, his

9 Ibid 25–26.
10 Ibid 23.
11 Ibid.
12 Ibid 13.
13 Higgins (n 1) 31.
14 *Ex Parte HV McKay* (1907) 2 CAR 1.
15 For an analysis of the origins of the living wage in Australia see: John Portus, *Australian Compulsory Arbitration, 1900–1970* (2nd edn Hicks Smith & Sons, Sydney 1971) 24–26. See also: Keith Hancock, 'The First Half Century of Australian Wage Policy' (1979) 21 J Indust Relations 129.

> essential human needs satisfied, and that among the human needs there must be included the needs of the family. Sobriety, health, efficiency, the proper rearing of the young, morality, humanity, all depend greatly on family life, and family life cannot be maintained without suitable economic conditions.[16]

Higgins' rationale for a basic wage incorporating workers' needs to sustain their living conditions was inextricably linked to his commitment to industrial peace. He reached the conclusion that 'one cannot conceive of industrial peace unless the employee has secured to him wages sufficient for the essentials of human existence'.[17]

For labour lawyers, Higgins' conviction that Australia's industrial relations system should be based upon a theory of industrial peace was important because it had tremendous influence upon the outcomes of the CAC. Higgins was not merely a legal scholar but the president of the institution at the apex of Australian industrial relations. According to McCallum, 'during this forty year reign, Higgins was able to set his mark on the nature and scope of interest arbitration in Australia. No other arbitrator has been held in such esteem, nor has any other tribunal member possessed such influence'.[18] Higgins' leadership, combined with the support of successive federal and state governments, saw Australia develop an institutional framework to maintain industrial peace. This framework was highly interventionist but not legalistic. It was prescriptive as to the manner of solving disputes but sufficiently flexible as to their outcome. The following section explores how the institutionalisation of industrial peace in Australia's labour laws evolved over time.

The institutionalisation of industrial peace

The desire to institutionalise industrial peace arose from the protracted industrial battles of the 1890s. At the conclusion of the nineteenth century, the outcome of these battles was that the striking unions lost: the employers had successfully asserted their right to agree to terms and conditions of employment directly with their workplace without third party intervention.[19] However, the employers' victory around a contractual model of labour relations was short-lived. They might have succeeded if not for patrician liberals like Higgins, Charles Kingston, William Pember Reeves and Bernard Ringrose Wise, who advocated the resolution of collective labour disputes by final and binding interest arbitration supported by the state.[20] In the constitutional debates of the 1890s, these figures were prominent in

16 Higgins (n 3) 38–39.

17 Henry Bourne Higgins, 'The Future of Industrial Tribunals' *The New Outlook* (Sydney 8–9 April 1922) 6.

18 Ron McCallum, 'The New Millennium and the Higgins Heritage: Industrial Relations in the 21st Century' [1996] JIR 294, 295.

19 William Spence, *Australia's Awakening: Thirty Years in the Life of an Australian Agitator* (The Worker Trustees, Sydney 1909) 47–241; James Sutcliffe, *A History of Trade Unionism in Australia* (2nd edn Macmillan, Melbourne 1971) 90–167.

20 For a description of who these liberals were, and the role they played in leading to the introduction of compulsory arbitration in Australia, see: Stuart Macintyre, 'Neither Capital nor

influencing the agenda so that the industrial relations power accorded to the federal government through the Constitution explicitly mandated a power to create a system of conciliation and arbitration for interstate disputes.[21] The aim of this constitutional power was to facilitate industrial peace through the use of labour courts that would attempt to solve disputes through conciliating the conflict between the parties; but where conciliation failed, the labour courts were empowered to utilise final and binding interest arbitration to impose fair and reasonable conditions of employment upon the parties.[22] The outcome of the conciliation and arbitration process was an 'award' which bound the parties and guaranteed minimum employment rights. Each award listed those parties (employers and unions) bound by it and in the event of a breach by one of the parties award conditions could be enforced through the courts. An observation made almost one hundred years after the Constitution's formation by Justice Kirby of the High Court reveals why this constitutional grant of power establishing a system of conciliation and arbitration through section 51(xxxv) was so significant:

> It imported a safeguard, restriction or qualification protective of all those involved in collective industrial bargaining: employer and worker alike. It provided an ultimate constitutional guarantee of fairness and reasonableness in the operation of any federal law with respect to industrial disputes, including for the economically weak and vulnerable. . . . [T]hese values profoundly influence the nature and aspirations of Australian society, deriving as they did from a deep-seated constitutional prescription.[23]

This importation of fairness and reasonableness into the Constitution was seen as the means by which to guarantee industrial peace, culminating in the enactment of the *Conciliation and Arbitration Act 1904* (Cth). The primary rationale for the introduction of arbitration was to manage conflict in the wake of the protracted industrial battles of the 1890s.[24] As Prime Minister Alfred Deakin

---

Labour: The Politics of the Establishment of Arbitration' in Stuart Macintyre and Richard Mitchell (eds), *Foundations of Arbitration: The Origins and Effects of State Compulsory Arbitration, 1890–1914* (OUP, Melbourne 1989) 186–87; See also: Tim Rowse, 'Elusive Middle Ground: A Political History' in Joe Isaac and Stuart Macintyre (eds), *The New Province for Law and Order* (CUP, Sydney 2004).

21 *The Constitution* 1901 s 51(xxxv). Higgins proposed its wording at the Constitutional Convention of 1897. Although it was initially rejected at this convention, it was accepted at the Constitutional Convention of 1898. For more, see B Creighton and A Stewart, *Labour Law* (4th edn Federation Press, Sydney 2010) 33.

22 Orwell Foenander, *Industrial Conciliation and Arbitration in Australia* (Law Book Company of Australasia, Sydney 1959) ch 1.

23 *New South Wales and Others v Commonwealth* [2006] HCA 52 [530] (Kirby J).

24 DH Plowman, 'Forced March: The Employers and Arbitration' in Stuart Macintyre and Richard Mitchell (eds), *Foundations of Arbitration: The Origins and Effects of State Compulsory Arbitration* (OUP, Melbourne 1989) 135; Robert Drago, Mark Wooden and Judith Sloan, *Productive Relations? Australian Industrial Relations and Workplace Performance* (Allen & Unwin, Sydney 1992) 10–11.

observed in his second reading speech on the Conciliation and Arbitration Bill 1904, the realisation of industrial peace was a long-term objective of the conciliation and arbitration mechanism:

> It is not a matter of today or tomorrow – of the success of a single measure or device. It is the introduction of a new principle, which, when it has found its proper means of working and exerting its influence, will comprehend necessarily as great a transformation in the features of industrial society as the creation of the King's Peace brought about in civil society.[25]

This Act established the CAC, which was specifically charged with effecting reconciliation between parties to industrial disputes, with preventing and settling such disputes by amicable agreement and, if this were not reached, with preventing and settling such disputes by conciliation and arbitration.[26] The Australian Labor Party was also pivotal to the institutionalisation of industrial peace during the early years of the Federation, as it held the balance of power in several of the state and federal Parliaments and threw its support behind governments that advocated compulsory arbitration.[27] The appointment of Justice Higgins as the second president of the CAC in 1907 was also critical. Justice Higgins believed that freedom of contract was a 'misnomer' when applied to the individual contract between an employer and individual employee.[28] He developed a line of the Court's jurisprudence that explicitly accepted an inherent power imbalance in the employment relationship that could be remedied through recognition of collective organisations.[29]

Industrial peace came to be inextricably linked with the concept of industrial fairness. Key decisions of the CAC cemented the Court's role in the Australian psyche as safeguarding the lot of working people. This can be traced back to the decision of Justice Higgins in the *Harvester Case*, which had a profound effect on the wages and conditions of Australian workers and their families.[30] Whilst this decision has since been criticised for its institution of the male breadwinner model,[31] it was important in signifying recognition by the Court of the obligations of employers to provide decent and fair conditions at work, recognising that labour is not just like any other commodity but that workers have social

25 Commonwealth, *Parliamentary Debates*, House of Representatives, 22 March 1904, 2864 (Alfred Deakin).

26 *Conciliation and Arbitration Act 1904* (Cth) s 23(2).

27 Ray Markey, 'Trade Unions, the Labor Party and the Introduction of Arbitration in New South Wales and the Commonwealth' in Stuart Macintyre and Richard Mitchell (eds), *Foundations of Arbitration: The Origins and Effects of State Compulsory Arbitration* (OUP, Melbourne 1989).

28 Higgins (n 3) 25.

29 Higgins (n 1) 121–44.

30 *Ex Parte HV McKay* (1907) 2 CAR 1.

31 See eg, Keith Hancock and Sue Richardson, 'Economic and Social Effects' in Joe Isaac and Stuart Macintyre (eds), *The New Province for Law and Order* (CUP, Sydney 2004) 146–47.

and family responsibilities too.[32] Other decisions were of a similarly egalitarian nature, emphasising industrial fairness concerning standard hours of work,[33] the development of the principle of equal pay for women workers,[34] the introduction of bereavement or compassionate leave entitlements[35] and the removal of discriminatory employment conditions for Indigenous Australians.[36] In the decision introducing paid annual leave for all award workers, the full bench of the Court explicitly recognised a need for employers to provide for their staff to have a break from continuous work, stating, 'a standard of living consists not only of the capacity to participate in the fruits of material production and services but comprehends also a reasonable period of respite from toil with the enjoyment of the cultural, social and recuperative benefits which respite permits'.[37]

Eventually, this developing notion of industrial fairness as the formula for achieving industrial peace culminated in the official recognition of the uniquely Australian phenomenon of the 'fair go'. Macintyre notes that the emphasis of the Constitution's framers and the Conciliation and Arbitration Court's early members was on egalitarianism and 'shaping the political economy according to the national ethos of the fair go'.[38] While seemingly a colloquialism, the 'fair go' became deeply embedded in Australia's labour laws and jurisprudence. According to Riley:

> The 'fair go' is an idiomatic expression of the Australian commitment to an egalitarian democracy which respects the autonomy and dignity of its citizenry. Those who engage workers and those who work are all working citizens, and as such they are entitled to equal respect and consideration in the determination of matters affecting their working lives.[39]

In Australian labour law this notion of the 'fair go' has been developed over time. Owens, Riley and Murray argue that the judicial decision in the *Harvester Case* gave content to the notion of fairness by holding that 'the law should ensure that workers are treated in a way that regards them as human beings'.[40] Additionally,

32 Orwell Foenander, *Towards Industrial Peace in Australia* (Melbourne University Press, Melbourne 1937) 69–72.
33 *Australian Timber Workers' Union v John Sharp and Sons Ltd* (1920) 14 CAR 811; (1921) 15 CAR 836 and (1922) 16 CAR 649; *Amalgamated Engineering Union v J Alderdice & Co Pty Ltd* (1927) 24 CAR 755; *Australian Railways Union v Victorian Railways Commissioners* (1937) 37 CAR 937 [938].
34 *National Wage Cases* (1967) 118 CAR 655 [660]. See *Equal Pay Cases* (1969) 127 CAR 1142; *National Wage and Equal Pay Cases* (1972) 147 CAR 172.
35 *Commonwealth Hostels Award* (1962) 100 CAR 755.
36 *Cattle Station Industry (Northern Territory) Award* (1966) 113 CAR 651; *Pastoral Industry Award* (1967) 121 CAR 454 [457]–[458].
37 *Annual Leave Case* (1945) 55 CAR 598.
38 Stuart Macintyre, 'Arbitration' in Graeme Davison, John Hirst and Stuart Macintyre (eds), *The Oxford Companion to Australian History* (OUP, Melbourne 2001) 31.
39 Joellen Riley, 'Good Faith Performance' in Mordy Bromberg and Mark Irving (eds), *The Australian Charter of Employment Rights* (Hardie Grant Books, Melbourne 2007) 13.
40 Rosemary Owens, Joellen Riley and Jill Murray, *The Law of Work* (OUP, Melbourne 2011) 18; see also, *Ex parte HV McKay* (1907) 2 CAR 1.

in the decision of *FEDA v Robe River Iron Association* the Industrial Relations Commission explained it in the following terms: 'managerial prerogative is not a sword that can be wielded in wanton disregard of the industrial consequences nor is it a shield to hide behind. An employer has a responsibility to manage fairly.'[41] Despite the substantial changes that have occurred in Australia's labour laws in the last two decades,[42] the uniquely Australian concept of the 'fair go' still endures and has even made it into federal legislation governing unfair dismissal[43] and into the names of the federal labour law statute[44] and the institution charged with resolving disputes between employers and employees.[45] Notwithstanding scholarly criticism of its use,[46] the stem word 'fair' is used seven times within the stated objects of the *Fair Work Act 2009* (Cth) and is the most common substantive descriptive word used in this section.[47] In 2015 Australia's Productivity Commission acknowledged the importance of fairness to Australia's workplace relations framework, recognising that 'labour differs from other inputs, and that a sound workplace relations system must give primacy to the wellbeing of employees (and would-be employees), and take account of community norms about the fair treatment of people'.[48] Thus, the uniquely Australian concept of the 'fair go' still endures. In a speech in 2010, the president of the New South Wales Industrial Relations Commission observed that the 'notion of a fair go is a profound one, firmly rooted in the Australian psyche'.[49] While this principle of industrial fairness or of a 'fair go' was initially embedded within Australia's industrial peace tradition, as I will explain later in this chapter, this notion became central to the construction of the uniquely Australian formulation of 'industrial justice' within the unfair dismissal system.

The achievement of industrial peace was made possible through the placement of industrial tribunals at the apex of Australia's institutional labour law framework. The establishment of the Conciliation and Arbitration Court in 1904 was matched by the creation of tribunals and wage boards in each of the Australian states.[50] These tribunals were primarily charged with dispute settlement via a process of setting minimum wages and conditions across Australia.

41 *FEDA v Robe River Iron Association* [1987] AILR 131.
42 For an overview, see Owens, Riley and Murray (n 41); Creighton and Stewart (n 22).
43 *Workplace Relations Act 1996* (Cth) s 170CA(2); *Fair Work Act 2009* (Cth) s 381.
44 *Fair Work Act 2009* (Cth).
45 The Fair Work Commission.
46 For example, Graeme Orr argues that the use of the term 'fair work' in the context of the *Fair Work Act 2009* (Cth) tends to be sloganistic rather than meaningful: Graeme Orr, 'The Fair Work Act and Other Names of Shame' (2009) 16 Aust J Lab Law 74, 75.
47 *Fair Work Act 2009* (Cth) s 3.
48 Productivity Commission, 'Inquiry into the Workplace Relations Framework' (Inquiry Report, Commonwealth of Australia 2015) 4.
49 Justice Roger Boland, 'In Defence of Industrial Tribunals' (paper presented to the National Conference of the Industrial Relations Society of Australia, Sydney, May 2010).
50 Richard Mitchell, 'State System of Conciliation and Arbitration: The Legal Origins of the Australasian Model' in Stuart Macintyre and Richard Mitchell (eds), *Foundations of Arbitration* (OUP, Melbourne 1989).

It was believed that the use of a neutral third party to set minimum standards according to principles of fairness would aid better relations between employers and unions, thereby minimising the threat of industrial action and, in so doing, would 'augment the prosperity and harmony of the nation'.[51] The role of the federal industrial tribunal was so strongly embedded and supported by the community that the few attempts to reduce its role have resulted in electoral oblivion for those making the attempt. At the federal level there has been only one direct attempt to abolish the industrial tribunal, and that was in 1929. The result was that the prime minister, Stanley Bruce, lost his seat and his government resoundingly lost the election.[52] According to Macintyre, 'the decisive defeat of the government on this issue in the national election of 1929 demonstrated public support for arbitration'.[53] The Commonwealth Government's *Workplace Relations Amendment (Work Choices) Act 2005* (Cth) did not have as its aim the abolition of the Australian Industrial Relations Commission (AIRC), but the tribunal's powers were severely weakened and the reforms were predicated upon a more individualised notion of the employment relationship. The conventional wisdom seems to be that the Work Choices legislation was a significant factor in the defeat of the coalition government in 2007, where Prime Minister John Howard lost his seat; only the second time a sitting prime minister has ever lost his seat.[54] These two events, so many years apart, suggest strong community support for an active, well-resourced industrial umpire able to bring fairness into the work relationship so as to achieve industrial peace.

Another aspect of the endeavour to secure industrial peace was the recognition and legitimisation of the unions as the exclusive voice for working people by the conciliation and arbitration system. The 1904 Act enabled unions to be registered and conferred a right to represent particular groups of workers in proceedings before the CAC. The High Court made a key decision which increased the role and power of unions in the *Burwood Cinema Case*.[55] This decision recognised that industrial disputes could exist between trade unions and employers who did not currently employ any trade union members over the employment of future trade union members. Additionally, the development by the High Court of the 'Metal Trades doctrine' a decade later gave unions coverage of all employees working in the industry.[56] Under this doctrine, employers were required to pay

51 Macintyre (n 21) 195.
52 Macintyre (n 39).
53 Ibid.
54 Dennis Woodward, 'WorkChoices and Howard's Defeat' (2010) 69 AJPA 274; Michael Bachelard, 'Burned by IR, Howard's Battlers Exact Revenge' *The Age* (Melbourne 26 November 2007); Judith Brett, 'Exit Right: The Unraveling of John Howard' (2007) 28 Quarterly Essay; Frank Bongiorno, 'Howard's End: The 2007 Australian Election' (2008) 97(397) The Round Table 589; Kathie Muir, *Worth Fighting For: Inside the Your Rights at Work Campaign* (UNSW Press, Sydney 2008).
55 *Burwood Cinema Ltd v Australian Theatrical and Amusement Employees Association* (1925) 35 CLR 528.
56 *Metal Trades Employers Association v Amalgamated Engineering Union* (1935) 54 CLR 387.

the same wages to their non-union employees, even though their non-unionised employees were not parties to the award.[57] The rationale for this approach was to prevent employers from using non-union labour to undercut awards.[58] Under the many different means through which unions achieved recognition, awards were able to cover most of the Australian workforce. This saw union membership swell to 51.6 per cent by 1921, growing from 6.1 per cent at the start of the century.[59] By channelling union activity into the conciliation and arbitration system rather than into industrial action, Australia's labour laws enabled unions to achieve their agenda whilst minimising the opportunity for industrial disruption. Even in 1990, when trade union membership had fallen to 46 per cent,[60] awards and agreements instituted by unions still covered 80 per cent of the Australian workforce.[61] The state was committed to promoting unionism in the conciliation and arbitration system because unions were viewed as essential to achieving industrial peace.

Another key mechanism for fostering industrial peace were the myriad federal and state laws seeking to squash industrial action. Prime Minister Alfred Deakin declared in the second reading speech that after the passage of the *Conciliation and Arbitration Act 1904* (Cth) there would be 'no more strikes or lockouts'.[62] The chief objects of the Act stated this goal,[63] and the prohibition against industrial action was contained in section 6, which expressly prohibited all strikes or lockout conduct occurring within the jurisdiction of the Act. While prevention of industrial action was a central component of the Act, the enduring significance of this legislation lay in the establishment of the mechanisms of conciliation and arbitration to facilitate industrial peace.

Nonetheless, despite the institutionalisation of industrial peace as the guiding principle of Australia's labour law system, in practice industrial conflict remained prevalent. Despite section 6, strike action had not been prevented. In 1912 an anonymous Australian contributor to *Round Table* noted: 'the prevalence of strikes in Australia has become almost a byword . . . the tendency to secure redress of grievances by refusing to work until they are redressed goes on apparently unmodified in spite of all the elaborate machinery for preventing it'.[64] The

57 Michael Kirby and Breen Creighton, 'The Law of Conciliation and Arbitration' in Joe Isaac and Stuart Macintyre (eds), *The New Province for Law and Order* (CUP, Sydney 2004) 106–8.

58 For comment on recent aspects of the Metal Trades doctrine, see Karen Wood and Ron McCallum, 'Crafting the Law: The High Court and Superannuation as an Industrial Matter' (1995) 8 Aust J Lab Law 121.

59 Australian Bureau of Statistics, *Trade Union Statistics December 1995* (Cat no. 6323.0.40.001, 1995).

60 Ibid.

61 Australian Bureau of Statistics, *Award Coverage, Australia, May 1990* (Cat no. 6315.0, 1990).

62 Commonwealth, *Parliamentary Debates*, House of Representatives, 22 March 1904, 765 (Alfred Deakin).

63 *Conciliation and Arbitration Act 1904* (Cth) s 2.

64 'Australia: Strikes and Legislation' [December 1912] *Round Table* 152, 152–53.

hoped for 'substitution of the might of the State' for the rude and barbarous processes of strike and lockout had not resulted in a general surrender of the weapon of industrial action by trade unions. The years 1916–29 were strike prone and included two widespread and prominent strikes in 1919 and 1929.[65] Notably, the section 6 prohibition on industrial action did not play a significant role in the resolution of the major industrial conflicts of the time. Nonetheless, there was never a return to the national strikes of the 1890s that had brought industry to a standstill; after 1904 it was extremely rare for a strike to extend beyond state boundaries, and stoppages tended to be of short duration.[66] As Justice Higgins noted proudly in 1915, 'those who are old enough to recall the terrible shearers' strike and seamen's strike of the "nineties", with their attendant losses and privations, turbulence and violence, will realise how much ground has been gained. The strikes which still occur are strikes within a single State.'[67]

The legislature maintained its efforts to eradicate strikes. The *Industrial Peace Act 1920* (Cth) provided for the establishment of special tribunals in different industries to deal with disputes independently of the CAC.[68] Amendments to the *Conciliation and Arbitration Act* in 1920 inserted section 6A, making it illegal for any person or organisation bound by an award or entitled to the benefit of an award to engage in a lockout or strike.[69] This largely unnecessary amendment (given that such action was already illegal under section 6) was a reassertion of the trade-off in the Act between strike action and access to compulsory arbitration. Further ad-hoc legislative measures against industrial action were passed in the 1920s. The *Immigration Act 1925* (Cth) authorised the deportation of persons who had not been born in Australia and who had been involved in 'serious industrial action',[70] amendments to the *Crimes Act 1916* (Cth) in 1926 inserted sections 30J and 30K to deal with serious industrial disturbances and boycotts of Commonwealth services or international trade[71] and the *Transport Workers Act 1928* (Cth) authorised licensing of transport workers to replace those on strike.[72] Additional amendments to the *Conciliation and Arbitration Act* in 1928 bolstered the prohibition against industrial action by tightening controls over the

65 DW Oxnam, 'The Incidence of Strikes in Australia' in JE Isaac and GW Ford (eds), *Australian Labour Relations Readings* (2nd edn Sun Books, Melbourne 1973) 19, 27. For discussion of the 1919 seamen's strike see Richard Morris, 'Mr Justice Higgins Scuppered: The 1919 Seamen's Strike' [1972] LH 52. For discussion of the 1929 miners' strike see Laura Bennett, *Making Labour Law in Australia: Industrial Relations, Politics and the Law* (LBC, Sydney 1994) 24.

66 Creighton and Stewart (n 22) 37. For more, see Shae McCrystal, *The Right to Strike in Australia* (Federation Press, Sydney 2010).

67 Higgins (n 3) 37.

68 *Industrial Peace Act 1920* (Cth) s 13. In response to the passage of this Act Justice Higgins resigned from the Conciliation and Arbitration Court, declaring that 'a tribunal of reason cannot do its work side by side with executive tribunals of panic', quoted in Portus (n 16) 9.

69 *Commonwealth Conciliation and Arbitration Act 1920* (Cth) s 3.

70 *Immigration Act 1925* (Cth) s 7.

71 *Crimes Act 1926* (Cth) s 17.

72 *Transport Workers Act 1928* (Cth) s 3.

internal affairs of trade unions, strengthening union responsibility for the actions of union officials and encouraging union discipline by allowing for reduced fines if unions actively sought to halt unlawful strike action by members.[73]

The adoption of industrial peace as the basis of Australia's labour laws occurred via complex institutional arrangements whereby compulsory, collective and cooperative dispute resolution was reaffirmed at every level. Through the establishment of a national CAC and tribunals or wage boards in each of the states, it became clear that Australia's industrial relations system was predicated upon the involvement of a state-initiated, neutral third party to ensure the fair settlement of differences between labour and capital. The aim was to avoid the protracted industrial battles of the 1890s. The model was one of institutions guaranteeing dialogue rather than strikes and lockouts. The outcome was the proliferation of union-negotiated awards and agreements, developed via the mechanism of conciliation and arbitration and governing the industrial lives of over four fifths of the Australian labour force. The notion of industrial peace was extremely influential and was so firmly embedded that the protection of individual rights such as through remedies for unfair dismissal were ignored for most of the twentieth century in the federal jurisdiction. Violation of the rights of individuals was seen as less threatening to industrial peace, as without collective support industrial action would not occur. Moreover, the notion of industrial peace was sufficiently robust that the Australian industrial relations system managed without a federal unfair dismissal system for a significantly longer period than in the United Kingdom, which developed its system over twenty years earlier, although, as the following section will explain, inroads were beginning to be made at the state level from the 1970s.

The impact of the industrial peace doctrine on the regulation of dismissals

An understanding of the origins and the apparent tardiness of the Australian unfair dismissal legislation compared with the spread of unfair dismissal protection abroad lies in an appreciation of how it sits uneasily with the dominant labour law policy of successive Australian federal governments during the twentieth century. Australia's traditional federal labour law was built upon the achievement of industrial peace. This commitment to industrial peace had far-reaching implications for the structural and substantive development of unfair dismissal law in Australia prior to the enactment of a federal statutory scheme in 1993. Firstly, the prevailing theory of industrial peace delayed the development of a statutory remedy for unfair dismissal in the federal system, as the priority of Australia's national labour law system was to minimise the potential for disruption by collective disputes between unions and employers. A trade-off was made between union security and job security, with the conciliation and arbitration system prioritising the former. Secondly, the industrial peace doctrine was sufficiently robust that even

73 *Commonwealth Conciliation and Arbitration Act 1928* (Cth).

when conciliation/arbitration was losing the support of the parties, there was a shared willingness to experiment with another collective method for regulating disputes between unions and employers premised upon industrial peace. During this period of experimentation in the 1980s, few inroads were made in developing a federal statutory remedy for unfair dismissal as industrial peace was still the dominant approach. At the federal level, it was only when the prevailing theory of industrial peace was dismantled more generally as the basis of Australia's labour laws that unfair dismissal law began to be reformed. The introduction of a federal statutory remedy for unfair dismissal was based upon the primary policy rationale, developed initially at the state level, of industrial justice. Throughout the period of federal inaction on the unfair dismissal front prior to 1993, more interesting developments were occurring within the state jurisdictions. This section will explore how these state systems evolved so that by 1993 a new federal statutory unfair dismissal system drew upon developments at the state level.

The development of state unfair dismissal systems

Three of the state tribunals developed unfair dismissal jurisdictions based upon the perceived utility of adjudicating dismissal disputes in order to achieve industrial peace. Unlike their federal counterpart, industrial tribunals in three states took a liberal view of their authority to make binding orders of reinstatement for workers whom they believed had been unfairly dismissed under a state award. The earliest recorded reinstatement order made in Australia was in 1902 handed down by the predecessor to the NSW Industrial Commission.[74] From this point, arbitrators in New South Wales,[75] Western Australia (WA)[76] and South Australia (SA)[77] chose to interpret their industrial dispute resolution power in a broad, instrumental fashion in order to create de facto reinstatement jurisdictions. By 1970 tribunals in all three states had fully institutionalised the review of collectively initiated applications for reinstatement with minimal statutory support.[78] This review of unfair dismissals was justified on the basis that the tribunals were fostering industrial stability by ensuring that a dismissal dispute concerning an individual worker did not escalate into a large-scale collective dispute. In each of these three states, access to the tribunals was largely controlled by unions that would make claims on behalf of individual members. By way of contrast, in Victoria there was considerable controversy as to whether reinstatement could be ordered as a remedy, with the Supreme Court of Victoria refusing to recognise

74 *Newcastle Wharf Labourers Union v Newcastle & Hunter River Steamship Co Pty Ltd* [1902] AR 1.

75 *Re: Bank Officers (State) Board* (Rawson case) [1921] AR 138 [145] (Roland J).

76 *Kwinana Construction Group v Electrical Trades Union* (1954) 34 WAIG 51 [52] (President Jackson).

77 *Guymer v Department of Tourism* (1969) 36 SAIR 52 [57] (President Bleby).

78 AP Davidson, 'Reinstatement of Employees by State Industrial Tribunals' (1980) 54 Aust LJ 706.

the existence of any jurisdiction to hear a claim for reinstatement, although this was later circumvented by legislation and overturned by the High Court.[79]

The constitutional chalk lines which had hamstrung the development of a statutory remedy for unfair dismissal at the federal level, and which will be explored in more detail in the next section, worked in favour of state legislatures that held constitutional power over all remaining industrial matters so long they did not do so in a manner which was inconsistent with a valid law of the Commonwealth.[80] In the 1970s and 1980s state governments began to enact legislation pertaining to the adjudication of unfair dismissal disputes. In South Australia, the Dunstan government passed the *Industrial Conciliation and Arbitration Act 1972*, which established the first individually initiated, justice-oriented system of employment termination review in Australia.[81] Section 15(1)(e) of this Act empowered the Industrial Court 'to hear and determine any question as to whether the dismissal from his employment of an employee . . . was harsh, unjust or unreasonable and the Court may, if it thinks fit, direct the employer of that employee to re-employ that employee in his former position'.

This section gave the South Australian Industrial Court the power to hear unfair dismissal claims and to order reinstatement of an employee to his or her former position. The 1972 Act was subject to major revision in 1984, and the insertion of a new section 30 transferred the Court's jurisdiction to the Industrial Commission and introduced a power to award compensation in lieu of reinstatement.[82] The South Australian system represented a break with the traditional arbitral approach to unfair dismissal predicated upon industrial peace, as the commission's jurisdiction was triggered by an application from an individual worker who was dismissed rather than by notification of an industrial dispute. The commission's decision-making power was not concerned with how to achieve industrial stability but required an examination of whether there was an infraction of the individual employee's rights because the dismissal was 'harsh, unjust or unreasonable'.

Western Australia followed suit, leading to the creation of two unfair dismissal jurisdictions operating side by side, one system predicated upon industrial peace, and the other upon industrial justice. While these two philosophies are not dichotomous and the argument of this chapter is that the industrial justice notion is derived from a strand of the industrial peace tradition, the creation of two separate unfair dismissal jurisdictions in Western Australia illustrates that policymakers were wrestling with how to accord individual employees with the right to challenge the fairness of their dismissal from within a traditional system

79 *Slonim v Fellors* (1984) 154 CLR 505. For more on this, see B Creighton and A Stewart, *Labour Law* (1st edn Federation Press, Sydney 1990) 160.

80 *The Constitution* s 109.

81 The forerunner to this provision was s 26(2) of the *Industrial Code 1967* (SA). For more on the South Australian system, see Andrew Stewart, 'The New Unfair Dismissal Jurisdiction in South Australia' (1986) 28(3) J Indust Relations 367; Andrew Stewart, *Unfair Dismissal in South Australia* (Corporate and Business Law Centre, Adelaide 1988).

82 *Industrial Conciliation and Arbitration Act Amendment Act 1984* (SA) ss 8(a), 21.

which had only ever accorded the right to challenge managerial decision making to unions. The industrial peace system was the traditional one that had existed in WA and was maintained to allow the tribunal to hear collectively initiated complaints about an individual's dismissal. However, this was supplemented by the establishment of a separate parallel cause of action for individually initiated claims under the *Industrial Relations Act 1979* (WA). This decision to introduce an individually initiated wing to the Western Australian unfair dismissal system was recognition that industrial justice for individuals needed to be achieved by the system as well as the traditional goal of industrial peace overseen by the collective. Victoria adopted an unfair dismissal system based upon the South Australian model in 1983 as jurisdiction was conferred upon the Victorian Conciliation and Arbitration Board to scrutinise individually initiated unfair dismissal jurisdictions and to order compensation or reinstatement if the dismissal was found to be 'harsh, unjust or unreasonable'.[83] In each of the three states to develop justice-oriented unfair dismissal systems, the rationale of industrial justice was primarily concerned with achieving justice through guaranteeing universal access to the system to all individuals, regardless of whether they had union affiliation.[84]

A different approach occurred in the state of New South Wales, which sought to defend the sanctity of its industrial peace model by mandating the resolution of unfair dismissal disputes through union monopoly.[85] Unlike in other jurisdictions where provision was made for individually initiated dismissal disputes, in NSW unions retained their right to act as the gatekeeper to the conciliation and arbitration system for industrial disputes, including disputes relating to individuals. An individual employee was not able to initiate proceedings without the support of a union, or alternatively a group of aggrieved fellow workers, because the unfair dismissal application had to be signed by the union secretary or the employer.[86] The rationale for union monopoly was that the best way to guarantee industrial peace was through unions vetting unfair dismissal applications and only pursuing those of merit. It also was a way of ensuring that only dismissals that could give rise to industrial disruption were dealt with by the NSW conciliation and arbitration mechanism. This had the practical effect, however, that if an individual had a legitimate unfair dismissal claim but was unable to secure union support because pursuing the individual's claim did not complement the union's broader agenda or undermined its relationship with the employer, then that individual had no

83 *Industrial Relations (Further Amendment) Act 1983* (Vic).

84 Although Queensland was slower than SA, WA and Victoria to develop a system allowing individual employees to initiate unfair dismissal claims, in 1994 it introduced legislation to this effect, largely modelled on the South Australian legislation: *Industrial Relations Act 1990* (Qld) pt 11 div 4.

85 Similarly, in Tasmania the *Industrial Relations Act 1984* (Tas) did not allow individual employees to initiate an unfair dismissal claim, as only a union could notify an 'industrial dispute' under s 3(1). This meant that in practice, union support was a necessary precondition to being able to access a remedy of reinstatement for an unfair dismissal.

86 *Roberts v Mona Vale District Hospital* [1975] 2 NSWLR 132, 138 (Court of Appeal); *Industrial Arbitration Act 1940* (NSW) s 74.

opportunity for redress. In contrast, dismissal of a union official was much more likely to receive adjudication by the conciliation and arbitration system, as such a claim would naturally attract union support.[87] The remedy awarded by the NSW Industrial Relations Commission (IRC) depended more upon maintaining industrial peace than achieving justice for the individual concerned. As Stewart observes, 'the likelihood of a remedy being secured is often directly related to the industrial muscle of the relevant union and to its willingness to act as an enforcer of any order made'.[88] This is because the primary task of the NSWIRC was to settle disputes in order to promote industrial harmony and the application of this task, usually aimed at collective disputes, to individual dismissal disputes meant that remedies could be awarded on the basis of averting sympathy strikes rather than whether the dismissal breached defined standards of employer behaviour. Despite the obvious criticisms that can be made against the NSW system because of union monopoly, Stewart does note that the emphasis on industrial peace led to the elevation of conciliation as the primary method for resolving dismissal disputes and resulted in the resolution of the vast majority of disputes at this stage.[89] It took until 1991 for this to change, following the recommendation of the Niland Report that there should be a right of individual application as a matter of general principle,[90] when a Liberal government gave workers in NSW the right to lodge their own complaint of unfair dismissal.[91]

Even in NSW, which remained staunchly committed to industrial peace as the governing objective of the state unfair dismissal system, key arbitral decisions refined the notion of a 'fair go' or 'industrial fair play' in the context of unfair dismissal disputes. The first judgment to assess the matrix of factors impacting upon whether a dismissal was fair was the judgment of Justice McKeon in *Western Suburbs District Ambulance Committee v Tipping*.[92] While this was a dissenting opinion, the statement of principles contained within the judgment has been widely regarded as authoritative.[93] Justice McKeon characterised the employer's right to dismiss as clear and fundamental and placed the burden on the individual employee to prove the unfairness of the dismissal. He suggested that in deciding whether to order reinstatement, the question the court should ask is whether there had been oppression, injustice or unfair dealing on the part of the employer. This discussion of justice in dismissal was extended by the significant decision of the NSWIRC in Loty & Holloway v Australian Workers Union,[94]

87 Andrew Stewart, 'Employment Protection in Australia' [1989] CLL 27.
88 Ibid.
89 Ibid 27–28. See also: MR Sherman, 'Unfair Dismissal and the Remedy of Re-employment' (1989) 31 J Indust Relations 212.
90 J Niland, 'Transforming Industrial Relations in New South Wales: A Green Paper' Vol 1 (NSW Government Printing Office, Sydney 1989) [413].
91 Andrew Stewart, 'A Quiet Revolution: Unfair Dismissal in New South Wales' (1992) 5 Aust J Lab Law 69.
92 [1957] AR (NSW) 273.
93 See *North West County Council v Dunn* [1970] CLR 247 [263] (Walsh J); see also *In Re Coccia and Australian Iron and Steel Pty Ltd* [1971] AR (NSW) 111 [115] (Sheldon J).
94 [1971] AR (NSW) 95.

which concerned an application for reinstatement of two employees dismissed from their positions in a union after a change in the composition of the union executive. In determining whether to make awards providing for their reinstatement, Justice Sheldon asked whether the employees had 'received less than a fair deal'.[95] Justice Sheldon also referred to the objective of the unfair dismissal jurisdiction as being to provide 'industrial justice' by reference to a number of factors, including the inviolability of the right of the employer to manage his business, the nature and quality of the work in question, the circumstances surrounding the dismissal and the likely practical outcome if an order of reinstatement is made. Justice Sheldon affirmed an earlier statement of a commissioner that the purpose of the exploration into the individual's dismissal by the NSWIRC was to ascertain whether there had been a 'fair go all round'.[96]

The idea of industrial justice that emerged in these state jurisdictions was heavily tied to principles of access and fairness. Because of the disputes over whether unions should control access to the conciliation and arbitration system by individuals wishing to challenge the fairness of their dismissal, access to the jurisdiction became an important issue in the Australian context. The tradition of a 'fair go' or industrial fair play which developed as a means of guaranteeing industrial peace also came to be incorporated in the expression of industrial justice by state tribunals. This understanding of fairness in dismissal involved weighing up the circumstances of dismissal and assessing whether these amounted to some degree of oppression, injustice or unfair dealing. Thus, industrial justice, as it developed as a notion within the state jurisdictions, tended to focus on the practicalities of dismissal rather than a more highly theorised understanding of precisely where and why this notion of justice is relevant.

The development of the federal unfair dismissal system

Federally, the fixation with industrial peace delayed the development of a statutory remedy for unfair dismissal law, as the priority of the Australian labour law system was to minimise the potential for disruption by collective disputes between unions and employers. Industrial peace proved to be a rather robust doctrine. Even when the conciliation and arbitration system was under threat or international jurisdictions were developing statutory remedies for unfair dismissal, the Australian system maintained its commitment to achieving industrial peace, and the policy prescriptions that naturally flowed on from this position tended to inhibit the advancement of unfair dismissal law. Other factors too were relevant to the comparatively late arrival of unfair dismissal law in Australia. The Constitution's conciliation and arbitration power[97] was perceived as a significant constraint upon the federal development of a statutory remedy for unfair dismissal.[98] Another factor pertinent to the delayed arrival of unfair dismissal law in

95 Ibid [99].
96 Ibid.
97 S 51(xxxv).
98 B Creighton and A Stewart, *Labour Law* (2nd edn Federation Press, Sydney 1994) 201–2.

Australia was that until the oil price driven 'stagflation' of the 1970s, and excepting the Depression era of the 1930s, full employment or something close to it tended to be the norm in Australia. This meant there was less urgency for unions to lobby for unfair dismissal reform because arbitrarily dismissed employees could find other work with little difficulty. Despite the existence of these other factors, three phases can be identified in the evolution of industrial peace as a doctrine influencing the maturation of federal unfair dismissal law. The first phase was characterised by the dominance of industrial peace between 1901 and 1982, which saw little support for introducing unfair dismissal law, as there was a trade-off between job security and union security. The second phase was marked by growing dissatisfaction with the ability of conciliation and arbitration to deliver favourable economic outcomes for Australia coupled with an unwillingness to move away from industrial peace. This saw a novel attempt to circumvent the conciliation and arbitration system, which did not encompass the development of a statutory remedy for unfair dismissal. Finally, the third phase was the introduction of a comprehensive federal unfair dismissal system in 1993 which saw the prevailing theory of industrial peace transmogrify into a new concern with achieving industrial justice. In this third phase, the Commonwealth government drew upon the experiences of the state unfair dismissal systems to create a federal system to provide an individual statutory remedy for unfair dismissal.

1901–1982

This first phase in the evolution of Australia's federal unfair dismissal system was marked by an unwillingness to provide a statutory remedy for unfair dismissal because of the dominance of industrial peace as the basis of Australia's labour laws. The national conciliation and arbitration system introduced in 1904 was explicitly concerned with preventing disputes that had the potential to become large-scale disruptions like that which occurred in the mining, maritime and shearing industries in the 1890s. Within the Australian federal tradition, disputes involving the dismissal of an individual did not usually hold the potential to threaten industrial peace and moreover were of a local nature and could not be characterised as an 'interstate' dispute for which the federal Conciliation and Arbitration Court possessed jurisdiction.[99] Higgins justified the federal system's focus on the collective on the basis that:

> It is of course, better for an employer that he should not be worried by complaints of individual employees and that any complaints should be presented collectively by some responsible union. He has then the advantage of being able to deal with his employees on a consistent scheme, equitable all round the service, and his time is not taken up by petty complaints or individual fads.[100]

99 *R v Gough; ex parte Cairn Meat Export Co Pty Ltd* (1962) 108 CLR 343; *In Re Stanton; ex parte Associated Airlines* (1978) 52 ALJR 454; *In Re Staples and another; ex parte Australian Telecommunications Commission* (1980) 54 ALR 507.

100 Higgins (n 3) 23.

In fact, the hallmark of Australia's traditional industrial relations system was the substantial degree of security accorded to collectively organised labour, namely the explicit recognition and preference given to unions within the conciliation and arbitration mechanism. This propensity for delivering union security was seen as the best way of achieving security for individual workers, although this meant that job security was not statutorily protected, as it was a minor part of the union movement's agenda for much of the twentieth century. Whilst not necessarily explicitly stated, unions tended to be more preoccupied with making inroads into the traditional industrial concerns of wages, conditions and working hours.

Another reason for the lack of momentum for a statutory system protecting unfair dismissal rights was perhaps the prevailing view of the parties that the conciliation and arbitration machinery did not allow individual workers to be arbitrarily deprived of their employment. Stemming from the influence of Higgins was an enduring belief in the need for management to provide job security by resolving staff problems within the workplace rather than resorting to dismissal.[101] Higgins viewed unemployment as an 'industrial sore' and wrote that 'it is impossible to overstate the evil effects, moral and physical, on the worker and on the community' of a person having no job.[102] This view, held by the most influential president of the Conciliation and Arbitration Court, meant that the arbitration system favoured keeping workers in their jobs and viewed dismissal as a last resort.[103] Stewart claims that unions were confident of their ability to deal with job security with employers directly rather than through the conciliation and arbitration system.[104] Foenander makes a similar observation, noting that the award system operated in practice to ensure that individual employees were not arbitrarily deprived of their jobs:

> The great majority of Australian employees are now working under conditions of weekly hiring, with no real fear that their employment will be terminated at short notice unless they are guilty of incompetence, neglect or dereliction of duty, malingering on the job or other conduct or offence that permits, under the relevant award or determination, of their summary or instant dismissal. In the case of professional and staff employees the guaranteed term of employment is invariably longer. Tenure is just as important as other conditions of employment, and as the wage rate.[105]

Little political will existed during this first phase to challenge the perceived constitutional constraints limiting the establishment of a statutory remedy for unfair dismissal. It was believed that the Conciliation and Arbitration Court, later the Conciliation and Arbitration Commission, had no jurisdiction to order the reinstatement of a dismissed worker. This is because under the conciliation and arbitration power, a dispute between a union and an employer needed to extend

101 Higgins (n 1) 160–62.
102 Ibid 160.
103 Ibid.
104 Stewart (n 88) 25.
105 Foenander (n 23) 45.

beyond the boundaries of one state, and an unfair dismissal dispute involving an individual does not meet this criterion. This jurisdictional difficulty was perceived to exist despite the fact that the *Conciliation and Arbitration Act 1904* (Cth), in its definition of industrial matters that the Court had purview over, included 'the right to dismiss or to refuse to employ, or the duty to reinstate in employment, a particular person or class of persons'.[106] However, this was not seen as enough to trump the interstate requirement explicit in section 51(xxxv) of the Constitution. As one member of the High Court remarked about the conflict between these two conferrals of power, 'Be it so. You must still have an industrial dispute about that matter extending beyond one State'.[107] However, despite the constraints of the constitutional arrangements establishing the conciliation and arbitration system, no serious attempts were made to introduce an individual remedy for unfair dismissal within the federal system, as it was generally believed that the ability of the system to achieve industrial peace took precedence and that the commission's de facto jurisdiction sufficed. This period was characterised by the willingness of the parties, particularly unions, to support the conciliation and arbitration system federally because the industrial peace doctrine was sufficiently robust and institutionally embedded to be challenged. The parties accepted that individuals could not make a claim even when their individual rights had been infringed because of the benefit guaranteed by industrial peace that unions were legitimised by the system and could make claims to improve the collective position of working people.

Thus, although constitutional constraints stymied the introduction of federal unfair dismissal legislation for much of the twentieth century, an extensive de facto unfair dismissal jurisdiction was exercised by the federal tribunal which provided protection against arbitrary dismissal based upon an idea of external and independent scrutiny of the employer's dismissal decision. Strictly speaking, the Australian Conciliation and Arbitration Commission had no statutory power to regulate unfair dismissals but relied upon the referral of cases by unions and/or employers. Where the employer consented, the commission would scrutinise the dismissal decision and hand down a 'non-binding' recommendation.[108] The effectiveness of this was constrained by the need for employers to consent to the commission's jurisdiction.[109]

1983–1992

The second phase in the evolution of industrial peace as a doctrine influencing the development of federal unfair dismissal law occurred during the period 1983–93 when there was a new attempt to move away from Australia's conciliation and

106 *Conciliation and Arbitration Act 1904* (Cth) as amended s 4.

107 *R v Gough; ex parte Cairns Meat Export Co Pty Ltd* (1962) 108 CLR 342 [350] (Dixon J). See also *R v Portus; ex parte City of Perth* (1973) 129 CLR 312.

108 See J O'Donovan, 'Reinstatement of Dismissed Employees by the Australian Conciliation and Arbitration Commission: Jurisdiction and Practice' (1976) 50 Aust LJ 636.

109 For example, see *National Union of Workers v Pacific Dunlop Tyres Pty Ltd* (1992) 43 IR 201.

arbitration tradition. The Accord was agreed between the Australian Council of Trade Unions and the Australian Labor Party prior to the 1983 federal election.[110] The rationale for this policy shift was not purely about industrial relations, although certainly a key objective was to secure industrial peace and reduce the incidence of strikes and working days lost to strikes.[111] In addition, there was a shared belief that conciliation and arbitration had become unable to achieve important economic objectives of productivity gains and low inflation, so there was need for a national solution predicated upon securing agreement between the social partners.[112] During this time, the issue of a statutory remedy for unfair dismissal was not central to the mainstream political agenda because the primary concerns of the industrial relations and economic agenda were securing industrial peace and improving the international competitiveness of the Australian economy. As I will explain in this section, during this period unions sought to secure unfair dismissal reform from within the existing conciliation and arbitration paradigm by trying to insert a condition mandating fair dismissals into awards.

Australia's experiment with the Accord represented an attempt to move away from conciliation and arbitration whilst preserving a collective labour law model predicated upon industrial peace. The Hawke government was elected in 1983 against a backdrop of mounting economic problems, including increasing inflation, high wage costs and high industrial disputation.[113] At the National Economic Summit of April 1983 agreement was reached between the peak union body, the Australian Council of Trade Unions (ACTU) and employers on the need to address Australia's escalating economic and industrial relations challenges.[114] Consequently, in September 1983 there was a new national wage case before the Conciliation and Arbitration Commission,[115] and between 1983 and 1986 the central emphasis in wage fixing was on the achievement of controlled wage increases proportionate to increases in the cost of living and in national productivity.[116] Central to the Accord was the notion of union restraint, not just on wages, but on all costs associated with labour. The Accord emphasised the framing of wage claims with due regard to economic policy; no extra claims could be made except in exceptional and extraordinary circumstances, and bargaining to reduce working hours was tied to increases in productivity.[117] In return for the unions committing to wage restraint, the Labor government agreed to reforms aimed to benefit all working people: the establishment of a price surveillance

110 Rowse (n 21) 43.

111 Bill Harley, 'Managing Industrial Conflict' in Joe Isaac and Stuart Macintyre (eds), *The New Province for Law and Order* (CUP, Sydney 2004) 343.

112 Rowse (n 21) 44–45.

113 Malcolm Rimmer, 'Unions and Arbitration' in Joe Isaac and Stuart Macintyre (eds), *The New Province for Law and Order* (CUP, Sydney 2004) 205.

114 Gwynneth Singleton, *The Accord and the Labour Movement* (MUP, Melbourne 1990) 120–56.

115 Ibid.

116 Creighton and Stewart (1994) 38.

117 Harley (n 112) 343.

mechanism, tax restructuring, superannuation and free universal health care financed by a 1 per cent income tax levy.[118]

During the Accord years, the unions advocated for unfair dismissal reform from within the conciliation and arbitration system. In 1984 the Australian Council of Trade Unions launched a test case on the issue of job security before the Conciliation and Arbitration Commission. In the *Termination, Change and Redundancy Case*[119] the commission decided that the Metal Industry Award 1984 was able to include a clause that a dismissal must not be 'harsh, unjust or unreasonable' and that this clause could be flowed on to other federal awards. The decision in *Gregory v Phillip Morris Ltd*[120] determined that an award provision that a dismissal not be 'harsh, unjust or unreasonable' could be incorporated into individual employment contracts.[121] This approach was subsequently overruled by the High Court in a later case which confirmed that employers were not required under the contract of employment to accord both substantive and procedural fairness in making a decision concerning dismissal.[122]

In a parallel but unrelated development, during the late 1980s and early 1990s a series of High Court decisions established that the federal industrial tribunal had the capacity to deal with unfair dismissal claims, although, as Stewart notes, these were 'fraught with difficulties for unions and workers'.[123] These decisions confirmed that the term 'industrial matter' included an individual's claim for reinstatement and the commission could address a purely local dispute over a dismissal if this would mitigate the risk of the dispute escalating into an interstate dispute.[124] The High Court also determined that the commission could order reinstatement so long as this decision was reached according to what is 'industrially right and fair' rather than enforcing a pre-existing entitlement.[125]

1993–1996

By the early 1990s it had become clear that pressure was mounting for wholesale reform of Australia's traditional approach of relying on conciliation and arbitration to settle disputes as a mechanism for achieving industrial peace.[126] Instead, the

118 Tom Bramble, *Trade Unionism in Australia: A History from Flood to Ebb Tide* (CUP, Cambridge 2008) 123–56.

119 (1984) 8 Indus R 34; (1984) 9 Indus R 115.

120 (1988) 80 ALR 455.

121 See eg, *Bostik (Australia) Pty Ltd v Gorgevski* (1992) 36 FCR 20.

122 *Byrne v Australian Airlines Ltd* (1994) 120 ALR 274, see [813]–[815].

123 Andrew Stewart, 'And (Industrial) Justice for All? Protecting Workers Against Unfair Dismissal', (1995) 1 Flinders J Law Reform 85, 89.

124 *Re Ranger Uranium Mines Pty Ltd; ex parte Federated Miscellaneous Workers Union of Australia* (1987) 163 CLR 656; *Re Boyne Smelters Ltd; ex parte Federation of Industrial Manufacturing and Engineering Employees of Australia* (1993) 177 CLR 446; *Re Printing and Kindred Industries Union; ex parte Vista Paper Products Pty Ltd* (1993) 67 ALJR 604.

125 *Re Ranger Uranium Mines Pty Ltd; ex parte Federated Miscellaneous Workers Union of Australia* (1987) 163 CLR 656.

126 See eg, HR Nicholls Society, *Arbitration in Contempt* (HR Nicholls Society, Melbourne 1986); WB Creighton, 'Trade Unions, the Law and the New Right' in K Coghill (ed), *The*

momentum appeared to be in favour of preventing and settling disputes through direct bargaining at the enterprise level. This led the Labor government to introduce the *Industrial Relations Act 1993* (Cth) which marked a watershed in Australia's industrial relations, as it was the first attempt to regulate the employment relationship directly through reliance on a range of constitutional powers rather than the traditional usage of section 51(xxxv). This reform saw a statutory remedy for unfair dismissal being introduced into the federal sphere for the first time. The introduction of a federal statutory remedy occurred because of reliance on the concept, developed initially at the state level, of industrial justice.

The marginalisation of industrial peace as the central normative basis for Australia's labour laws resulted from the increasing pressure by the early 1990s to reduce Australia's labour law reliance on the traditional machinery of conciliation and arbitration. There were a number of key reasons for this. Firstly, the opening up of the Australian economy led to support for the deregulation of conciliation and arbitration and for abandoning industrial peace as the primary objective of the system. Key developments were the floating of the Australian dollar in 1983, the deregulation of the Australian financial system and the progressive removal of tariffs protecting Australian manufacturing. Secondly, Australia began to experience mounting problems associated with its balance of payments in the late 1980s and the economy went into recession. Unemployment was at record levels and the nature of the labour market was changing with decreasing employment in manufacturing, casualisation of 25 per cent of the workforce and increasing participation of women. Thirdly and perhaps most importantly, these economic changes led to increasing pressure by interest groups who argued that the prevailing government policy of deregulating product markets needed to be complemented by deregulation, or at least, decentralisation, of the labour market.[127] The recession, in particular, laid the groundwork for the removal of conciliation and arbitration, as it gave impetus to the argument that the setting of wages and conditions on an industry basis hamstrung Australia's productivity.

There was immense intellectual pressure to reduce centralised wage fixation predicated upon achieving industrial peace and economic objectives and move towards a focus on the enterprise – typified by both the Niland Report[128] and a report from the Business Council of Australia recommending a shift to enterprise bargaining at the workplace level.[129] Pressure for enterprise bargaining came not just from employer groups but also from unions who saw it as a means of fostering collectivism in the workplace. By April 1991 the commission was faced with

New Right's Australian Fantasy (McPhee Gribble/Penguin, Melbourne 1987); B Dabscheck, *Australian Industrial Relations in the 1980s* (OUP, Melbourne 1989); L Bennett, 'The American Model of Labour Law in Australia' (1992) 5 Aust J Lab Law 135.

127 Russell Lansbury and Mark Wescott, 'Collective Bargaining, Employment and Competitiveness: The Case of Australia' [2000] IJES 102.

128 Niland (n 91).

129 Business Council of Australia, 'Enterprise-Based Bargaining Unit: A Better Way of Working' (Report to the Business Council of Australia by the Industrial Relations Study Commission, 1989).

pro-enterprise bargaining submissions from all the major employer groups, the ACTU and all the then Commonwealth and state governments. When the AIRC initially opposed enterprise bargaining in its ruling, it faced almost universal criticism, with the Australian Labor Party (ALP) and the ACTU both deciding to launch an industrial campaign advocating enterprise bargaining.[130] Dabscheck argued that the commission's reluctance to reform the traditional processes of conciliation and arbitration by introducing enterprise bargaining meant it was out of step with the regulatory pressures placed by all the other parties.[131] Furthermore, the advent of globalisation meant that influential international organisations exerted pressure on Australia to abandon its conciliation and arbitration tradition and gave impetus to neo-liberal reformers within Australia to make the case for change.[132]

Thus, in 1993 the prevailing industrial peace doctrine embedded in a system of conciliation and arbitration was replaced by a new industrial relations order with new objectives, not necessarily contingent upon the primacy of industrial harmony. Interestingly, despite the dismantling of conciliation and arbitration and the extension of enterprise bargaining more generally, conciliation and arbitration machinery came to be of increasing importance in the area of unfair dismissals as the commission's machinery was chosen to conciliate unfair dismissal disputes, excepting for rare occasions where conciliation was deemed inappropriate.[133] The Labor government chose not to place the entire unfair dismissal system in the commission's jurisdiction and created the Industrial Relations Court, which was constituted by Federal Court judges and judicial registrars and was bound by legal rules of procedure. This decision was motivated by the Labor government's interpretation of the *Boilermakers' Case*,[134] which they viewed as preventing the commission from granting individual remedies, as this would involve the use of judicial power which could only be exercised by a court.[135] This meant the Industrial Relations Court was the first procedural point of call for unfair dismissal applications. All applicants had to lodge their application with

130 Chris Briggs, 'Australian Exceptionalism: Australian Trade Unions in the Emergence of Enterprise Bargaining' [2001] JIR 27.

131 Braham Dabscheck, 'The Slow and Agonising Death of the Australian Experiment with Conciliation and Arbitration' [2001] JIR 277.

132 For example, in an assessment of the Australian economy at the time, the IMF argued that decentralisation was not progressing fast enough and that lingering high levels of structural unemployment were the result: Lansbury and Westcott (n 128) 103.

133 *Industrial Relations Reform Act 1993* (Cth) ss 170EC–170ED.

134 *R v Kirby ex parte Boilermakers' Society of Australia* (1956) 94 CLR 254.

135 In the *Boilermakers Case* the High Court held that the Court of Conciliation and Arbitration created in 1904 could not exercise both the quasi-legislative function of making awards and the judicial functions of interpreting and enforcing them. Consequently, two new bodies were created: firstly, the Australian Industrial Relations Commission (before 1989 the Australian Conciliation and Arbitration Commission) to exercise the non-judicial power of conciliation and arbitration and secondly, the Industrial Division of the Federal Court to exercise strictly judicial functions. See Kirby and Creighton (n 58). See also: *Re Dingjan; Ex Parte Wagner* [1995] 183 CLR 323.

the IRC.[136] The IRC was then required to refer the matter to the commission for conciliation unless the IRC was satisfied that such a referral was inappropriate.[137] The commission's role was to inquire into the matter and help the parties reach settlement. If settlement did not occur within a reasonable period, the commission could produce a certificate stating that conciliation failed and the matter was remitted to the IRC for resolution.[138] Remedies that could be awarded by the IRC included compensation and reinstatement. Reinstatement was intended as the primary remedy and involved either reappointing the employee to her or his former position, or else appointing the employee to another position on terms and conditions no less favourable.[139]

Despite the marginalisation of industrial peace as an objective of Australia's labour laws after 1993, it was not replaced by a robust and cohesive ideal of industrial justice at the federal level. The introduction of unfair dismissal law was characterised by the Labor government as necessitated by Australia's obligations under international law, not because of a need within Australian workplaces.[140] In introducing the Bill into the Parliament, the federal minister for industrial relations, Mr Brereton, did not refer to any rationale other than giving effect to Australia's international obligations as the impetus for these provisions and a new object was added to the Act: 'the protection of wages and conditions of workers through awards and by ensuring that labour standards meet Australia's international obligations'.[141] The use of this single rationale was interesting because it meant that unlike in the United Kingdom, where the introduction of unfair dismissal laws was accompanied by robust discussion as to why such protection was needed in order to afford greater job security, in Australia this debate did not occur.

The reason the parliamentary debate took the form of assessing the merits of reliance on international conventions to introduce domestic reform on unfair dismissal was because the Labor government used the external affairs power in the Constitution to avoid the constraints of section 51(xxxv). The external affairs power[142] enables the federal government to make laws with respect to Australia's external affairs and was more expansively interpreted in a series of cases upholding federal laws giving effect to Australia's obligations under international treaties and conventions.[143] To utilise this power, the international instrument must be ratified by the executive arm of the Commonwealth

136 S 170EA.
137 S 170EC.
138 S 170ED.
139 S 170EE.
140 According to s 170CA, the division is intended to give effect to the ILO's Termination of Employment Recommendation 1982 (No 166).
141 Part 2, s 4(b).
142 S 51(xxix).
143 *Koowarta v Bjelke-Petersen* (1982) 153 CLR 168; *Commonwealth v Tasmania* (1983) 158 CLR 1; *Richardson v Forestry Commission* (1988) 164 CLR 261; *Polyukhovich v The Commonwealth* (1991) 65 AJLR 521.

government and the judicial test for assessing whether an Act is supported by section 29 is:

> The law must be capable of being reasonably considered to be appropriate and adapted to achieving what is said to impress it with the character of a law with respect to external affairs. . . . Implicit in the requirement . . . is a need for there to be a reasonable proportionality between the designated purpose or object and the means which the law embodies for achieving or procuring it.[144]

The key sections governing unfair dismissal were contained in part VIA division 3 of the *Industrial Relations Reform Act* and were founded upon the ILO Termination of Employment Convention 1982 (No 158), which was ratified by Australia in February 1993, and the associated Termination of Employment Recommendation (No 166). In some cases the wording of the Australian provisions pertaining to unfair dismissal were identical to those found in the ILO convention and recommendation.[145] The debate over the proposed unfair dismissal scheme focused upon the appropriateness of relying upon section 51(xxix) to introduce a domestic law based on a treaty that most of Australia's trading partners had not ratified. The use of section 51(xxix) instead of section 51(xxxv) to introduce federal unfair dismissal reform represented the use of a novel constitutional power with no affiliation with the traditional doctrine of industrial peace. This narrow parliamentary debate contributed to a fairly under-theorised notion of industrial justice as the basis of Australia's unfair dismissal law.

Conclusion

This chapter has charted the evolution of Australia's labour laws from the traditional conciliation and arbitration system predicated upon a normative preoccupation with the achievement of industrial peace until the introduction of a new system after 1993. This new system did not involve the complete overturning of tradition, as conciliation was chosen as the mechanism for resolving unfair dismissal disputes for most cases. The role of conciliation and arbitration was also to become more important, not less – a development we will turn to in the following chapter. This development saw the transformation of a tribunal system previously concerned with resolving collective disputes into one that was much more concerned with individual dispute resolution.

144 *Commonwealth v Tasmania* (1983) 158 CLR 1 [260] (Deane J).
145 See further, Creighton and Stewart (1994) 203.

5 Australia – Part II

The evolution and erosion of unfair dismissal law

Introduction

Australia's federal unfair dismissal law has been subject to persistent revision since its inception in 1993. Only eight weeks after the introduction of a statutory scheme for resolving unfair dismissal disputes, and then nearly every subsequent year up until 2009, an attempt was made to reform the federal unfair dismissal system through legislation.[1] Since the *Fair Work Act 2009* (Cth), unfair dismissal law has been relatively stable, although, as I will explain, this Act ushered in significant change. The Act was underpinned by objectives of simplicity and efficiency rather than the original normative foundation of federal unfair dismissal law, which was industrial justice.[2]

In each of the reform attempts, it is possible to identify the influence of employers' groups in making the case for reform and the increasingly overt preoccupation of policymakers with the protection of business efficiency and the control of regulatory burdens. In this chapter I examine the basis for reform to Australia's federal unfair dismissal law post-1993. Between 1993 and 2009 the Liberal-National Coalition sought to peel away statutory protection of unfair dismissal because of a belief in the illegitimacy of unfair dismissal law. Since the passage of the *Fair Work Act 2009* (Cth) by the Labor government and the more recent election of the Abbott and Turnbull Coalition governments since 2013, the Liberal-National Coalition has not publicly

1 *Industrial Relations and Other Legislation Amendment Act 1993* (Cth); *Industrial Relations Amendment Act 1994* (Cth); *Workplace Relations Act 1996* (Cth); Workplace Relations Amendment Bill 1997 (Cth); Workplace Relations Amendment Bill 1997 (No 2) (Cth); Workplace Relations Amendment (Unfair Dismissals) Bill 1998 (Cth); Workplace Relations Amendment (Unfair Dismissals) Bill 1998 (No 2) (Cth); Workplace Relations and Other Legislation Amendment (Small Business and Other Measures) Bill 2001 (Cth); Workplace Relations Amendment (Fair Dismissal) Bill 2002 (Cth); *Workplace Relations Amendment (Work Choices) Act 2005* (Cth).

2 This was aided by the decision of the subsequently elected Abbott Coalition government not to make any changes to unfair dismissal law under the *Fair Work Act 2009* (Cth) during its first term in office. See: Liberal-National Coalition, 'The Coalition's Policy to Improve the Fair Work Laws' (May 2013). A copy of this policy can be accessed at <http://lpaweb-static.s3.amazonaws.com/Policies/FairWork.pdf>.

articulated this argument and has actively distanced itself from its previous industrial relations platform.[3]

That the role and validity of unfair dismissal law was politically contentious after 1993 is unsurprising given that there was no bipartisan consensus for its introduction. The case for unfair dismissal law was characterised by the Labor government as being predicated upon international law. When the federal minister for industrial relations, Mr Brereton, introduced the Bill in Parliament, the only rationale he provided was Australia's international obligations. One of the objects expressed in the Act was: 'the protection of wages and conditions of workers through awards and by ensuring that labour standards meet Australia's international obligations'.[4] This emphasis on international obligations meant that there was little public discussion in Australia of the needs of workers or the importance of job security, unlike in the United Kingdom.

Why was the introduction of unfair dismissal law so much more politically divisive in Australia than in the United Kingdom? In my view a number of factors are relevant to understanding this dissonance. First, the divergent timing of legal change meant that the economic context for introducing unfair dismissal law was different. The United Kingdom in 1971 faced a very different economic climate to Australia in 1993, where unfair dismissal law was introduced subsequent to the Thatcher and Reagan administrations abroad, which had resulted in the proliferation of neoliberal ideology amongst policymakers. Economic rationalists argued that unfair dismissal law interfered with the efficiency of the market mechanism.[5] Second, the Labor government's decision to frame the introduction of unfair dismissal law as a requirement under international law meant that the Australian political debate hinged upon the suitability of applying international labour standards to Australia, whilst the British debate was more concerned with the need to provide job security and to prevent unofficial strikes. In the United Kingdom in the 1960s and early 1970s there was a more comprehensive reflection upon the investment that individual employees made in their jobs and the perceived need for the state to protect this investment from being arbitrarily taken away. This consideration culminated in the final report of the Royal Commission on Trade Unions and Employers' Associations published in 1969.[6] In Australia the Liberal-National Coalition opposed unfair dismissal law on the basis that business owners invest their livelihoods in their business, which was threatened by the increasing paper and compliance burden imposed by the statutory unfair dismissal system. Furthermore, in Australia

3 For example, whilst in opposition, the Opposition Leader Mr Abbott publicly signed a contract with the public stating that Work Choices was 'dead, buried, cremated'. See Patricia Karvelas, 'Tony Abbott Signs Contract on Work Choices but Muddles Message on Workplace Laws', *The Australian* (Sydney 19 July 2010).

4 *Industrial Relations Reform Act 1993* (Cth) pt 2 s 4(b).

5 Richard Epstein, 'In Defense of the Contract at Will' (1984) 51 U Chicago L Rev 947; Richard Epstein, 'The Common Law and the Labour Market' (HR Nicholls Publications, 2001).

6 Report of the Royal Commission on Trade Unions and Employers' Associations (Cmnd 3888, 1969) [528].

the Coalition characterised the introduction of unfair dismissal laws as part of an agreement between the union movement and the Labor government. During the second reading debates for the Workplace Relations Amendment (Work Choices) Bill 2005 (Cth), Prime Minister Howard stated:

> Of all the things that are contained in this legislation, none is more important than our commitment to repeal the unfair dismissal laws, which have not been part of our industrial scene since Federation; they have only been part of our industrial scene since 1994, and then only as a result of a secret deal made between the then Labor government and the trade union movement during the 1993 election campaign.[7]

Although the Abbott and Turnbull Coalition governments have not revived this idea, the Howard-led Coalition (both in opposition and government) was consistently opposed to unfair dismissal law since its inception, never relinquishing this idea of unfair dismissal law as a payback to the unions, and thus unjustified on policy grounds.

Against this backdrop of political division caused by the introduction of unfair dismissal law, I will examine the reforms to federal unfair dismissal law which occurred after its inception. In particular, this chapter addresses two regulatory themes: first, the changes made to the adjudicative mechanism and its capacity to provide independent scrutiny of an employer's dismissal decision, and second, the changes made to the application of unfair dismissal law to small business. Both of these reflect a reform agenda animated by a desire to reduce the regulatory burden on business whilst achieving the efficient administration of justice. Although, on the whole, federal unfair dismissal law has not faced a full-frontal assault and it has been fairly impervious to threats to its existence, the dilution of this law since 1993 has meant that its capacity to offer meaningful protection for job security has been somewhat constrained.

The role of the adjudicative mechanism

A foundational aspect of unfair dismissal law is the belief that an employer's dismissal decision should be capable of withstanding external scrutiny via an independent adjudicative mechanism. Although Australia's federal unfair dismissal scheme was initially anchored in the Industrial Relations Court, its role in adjudicating unfair dismissal disputes was soon taken over by the federal industrial tribunal, which to the present day has carriage over unfair dismissal claims made by 'national system employees'.[8] The bulk of the tribunal's role today concerns

7 Commonwealth of Australia, *Parliamentary Debates*, House of Representatives, 9 November 2005 (John Howard, Opposition Leader).

8 A 'national system employer' refers to the type of employer covered by the *Fair Work Act*. Employers and employees not covered by the *Fair Work Act* remain covered by the applicable state industrial relations system. See *Fair Work Act 2009* (Cth) s 13.

unfair dismissal.[9] This section examines how the role of the independent adjudicative mechanism in the federal system has changed over time and the effect this has had on the operation of the system and its achievement of job security protection.

The Industrial Relations Court

In 1993 the Labor government established the Industrial Relations Court (IRC) to deal with unfair dismissal applications made by individual employees and disputes between unions and an employer about secondary boycotts. A key aspect of the Howard Coalition government's argument against unfair dismissal law was its view that a special industrial relations court was unnecessary to regulate unfair dismissal disputes between employers and employees. As we will explain in this part, the Howard Coalition viewed the employment contract as analogous to any other contract regulated under the common law.

The creation of the IRC through the Labor government's *Industrial Relations Reform Act 1993* had long been in the pipeline. In 1987 the Hawke government proposed the creation of a separate labour court through the Industrial Relations Bill 1987 and the Industrial Relations (Consequential Provisions) Bill 1987. A highly controversial aspect of this legislation was the transfer of jurisdiction from the Industrial Registrar of the Federal Court to a new Labour Court, but the dissolution of Parliament in July 1987 meant that these Bills never became law. When the IRC was created in 1993, the Coalition was opposed to its existence right from its inception, arguing that the IRC's independence would be compromised. In its view, Labor's primary motivation in establishing a specialist labour court was to stack the court with judges sympathetic to the interests of unions and workers. The Coalition drew upon the notion of an 'Industrial Relations Club' to argue that the IRC would be a 'club court'. The term 'Industrial Relations Club' was coined in 1983 by Gerald Henderson, a prominent Australian journalist and executive director of the Sydney Institute, an influential policy think tank.[10] In his 1983 essay entitled 'The Industrial Relations Club', Henderson described what he called the rituals of a self-serving club comprising key unionists, Labor Party figures and others who fixed industrial relations outcomes with an ethos of complacency and self-congratulation. He opposed its reliance on 'consensus', 'negotiations' and 'doing deals . . . to secure industrial harmony' because 'economic realities take what is very much second place, if a . . . [decision needs to be] made according to tough-minded economic criteria'.[11]

Henderson's conception of an Industrial Relations Club was significant in solidifying the Coalition government's opposition to the idea of a specialist labour court. Henderson's key premise of an industrial relations system predicated on special

9 42.8 per cent of applications lodged before the FWC concern unfair dismissal. The second most significant number of applications concerns agreements (17.3 per cent): FWC, *Annual Report 2014–2015* (FWC, 2015) 9.

10 Gerard Henderson, 'Industrial Relations Club' *Quadrant* (September 1983).

11 Ibid 23–24, 29.

deals done behind closed doors was championed by Coalition members of Parliament and figured prominently in the debates over the unfair dismissal laws throughout the 1990s. In particular, the phrase was applied by Mr Howard, who was the key driver of the Coalition's industrial relations policy during its time in opposition:

> The Prime Minister is not doing the bidding of the average Australian family in this dispute. He is not doing the bidding of the tourist industry. He is not doing the bidding of the airlines. *He is doing the bidding of the mandarins of the industrial relations club.* That is why he is taking the attitude that he is taking [emphasis added].[12]

The second reading debates about the establishment of the IRC illustrate the Coalition's argument that 'specialist courts are always a little suspect because the concern is they will do special deals for special groups'.[13] The Coalition's view was that the common law courts should be used to regulate employment disputes. Mr Peter Costello, who later became the federal treasurer for the Coalition government argued:

> Normal courts tend to dispense equal justice. So we have a proposal to set up a whole new court, a whole new regime – the industrial relations court – a special court for special justice for special mates. We do not have a special court for corporations. We do not have a special court for men. We do not have a special court for women . . . but we have a special court for trade unions to make sure that people are appointed because of their understanding of their special problems.[14]

Nonetheless, the Labor government fiercely contested the Coalition's support for the common law courts regulating disputes in the workplace. Labor's view was that relying upon the common law courts to enforce rights under the contract of employment placed industrial justice beyond the capability of the individual. Labor argued:

> when individual workers are forced to go to the [common law] courts, how many of them can afford to pay the extraordinary fees which are levied on them when they go through the formal legal process? What we have under challenge is a total attack on the cost of industrial justice, placing it beyond the reach of individual workers.[15]

12 Commonwealth of Australia, *Parliamentary Debates*, House of Representatives, 5 September 1989 (John Howard).

13 Commonwealth of Australia, *Parliamentary Debates*, House of Representatives, 17 November 1993 (John Howard, Opposition Leader).

14 Commonwealth of Australia, *Parliamentary Debates*, House of Representatives, 22 November 1993 (Peter Costello, Shadow Treasurer).

15 Commonwealth of Australia, *Parliamentary Debates*, House of Representatives, 29 September 1999 (Kevin Rudd).

The Australian Industrial Relations Commission

Upon winning the federal election in 1996, the Coalition government did not abolish the statutory system of unfair dismissal and reinstate the law of wrongful dismissal enforced by the common law courts. At this stage and until after its victory in the 2004 election, the Howard government did not have a majority in the Australian Senate, which meant it had to negotiate with the minor parties in order to pass its legislation.[16] The Howard Coalition government eliminated the IRC's role by transferring the IRC's jurisdiction to the Federal Court of Australia.[17] Despite advocating a move away from conciliation and arbitration more generally,[18] the Howard Coalition government's first term reforms anchored the unfair dismissal system in the traditional processes of conciliation and arbitration, with the Australian Industrial Relations Commission (AIRC) appointed as the adjudicator of unfair dismissal disputes.[19] This occurred in 1996 and the Howard Coalition government never removed the AIRC's jurisdiction over unfair dismissal during its time in office. Although, as I will explain, the 1996 reforms did seek to reduce the number of claims under the federal unfair dismissal provisions and were aimed at moderating the outcomes of claims that did eventuate, there is an interesting question of why unfair dismissal law went against the Coalition government's dominant policy of dismantling conciliation and arbitration in this period.

A primary reason for relying upon conciliation and arbitration to resolve unfair dismissal disputes was the Coalition government's belief that the unfair dismissal system introduced by Labor was 'far too detailed, too prescriptive and too legalistic and hence a disincentive to employment'.[20] The IRC's jurisdiction was abolished with the intention of replacing what the Coalition viewed as a legalistic determination of unfair dismissal applications with the more commonsense approach of the AIRC and to strike a fairer balance between the interests of employers and employees. The Coalition government imposed the AIRC's long-standing arbitral principle of a 'fair go all round' into the jurisdiction of unfair dismissal in determining whether a dismissal was harsh, unjust or unreasonable. Section 170CA(2) contained an express statement of legislative purpose as being to provide a system to ensure a 'fair go all around' to

16 The Workplace Relations and Other Legislation Amendment Bill was originally introduced in the Parliament in May 1996. It became law in November of that year, following the agreement between the government and the Australian Democrats to secure its passage through the Senate.

17 The IRC was not abolished but it no longer had jurisdiction. It automatically ceased to exist when 'no person holds office as a Judge' of the Court: *Workplace Relations and Other Legislation Amendment Act 1996* sch 16 item 84.

18 John Howard, 'Radio Interview: PM', Australian Broadcasting Corporation, quoted in David Peetz, 'Coming Soon to a Workplace Near You – The New Industrial Relations Revolution' (2005) 31 Aust Bull Lab 90, 91; Peter Reith, Shadow Minister for Industrial Relations, 'Better Pay for Better Work' (Coalition Industrial Relations Policy, 1996) 1.

19 See further, A Chapman, 'Termination of Employment under the Workplace Relations Act 1996 (Cth)' (1997) 10 Aust J Lab Law 89.

20 Reith (n 18) 1.

the employer and the employee. This section noted that this arbitral principle stemmed from Justice Sheldon in a New South Wales (NSW) unfair dismissal case of *Re Loty and Holloway v Australian Workers Union*.[21] The use of this specific phrase in the *Workplace Relations Act 1996* (Cth) arose out of significant debate over the predecessor Act, which did not include this phrase. In the second reading debates, Mr Reith referred to the judgment of Justice Gray of the IRC and stated:

> They [Labor's unfair dismissal laws] proved to be totally biased against employers. Honourable members do not have to accept my view of that. Justice Gray, in one of the very many court cases we have had on these provisions, said, 'The former South Australian and the present State Act, like their counterpart in New South Wales, operate in the realm of the "fair go all round." . . . This is not a realm that this Court inhabits. The provisions of division 3 of part VIA of the federal Act are not directed to achieving some balance between the interests of employers and employees in particular cases. They constitute a charter of rights for employees. They are directed towards the protection of the existing jobs of employees.'[22]

In replacing the IRC's role in adjudicating unfair dismissal applications with the AIRC, the Coalition government chose to eschew the legalism that was perceived to be associated with the IRC's jurisdiction and instead reformed the federal system to mirror more closely the states' unfair dismissal laws developed on the South Australian model.[23]

By mandating that the commission consider the 'fair go all round' principle, the Howard Coalition government required the commission to consider the business's capacity to pay in its determination of the amount of compensation accorded to an individual after a finding of unfair dismissal. The 'fair go all round' principle originally emerged in Australian labour to protect employees, as they were seen as the disadvantaged party in the employment relationship.[24] Mr Mark Vaille, a key member of the government, characterised the introduction of the 'fair go all round' principle as being partially about the reinstatement of managerial prerogative and requiring the commission to consider fairness to the employer, not just the employee, in disputes about dismissal. He stated that

> the expression of a 'fair go all round' has been used to refer to the importance, but not inviolate ability, of the right of an employer to manage the employer's business, the nature and quality of the worker in question, the

21 [1971] AR (NSW) 95.

22 Commonwealth of Australia, *Parliamentary Debates*, House of Representatives, 30 August 1995 (Peter Reith, Minister for Workplace Relations).

23 B Creighton and A Stewart, *Labour Law* (3rd edn Federation Press, Sydney 2000) 313.

24 For an exploration of how the concept of a 'fair go all round' evolved in Australia see Chapter 4.

circumstances surrounding a dismissal and the likely practical outcome of an order being made.[25]

In this way, the 'fair go all round' principle underwent an ironic reversal during the Howard Coalition government's time in office. Its adoption of the 'fair go all round' principle in the unfair dismissal legislation was actually about rebalancing the system in favour of employers, whereas in its general inception and usage it was about the underdog, which was traditionally depicted as the Australian worker. This transformation of the 'fair go all round' principle was symptomatic of the government's efforts to recast the contract of employment as a relationship between equals, not as a relationship between the employee-as-underdog and the employer-as-master. In its view, at different times, both the employee and the employer could be disadvantaged through the contract of employment and providing for a 'fair go all round' was the appropriate way of ensuring that a balance between the interests of the parties was observed.

The Howard Coalition government's reliance on the AIRC was motivated by the view that the IRC accorded too much importance to procedural fairness. Under the predecessor Act a failure to provide due process could singlehandedly lead to a finding of unfair dismissal, but this was heavily criticised by the Coalition when they were in opposition. In debating the Labor government's 1995 amendments, the opposition repeatedly referred to cases where the IRC had overturned a dismissal that was not procedurally fair where this in their view seemed to fly in the face of common sense:

> A worker in a funeral parlour was dismissed for cremating the wrong body and then awarded $8000 as compensation. . . . There was a company that had a crackdown on people who were nicking stuff from work. One bloke was actually caught red-handed nicking stuff from work whilst the company had a campaign against pilfering. That guy was compensated and reinstated. In another case, the court found an employee's dismissal had been unfair even though his employer had given him three written warnings about unsatisfactory performance. . . . [I]n another case a manager was dismissed because of a $300 000 business deficit. He was reinstated because the deficit was not considered by the court to be conclusive evidence of a downturn in business. $300 000 in the red and that is not enough to prove a downturn in the business.[26]

Consequently, the Coalition government's reform package regulating termination of employment sought to dilute the role of procedural fairness in determining whether a dismissal was unfair. Under section 170CG(3) the AIRC was

25 Commonwealth of Australia, *Parliamentary Debates*, House of Representatives, 26 June 1996 (Mark Vaille, Minister for Trade).

26 Commonwealth of Australia, *Parliamentary Debates*, House of Representatives, 30 August 1995 (Peter Reith, Minister for Workplace Relations).

required to take into account the following factors in order to determine whether an unfair dismissal took place:

a) Whether there was a valid reason for the termination relating to the capacity or conduct of the employee or to the operational requirements of the employer's undertaking, establishment or service; and
b) Whether the employee was notified of the reason; and
c) Whether the employee was given an opportunity to respond to any reason related to the capacity or conduct of the employee; and
d) If the termination related to unsatisfactory performance by the employee – whether the employee had been warned about that unsatisfactory performance; and
e) Any other matters that the Commission considers relevant.[27]

Whilst these factors all appeared individually in the 1993 Act either expressly or by implication, the 1996 Act rearranged these matters as indicia under a single test: was the dismissal harsh, unjust or unreasonable? A failure by an employer to fulfil any one (or more) of the factors in section 170CE(1)(a)–(e) did not necessarily give rise to a contravention of the Act, as procedural fairness was only one consideration. The Explanatory Memorandum to the Bill explained that the intention was that undue weight would not be given to procedural defects in termination.[28] The government's reduction in the role of procedural fairness under the 1996 Act by making it one aspect of a multi-factor test was consistent with its decision to anchor the unfair dismissal system in the AIRC. Unlike the IRC, the AIRC was not constituted by legally qualified judges but instead comprised of members with industrial relations expertise.

The government's sole reliance on the conciliation and arbitration machinery of the AIRC by removing the IRC's jurisdiction was also accompanied by a desire to discourage disputes proceeding to arbitration. Whilst the first step for the AIRC was still to conciliate the dispute, if this failed the AIRC was required to issue a certificate stating that it was satisfied that all reasonable attempts to settle the matter had been or were likely to be unsuccessful and was then required to indicate the commission's assessment of the merits of the application.[29] This new provision was aimed to help the AIRC make a costs order against an applicant who elected to proceed to arbitration despite the dubious merits of his or her case. Once a certificate had been issued it was up to the applicant to determine the next move within the strict time frame of seven days – either to drop the application or proceed to the AIRC's arbitration wing (or in the case of unlawful termination, to a court). Arguably, seven days was not a long time for applicants to consider their options after receiving legal advice, especially given the complicated nature of section 170CF(2).

27 *Workplace Relations Act 1996* (Cth) s 170CG(3).
28 Workplace Relations and Other Legislation Amendment Bill Explanatory Memorandum [7.44].
29 S 170CF(2).

Perhaps another reason for the Coalition government's willingness to rely upon conciliation and arbitration of unfair dismissal applications, despite its policy of dismantling conciliation and arbitration more generally, is because the unfair dismissal system involved the determination of individual rights. Prior to the 1996 election, the Coalition's industrial relations policy 'Better Pay for Better Work' outlined the need for direct relations between employer and employee without the 'uninvited intervention' of trade unions.[30] This continued to be the focus of the Coalition government throughout its time in office as Work Choices provided strict controls over union activity which was intended to address 'a system where third parties of all stripes can insert themselves too easily into workplace processes to the detriment of cooperation between employers and employees'.[31] The traditional system of conciliation and arbitration was used to resolve collective disputes, and the determination of these disputes through the commission legitimised the role of trade unions. In contrast, the unfair dismissal system is concerned with providing individuals with a statutory remedy and the use of conciliation and arbitration in this system does not require a recognition or encouragement of trade unionism. Perhaps this was a key reason why conciliation and arbitration via the AIRC was permitted by the Coalition Howard government in the unfair dismissal system but marginalised in its policies regarding collective wage determination and collective dispute resolution.

Fair Work Australia

Upon its decisive victory in the federal election in 2007, the Labor government did not seek to recreate the IRC. Instead, Labor's policy was to establish 'a simpler unfair dismissal system which balances the rights of employees to be protected from unfair dismissal, with the need for employers to manage their workforce and to ensure a faster, less costly and less complex process for all'.[32] Although Labor's pre-election policy platform promised a 'fresh' unfair dismissal process involving 'conferences' conducted by an industrial umpire which Labor named 'Fair Work Australia' (FWA),[33] the legislative enactment of this promise left it to the Fair Work Commission's (FWC) discretion which dispute resolution mechanisms it relied upon.[34] Whilst the *Fair Work Act 2009* (Cth) does not require the FWC to conciliate unfair dismissal applications, the Act does require the FWC to conduct a conference or hold a hearing if the matter involves disputed facts.[35] Early after its inception, the FWC used its discretionary power to design a standard dispute

30 Reith (n 18) 1.

31 John Howard, 'Workplace Reform: The Next Logical Step' (Address to the Sydney Institute, Four Seasons Hotel, Sydney 2005).

32 Kevin Rudd and Julia Gillard, 'Forward with Fairness: Labor's Plan for Fairer and More Productive Australian Workplaces' (ALP, Canberra 2007) 19.

33 Hereafter, FWA will be referred to as the Fair Work Commission or FWC.

34 B O'Neill, 'General Manager's Report into the Operation of the First Three Years of the Fair Work Act 2009 (Cth) Unfair Dismissal System' (Commonwealth of Australia, December 2012) 30.

35 *Fair Work Act 2009* (Cth) s 397.

resolution process for unfair dismissals. This process continues to operate to the present day. Once an unfair dismissal application is made, it is provided to the employer in question requiring them to outline the reasons for dismissal and the employer's response to the applicant's allegations. At this stage the application is then analysed and either allocated to a member of the FWC or allocated to the conciliation support team. The large bulk of unfair dismissal applications are then listed for a voluntary telephone conciliation.[36] Where a matter is unable to be resolved with the assistance of the conciliator, or the employer makes a jurisdictional objection, the matter is listed before a commission member.[37]

Whilst the introduction of conciliation by telephone was a substantial break with the traditional unfair dismissal process, conciliation has usually been a precursor to arbitration in Australia's federal unfair dismissal system.[38] Under the *Workplace Relations Act 1996* (Cth), the AIRC was required to conciliate unfair dismissal matters.[39] These conciliations were conducted by commissioners and former commissioners in the first instance. Where a conciliation did not result in settlement of a matter, the matter could not proceed to arbitration unless the conciliator issued a report to the panel head who then issued a certificate stating that all reasonable attempts had been made to settle the matter.[40] The formal and legal nature of Australia's traditional conciliation process was a hangover from the early days of conciliation being carried out by the Conciliation and Arbitration Court. As it evolved, the conciliator was always a member of the commission, the parties stood when the commissioner entered the room, there were formal submissions and statements, and the conciliation generally took place at the tribunal's offices. The parties were compelled to attend the conciliation and only if it failed would the parties proceed to arbitration, which is when the commissioner made a determination that was legally binding. These features of the traditional conciliation process, used between 1901 and 1993 to determine collective disputes about wages and conditions, were applied to federal unfair dismissal law prior to the development of telephone conciliation following the passage of the *Fair Work Act 2009* (Cth). In the traditional process, the objective of conciliation was to encourage the parties to reach agreement, with the spectre of arbitration used to motivate settlement. As Justice Henry Bourne Higgins stated in his summary of the commission's role:

> But it ought to be more generally understood that the Court has no power to award, to make a compulsory award, except so far as it cannot secure

36 Telephone conciliation is voluntary, although most unfair dismissal applicants are unaware of this. The Fair Work Commission states on its website that it is a voluntary process. See <www.fwc.gov.au/at-the-commission/coming-the-commission/what-happens-at-conciliation>.

37 FWC (n 9) 70. An example of a jurisdictional issue is when an unfair dismissal claim is made out of time. Unfair dismissal claims can only be made within twenty-one days of the date of dismissal; *Fair Work Act 2009* (Cth) s 394.

38 See further, Marilyn Pittard, 'Fair Process in Unfair Dismissal Claims: Changing Landscape under the Fair Work Act' (2010) 17 Aust J Admin Law 199.

39 *Workplace Relations Act 1996* (Cth) s 650(1).

40 *Workplace Relations Act 1996* (Cth) s 650(2).

> agreement between the contending parties. Its first duty is to try to conciliate, to get an agreement. . . . But without the power to award in the final resort, there often could be no agreement procured. A few unreasonable employers could hold up a fair settlement, could indeed hold up the whole industry. . . . The ideal of the Court is to secure regulations such as would be fitting for a fair collective agreement; *and the power to award is held by the Court in reserve, as a whip over a horse* [emphasis added].[41]

Despite the long pedigree of conciliation in Australian labour law, conciliation by telephone was an innovation. Although conciliation by telephone had previously occurred on rare occasions to deal with disputes in remote areas, after 2007 the practice became the norm. It was intended to empty the conciliation process of legal rules of procedure, formal submissions and lengthy proceedings and achieve Labor's commitment to delivering 'a simpler, faster and less costly unfair dismissal process'.[42] The new telephone conciliation process meant that conciliation was no longer carried out by a member of the commission with security of tenure who had been appointed because of a distinguished career in industrial relations. Instead, the FWC appointed conciliators who were lay professionals with specialist experience in dispute resolution. Unlike an independent judiciary, which is not susceptible to performance management, FWC conciliators are accorded targets as to the number of conciliations they are required to carry out each week and how long these should take. By the FWC's own admission, the conciliator's role is an activist and interventionist one, aimed at finding a resolution to the dispute between the two parties.[43]

Undeniably, telephone conciliations have been successful in expediently processing claims and resolving disputes prior to arbitration, although the statistics do not show a vastly different picture to that which existed prior to the introduction of conciliation by telephone. The FWC argues that telephone conciliations have been successful in resolving unfair dismissal applications in a 'timely, informal, effective and efficient manner',[44] with the median time from lodgement of an application to the finalisation of an unfair dismissal conciliation dropping from 46 days in 2013–14 to 28 days in 2014–15.[45] That this median time frame is now less than a month evinces the efficient nature of the telephone conciliation process that has been implemented by the FWC. Nonetheless, although unfair dismissal disputes appear to reach conciliation more quickly, the overall time frame before the majority of disputes are finalised appears to be slightly longer under the present system of telephone conciliations. In 2014–15 it took

41 Henry Bourne Higgins, 'Industrial Arbitration' (address in Chapter House of St Paul's Cathedral, Melbourne, 22 March 1926), reprinted in (2001) 27 Aust Bull Lab 177, 187.

42 Rudd and Gillard (n 32) 3, 19.

43 Jennifer Acton, 'Where Have All the Cases Gone? Voluntary Resolution of Unfair Dismissal Claims' (ALLA National Conference, Adelaide, November 2010).

44 Ibid.

45 FWC (n 9) 70.

42 days from lodgement of an unfair dismissal application until the first conciliation,[46] whereas in 2008–09 it took 54 days.[47] However, in 2014–15 it took 133 days from lodgement of an application until finalisation of an unfair dismissal application,[48] whereas in 2008–09 it took only 106 days.[49] Thus, whilst conciliation by telephone appears to enable the dispute to be conciliated at an earlier point in time, overall the introduction of telephone conciliation has not greatly improved the timeliness of processing unfair dismissal applications.

A similar point can be made about the efficacy of telephone conciliation compared with the previous model of in-person conciliation in resolving disputes and helping the parties reach agreement. More than 11,000 matters were conciliated in 2014–15 and 79 per cent of matters referred to conciliation were resolved at this stage.[50] The conciliation process, combined with comprehensive case management processes post-conciliation, resulted in nearly 90 per cent of unfair dismissal applications being resolved without a need for a determination to be made by a commission member.[51] It should be noted, however, that in the year before telephone conciliations were introduced, conciliation by a commission member was successful in resolving claims, with 86 per cent of claims being resolved at or prior to conciliation, and with a further 13 per cent finalised prior to arbitrated orders being issued.[52]

In research commissioned by FWA in the year after telephone conciliations were introduced, most applicants and respondents reported a positive attitude towards the use of this mode of dispute resolution.[53] The research found that '78% of applicants [and] 81% of respondents . . . agreed or strongly agreed the conciliation of an unfair dismissal application by telephone conference works well'.[54] The vast majority of applicants and respondents felt that telephone conciliation was efficient and effective, and 72 per cent of applicants and 59 per cent of respondents reported that telephone conciliation was more comfortable than face-to-face conciliation. The research also found broad support for the conduct and performance of conciliators.[55]

Nonetheless, there are potentially a number of concerns arising from this shift towards telephone conciliations. A key difference between the previous model, which relied on a tribunal member to conciliate the dispute, and the use of a specialist lay conciliator is that the latter may be under greater pressure to achieve a settlement. Whilst a tribunal member is a judicial officer with security of tenure, a

46 FWC (n 9) 79. This statistic concerns 90 per cent of matters.

47 Australian Industrial Relations Commission, *Annual Report 2008–2009* (AIRC, 2009) 47. This statistic concerns 85 per cent of matters.

48 FWC (n 9) 79. This statistic concerns 90 per cent of matters.

49 Australian Industrial Relations Commission (n 47) 47. This statistic concerns 85 per cent of matters.

50 FWC (n 9) 72.

51 Ibid.

52 Australian Industrial Relations Commission (n 47) 9.

53 Fair Work Australia, 'Unfair Dismissal Conciliation Research' (TNS Social Research 2010) 5.

54 Ibid.

55 Ibid 37–44.

lay conciliator is a public servant whose work is subject to key performance indicators.[56] The duty of the conciliation officer to achieve settlement over the phone to avoid the case going to arbitration could prevent the conciliator from adopting a truly impartial stance. There is significant time pressure upon the conciliation officer to negotiate an agreement between the parties, as the conciliator is required to conduct up to three conciliations per day. This target allows each conciliation to last for about one and a half hours, although there is scope for the conciliator to make follow-up phone calls to the parties. Given that over the phone there is more opportunity for misunderstanding to occur and often more time needs to be spent explaining, a conciliator may struggle to uncover the truth of a situation in that time frame. In this context, it is possible that it is more difficult to achieve a just outcome. In a case where an employee has been unfairly dismissed, a conciliator is likely to encourage an employee to accept an employer's offer or, in the case of a fairly vexatious or trivial claim, an employer may be persuaded to offer a minimal amount to stop the complaint proceeding to arbitration and to ensure its resolution. Despite there being no powers to compel the parties to reach agreement, an FWC conciliator is still able to use all his powers of persuasion, knowledge and experience to encourage settlement. This is a considerable advantage considering this is likely to be the first unfair dismissal conciliation an employee has been involved in, and one of only a handful that an employer has participated in. Although the parties may have other motivations for reaching a settlement, such as a desire to reduce costs or to end the dispute so that the parties can move on, a conciliator's role is a powerful one in helping the parties reach an agreement.

Another concern is that the move to resolve unfair dismissal disputes via telephone conciliation means that priority is given to resolving disputes *quickly* rather than resolving disputes *fairly*. The two are not necessarily mutually exclusive but certainly a preoccupation with the former and with achieving the settlement of claims means that a conciliator has less of an interest in ensuring that industrial justice is achieved. In fact, this is not a strong focus of a conciliator's role: the FWC's Procedures Manual emphasises that a conciliator's key objectives are to maximise flexibility and informality, to be independent and impartial and to encourage settlement of disputes.[57] Collins, writing about conciliation in the British context, articulates a drawback of the conciliation process in its ability to deliver procedural justice.[58] He argues that during conciliation the primary concern of the conciliator is to encourage the parties to resolve the substantive aspects of the case, which usually results in the employer putting down a modest sum which reflects the merits of the case but does not account for a breach of the standards of fair procedure.[59] This observation is even more pertinent in

56 For an example of these, see the Key Performance Indicators targets recorded in the FWC's 2013–14 Portfolio Budget Statements.

57 Fair Work Commission, 'Procedures Manual' app 38: Conciliator Code of Conduct.

58 Hugh Collins, *Justice in Dismissal: The Law of Termination of Employment* (Clarendon Press, Oxford 1992) 137–39.

59 Ibid 138.

the Australian context of telephone conciliations, where the time pressure to resolve the dispute over the phone and in the days after the telephone conciliation affords less time to draw attention to the potential procedural defects of the employee's dismissal. Bedford and Creyke note that many tribunals must carry out their functions in a way which is 'fair, just, economical, informal and quick'.[60] It could be argued that telephone conciliations with their reliance on lay conciliators prioritise the latter three of these objectives at the expense of the former[61] and that, in so doing, telephone conciliations mean that Australia's unfair dismissal laws continue to allow the payment of 'go away money'. 'Go away money' refers to the practice of employers offering money to settle marginal, or on occasion what they perceive as groundless, unfair dismissal claims. The Labor government's 'Forward with Fairness – Policy Implementation Plan' promised effectively to end the payment of 'go away money' by employers.[62] However, submissions to the Fair Work Act Review[63] and to the Productivity Commission inquiry into the Australian workplace relations framework[64] indicate that some employer groups still consider this to be a significant problem under the *Fair Work Act* 2009 (Cth).[65] The Productivity Commission's inquiry report found that 'while anecdotal evidence suggests that "go away" money is still paid, the exact share of settled cases falling into this category is not clear'.[66] The Productivity Commission also noted the evidential difficulty in ascertaining the extent of 'go away' money being paid to employees because there is no independent party to assess whether the amount of money paid to a former employee is appropriate in the circumstances of the matter.[67] The commission

60 N Bedford and Robin Creyke, *Inquisitorial Processes in Australian Tribunals* (Australian Institute of Judicial Administration, Melbourne 2006) 33.

61 Ibid.

62 Julia Gillard and Kevin Rudd, 'Forward with Fairness – Policy Implementation Plan' (Canberra: ALP, 2007) 18.

63 The Fair Work Act Review was conducted by a panel of eminent Australians, comprising Reserve Bank Board Member Dr John Edwards, former Federal Court Judge the Honourable Michael Moore, and noted legal and workplace relations academic Professor Emeritus Ron McCallum AO. The Fair Work Act Review Panel's final report, 'Towards More Productive and Equitable Workplaces: An Evaluation of the Fair Work Legislation', was released on 2 August 2012.

64 On 19 December 2014 the Australian government asked the Productivity Commission to undertake an inquiry into the Australian workplace relations framework. The Productivity Commission handed its final report to the Australian government on 30 November and it was publicly released on 18 December 2015: Productivity Commission, 'Inquiry into the Workplace Relations Framework' (Inquiry Report, Commonwealth of Australia 2015).

65 For example, see Anthony Forsyth and Andrew Stewart, Submission to Fair Work Act Review, February 2012, 32–33; Council of Small Business of Australia, Submission to the Fair Work Act Review, February 2012, 7. See also the submissions of the Australian Hotels Association and Accommodation Association of Australia (submission no 164) and Queensland Industry (submission no 150) which raise concerns about the payment of 'go away money'.

66 Productivity Commission (2015) 580.

67 Ibid.

considers recent reforms to dissuade the payment of 'go away money' as a 'step in the right direction'.[68]

Conclusion

This section began with an analysis of the Howard Coalition government's opposition to the idea of specialist labour courts and its decision to anchor the federal unfair dismissal system within the conciliation and arbitration mechanism undertaken by the federal tribunal. This gave way to an analysis of the Rudd and Gillard Labor governments' subsequent decision not to revive the IRC but to rename the federal tribunal and to encourage a dispute resolution process which prioritised the timely and efficient processing of unfair dismissal claims. Labor's reforms have survived the subsequent election of the Abbott and Turnbull Coalition governments, with conciliation by telephone now firmly implanted as the primary mechanism by which unfair dismissal claims are processed.[69] Although telephone conciliation does appear to provide an efficient and timely mechanism for resolving unfair dismissal claims, and has no doubt decreased the costs of the process to the FWC and to the parties, the FWC's performance in this regard does not appear to be substantially different since the introduction of conciliation by telephone compared with the year prior to the introduction of this reform. Additionally, there is a genuine concern as to whether the use of telephone conciliations dilutes the quality of the scrutiny of an employer's dismissal decision provided by the external adjudicative mechanism.

Small business exceptionalism as a challenge to unfair dismissal law

That the Howard Coalition government desired to exempt small business from unfair dismissal law is clear. Eleven unsuccessful legislative attempts were made between 1996 and 2005 to remove small business from the unfair dismissal system on the basis that these businesses do not have specialist human resources personnel.[70] During its fourth term, the Howard Coalition government was finally successful in its intention to exempt small business from the unfair dismissal

68 Ibid 589. In brief, these reforms included increased powers for the FWO to dismiss applications where it was satisfied the applicant had behaved unreasonably (s 399A); to make an order for costs against a party if their unreasonable act or omission caused the other party in the matter to incur costs (s 400A); and to impose cost orders on lawyers and paid agents where the tribunal is satisfied that they encouraged speculative claims (s 401(1A)).

69 Telephone conciliation is also likely to be extended into other areas of the FWC's practice – for example, the 2015 pilot trial of the use of telephone conciliations for general protections claims has concluded and from 2016 telephone conciliations will become the norm for all general protections applications involving dismissal: FWC (n 9) 2.

70 These attempts to make amendments included two via regulations, both of which were unsuccessful and ten Bills, nine of which were unsuccessful, while the tenth Bill (which ultimately became Work Choices) was successful: Steve O'Neill, 'Unfair Dismissal and the Small Business Exemption' (Parliament of Australia Library, 2008).

system. Its *Workplace Relations Amendment (Work Choices) Act 2005* (Cth), which came into effect in 2006, removed businesses with less than 100 employees from the unfair dismissal jurisdiction.[71] Prior to this reform, the only threshold numbers that had been discussed by the government were fifteen or twenty. The increased threshold was described as 'the single biggest surprise' of the Work Choices reforms.[72] Nevertheless, leaving aside the well-trodden arguments about the adequacy of this numerical figure in defining a small business, my concern here is whether the Howard Coalition government's argument about needing to inoculate small business from unfair dismissal law is made out. This section will consider the Howard Coalition government's argument that a small business owner enters into an employment contract with an employee in a relationship of equal power, thereby undermining the argument that the employment contract is a special type of contract necessitating statutory intervention to remedy the disadvantaged position of the employee.

The case for regulatory tiering

Regulatory tiering is lighter regulatory treatment for small businesses, which they are seen to deserve by virtue of their small size.[73] In the specific context of unfair dismissal law, small businesses are often viewed as deserving of special solicitude because the immense pressure of running a small business means that small business owners lack the time or resources to acquaint themselves with how to comply with statutory dismissal standards. Small employers are also seen to be less equipped during the recruitment process for new employees and therefore deserving of special leniency if their hiring decisions turn out to be incorrectly made. There is also a belief that small businesses tend to be more constrained with regard to liquidity, so that an unexpected financial cost like that which can arise from an unfair dismissal claim has a greater impact on their viability.

During its four terms in government between 1996 and 2007, the Howard-led Coalition consistently argued that the small business case challenges the traditional labour law characterisation of the employment contract as an unequal bargain between an employer and employee. Traditional labour law views the assumption of freedom to contract as problematic because of a belief that the parties are unequally matched. As Higgins famously opined, 'the "haggling of the market" for labour, with the pressure for bread on one side and the pressure for profits on the other' is usually an unequal contest.[74] In his view 'despotism in contract' is more common than freedom of contract in employment relationships.[75] The

71 *Workplace Relations Amendment (Work Choices) Act 2005* (Cth) (hereafter '*Work Choices Act*').
72 Peetz (n 18).
73 For more on this notion of regulatory tiering, see eg, William A Brock and David S Evans, 'The Economics of Regulatory Tiering' (1985) 16(3) Rand J Eco 398. See also, Productivity Commission (n 66) 222.
74 *Ex Parte HV McKay* (1907) 2 CAR 1, 3.
75 *Federated Engine Drivers and Firemen's Association of Australasia v Broken Hill Proprietary Co Ltd* (1911) 5 CAR 9, 28 (Higgins J).

Howard Coalition government challenged this traditional notion of labour versus capital through honing in on the relationship between the small business owner and the employee. In its view the actual workings of the contract of employment in this context reveal a very different power relationship to the traditional imbalance of power characterised in academic literature. The Howard Coalition government depicted a small business owner as part of the 'engine room of the Australian economy', who works on behalf of the national prosperity, investing their time, energy and resources into making their business a success.[76] As Prime Minister Howard noted, 'we remain, unapologetically, a party that supports and encourages the 1.9 million small businesses in Australia. I grew up believing that the best thing you could do in life was to start a business, work hard, take risks, employ people and pass on that legacy to your children.'[77] His government believed that the ability of the small business owner to succeed was hampered by unfair dismissal law, which sets up 'procedures, rules and regulations surrounding relationships between employers and employees' and as a result shrouds 'the whole relationship with legalism and procedural arguments'.[78] The Howard Coalition government viewed unfair dismissal law as unnecessary because the employee was seen as a valued member of the small business whose direct relationship with the owner enabled the employer to assess the employee's performance accurately. According to this perspective, small business owners were deterred from dismissing employees arbitrarily because they invested heavily in the recruitment process and the ongoing employment relationship in order to employ and retain quality staff. The Howard Coalition government also argued that small business owners could be disadvantaged in the employment relationship because of the investment of not just their work but their livelihood in the business, often referring to a belief that 'in many small businesses the employees are taking home more pay than the employers'[79] and observing that 'employers are never compensated when their valued employees leave'.[80] This personalisation of the parties entering into the employment contract was a strong feature of the Coalition's argument against the introduction of unfair dismissal laws by the Labor government in 1993. In contesting this reform, the Howard Coalition government argued the importance of enabling small business owners to enter into direct relationships with their employees because they are 'good people of principle, who want that freedom, as employers, to agree with their employees, man to man, woman to woman, *equal to equal* . . . and to get on with business without this paraphernalia'.[81]

76 John Howard, 'The Challenge of Economic Management' (Canberra: Menzies Research Centre, 2007).

77 Ibid.

78 Commonwealth of Australia, *Parliamentary Debates*, House of Representatives, 9 June 1994 (Bob Charles).

79 Commonwealth of Australia, *Parliamentary Debates*, House of Representatives, 9 June 1994 (Peter Slipper).

80 Commonwealth of Australia, *Parliamentary Debates*, House of Representatives, 31 August 1995 (Wilson Tuckey).

81 Commonwealth of Australia, *Parliamentary Debates*, House of Representatives, 22 November 1993 (Peter Costello, Shadow Treasurer).

During its period in opposition, Labor fiercely contested the Howard Coalition government's notion of small business disadvantage counterbalancing employee disadvantage in the employment contract. Labor's view was that the employment contract was different from a commercial contract because 'the thing being sold is indivisible from the seller and thus associated with a complex dynamic web of social interactions which lie outside the simple market transaction'.[82] Labor's view was that there is an imbalance of power in the employment contract that is remedied by statutory intervention. As Senator Beahan observed during the parliamentary debates about the unfair dismissal laws:

> The term bargaining is used to disguise what is in truth the imposition of terms and conditions over which most individual employees will have no control. 'Flexibility' in the Liberal lexicon is code for wholesale reduction in wages and conditions and the restoration of employer control over every aspect of the workplace – or the return to the old and outdated concept of managerial prerogative.[83]

Both prior to and during the term of the Howard Coalition government, Labor did not agree that small businesses should be exempt from unfair dismissal law. In the second reading debates for the Industrial Relations and Other Legislation Amendment Bill 1995, Labor's minister for industrial relations explicitly recognised that the unfair dismissal system involved a cost for employers. He stated that whilst 'it is true that the unfair dismissal provisions do put certain burdens on employers who wish to dismiss employees, there is no doubt that we are proud that those burdens are there. We say that the burden is entirely commensurate with the importance of the decision to the employee.'[84] Thus, the debate over the application of Australia's unfair dismissal laws to small business revealed a clear point of demarcation between the major political parties. During its time in opposition between 1996 and 2007, the Labor Party consistently repudiated the Coalition's argument that the contract of employment represented an equal bargain that adequately regulated the dismissal of an employee.

Reform attempts affecting small business by the Howard Coalition government between 1996 and 2007

The Howard Coalition government's belief in the equal ability of small business owners and employees to enter into the employment contract led to numerous attempts to remove small business from the unfair dismissal jurisdiction. The government advocated a return to the common law of wrongful dismissal for

82 Commonwealth of Australia, *Parliamentary Debates*, House of Representatives, 7 December 1993 (Lindsay Tanner).

83 Commonwealth of Australia, *Parliamentary Debates*, Senate, 7 December 1993 (Michael Beahan).

84 Commonwealth of Australia, *Parliamentary Debates*, House of Representatives, 18 September 1995 (Laurie Brereton, Minister for Industrial Relations).

small business owners, as this provided both employers and employees with rights under the contract. Its argument was that the contract 'guaranteed an employee certain rights, on the other hand they left the employer to run his own business as he wished, within reasonable limits, and to hire and fire'.[85] Upon winning the federal election in 1995, the Coalition government commissioned a task force to investigate the compliance and paper burden on small business.[86] A key finding of this task force was the perception that the unfair dismissal laws were 'the final nail in the coffin for a segment of the society that has now felt besieged for more than a decade'.[87] According to the task force's final report, small business owners raised the unfair dismissal laws time and again even though only a small number reported having been directly affected.[88] This report set the background for the Howard Coalition government's endeavour to exempt small business from the unfair dismissal system. Between 1997 and 1998, six Bills were passed through the House of Representatives seeking to extract businesses with fewer than fifteen employees from the unfair dismissal laws. These failed to get through the Senate where the Coalition government did not have a majority, as the government was unable to garner the support of the minor parties who held the balance of power. For a Bill to become law in Australia, a majority in the House of Representatives and the Senate must pass it. Between 2001 and 2004 the government attempted on five further occasions to pass laws exempting businesses with more than twenty employees from the unfair dismissal system. Again, these Bills failed to become law.[89] Nonetheless, the government was able to secure the passage of the *Workplace Relations Amendment (Termination of Employment) Act 2001* (Cth) which added some further factors to those already existing in section 170CG(3) in deciding whether a dismissal was unfair, unjust or unreasonable. These were:

> (da) the degree to which the size of the employer's undertaking, establishment or service would be likely to impact on the procedures followed in effecting termination; and
>
> (db) the degree to which the absence of dedicated human resource management specialists or expertise in the undertaking, establishment or service would be likely to impact on the procedures followed in effecting the termination.

In the first case to examine these factors, Senior Deputy President Lacy of the AIRC indicated the reluctance of the commission to modify the standard required of dismissal processes because a business was small in scope:

85 Commonwealth of Australia, *Parliamentary Debates*, House of Representatives, 9 June 1994 (Peter Slipper).

86 Small Business Deregulation Task Force, 'The Bell Report, Time for Business, Report of the Small Business Deregulation Task Force' (Small Business Deregulation Task Force, 1996).

87 Kirsten Falconer and Fadil Pedic, 'Small Talk – Group Discussions with Small Business about Paper and Compliance Burden' (Small Business Deregulation Task Force, 1996) 29.

88 Small Business Deregulation Task Force (n 86) 15.

89 See further, Marilyn Pittard, 'Unfair Dismissal Law: The Problem of Application to Small Business' (2006) 19 Aust J Lab Law 255.

> While the significance of the absence of the human resource management specialists or expertise in an undertaking in relation to the procedures for effecting termination of employment are reasonably evident, the same cannot be said of the size of the employer's undertaking in relation to such procedures. Employees who are about to lose their employment are entitled to expect a fair go, regardless of the size of the employer's undertaking.[90]

A watershed in Australia's unfair dismissal laws occurred in 2006 with the enactment of the Coalition government's Work Choices reforms.[91] After a decade in office and finally with a majority in both Houses of Parliament, the *Work Choices Act* represented the government's bold attempt to establish a largely national system of labour relations in the Australian private sector and represented the most fundamental change to the Australian labour law landscape for more than 100 years. The case for Work Choices was premised upon the need for Australia to compete in a globalised world by improving the productivity of the labour force. A key aspect of the government's agenda was to provide a framework for business to increase their international competitiveness. The small business exemption which the government was finally able to introduce had the effect of removing unfair dismissal rights for three million Australian employees.[92]

The *Work Choices Act* excluded employees of businesses with a labour force of 100 or fewer from unfair dismissal protection. The government argued that this would allow a 'small' business to hire new employees without the threat of an unfair dismissal claim if that employee is let go. The decision to use 100 employees as the threshold number for a small business was surprising, as in its previous discussions of small business exemptions the government had suggested limits of 15 or 20 employees. There was no policy document outlining why 100 was chosen, and debate around this number was scant. The decision to use 100 as the threshold number exempted small business as well as medium to larger employers from the unfair dismissal laws.[93] The Australian Bureau of Statistics estimated that at the time the *Work Choices Act* was introduced, over 90 per cent of Australian businesses employed 100 staff or fewer.[94]

The 100 employees rule increased confusion and the administrative burden upon businesses as the task of determining the number of employees was not

90 *Pergaminos v Thian Pty Ltd t/as Glenhuntly Terrace*, Print 920123 (16 July 2002) 10.

91 In late 2005, the Australian Parliament enacted the *Work Choices Act*, which made very significant amendments to, and re-numbered the sections of, the *Workplace Relations Act 1996* (Cth).

92 Fair Work Bill 2009 (Cth), Explanatory Memorandum, 212.

93 Marilyn Pittard, 'Back to the Future: Unjust Termination of Employment under the Work Choices Legislation' (2006) 19 Aust J Lab Law 225.

94 Australian Bureau of Statistics, *Characteristics of Small Business* (Cat no. 8127.0, 2004), cited in Sarah Haining and Jan Schapper, 'Unfair Dismissal: Perception and Reality' (Monash University, 2006) <http://pegsnet.pegs.vic.edu.au/studentdownloads/Economics/Students/Year%2012%20Folder/Microeconomics/unfair-dismissal%20laws.pdf> accessed 10 January 2011.

as straightforward as first appeared. Only full-time, part-time and regular casuals were included in the headcount of employees, but employees who were employed by a 'related body corporate' could also be included. What determined a 'related body corporate' was stipulated in section 50 of the *Corporations Act 2001* (Cth). The *Triangle Cables Case* exemplified the difficulty in determining whether the 100 employees rule applied to a particular company.[95] In order to ascertain whether the sacked employees could claim that their dismissal was unfair because there were less than 101 employees, the commission underwent a very detailed examination of the company's relationship with related companies in Thailand, Germany, the USA, Italy and the Netherlands, as well as scrutiny of employees who worked at Triangle Cables but were employed by labour hire companies.[96] This was a very complex and time-consuming process, undermining the simplicity of the reform as well as putting immense pressure on employers seeking to rely upon the exemption to ensure they had made a correct headcount before terminating an employee.

The removal of unfair dismissal rights for three million Australian employees via the 100 employees rule begs the question: was the real intent of the Coalition government to remove the unfair dismissal laws altogether and to return to the common law of wrongful dismissal? Certainly the government's sudden decision to increase the threshold for the exemption from 15 or 20 to 100 adds credence to this argument given that this number did not seem to reflect community norms around the size of a small business. In the second reading speech introducing the Work Choices Bill into Parliament, the minister for workplace relations assured the House that 'Work Choices will take the unfair dismissal monkey off the back of business' and 'whatever their intended purpose, unfair dismissal laws have acted as a brake on job creation. . . . [T]hey have fostered a climate of complaint and litigation . . . to the point where some firms go to any lengths to avoid hiring extra staff'.[97] Nothing in this speech or in any of the public statements issued by members of the Coalition government during its fourth term indicated any support for the existence of a statutory right not to be unfairly dismissed. The following quotation from Prime Minister Howard's speech to the small business community in 1996 illustrates the strength of the anti-unfair dismissal law rhetoric that characterised the government's approach throughout its eleven years in office:

> I want to assure all of you that we will not weaken or tire in our efforts to secure the passage through the Senate of further reforms of the unfair dismissal laws. They remain to me one of the greatest blots on the escutcheon of small business. I hold strongly to the belief that if we could get rid of the

95 *Baldacchino and Ors v Triangle Cables (Aust) Pty Ltd* (Australian Industrial Relations Commission, Smith C, 24 May 2006).

96 Ibid.

97 Commonwealth of Australia, *Parliamentary Debates*, House of Representatives, 2 November 2005 (Kevin Andrews).

restrictions we're trying to get rid of we will see more jobs created in the small business community.[98]

As the Howard Coalition government lost the subsequent federal election, one can only posit that its next legislative reform to the unfair dismissal laws might have been to abolish them altogether or preserve them for employees in a very small minority of businesses. However, this is just conjecture – what can be positively identified is the Howard Coalition's opposition to unfair dismissal law, its belief in the appropriateness of the employment contract to govern relations between employees and employers, and its willingness to advocate a special case of employer disadvantage for small business owners and to apply an exemption from unfair dismissal law to both small and medium-sized businesses.

Reform attempts affecting small business by the Labor government between 2007 and 2013

It is against this backdrop of the previous government's argument about small business exceptionalism that the Labor government introduced the Fair Dismissal Code (FDC), which represented Labor's attempt to balance the need to protect job security with the recognition that 'small businesses do not have the human resources support that larger businesses enjoy'.[99] So thus, whilst access to the unfair dismissal system was enlarged under the FDC, as a small business was defined as a business with fewer than fifteen employees,[100] the establishment of the FDC was intended to limit procedural fairness requirements and prevent substantive review of an employer's dismissal decision if the FDC was complied with,[101] although, as I will explain, in practice the process has been more complicated than intended. Furthermore, the introduction of the FDC illustrated the success of the Howard Coalition government in establishing the rights of small business as a legitimate focus of the unfair dismissal system justifying regulatory tiering and the willingness of the Labor government to accept this argument.

The FDC is found in part 3–2 of the *Fair Work Act 2009* (Cth).[102] That part's objects include establishing a framework for dealing with unfair dismissal that

98 John Howard, 'The Challenges Facing Small Business' (Speech to the Council of Small Business Organisations of Australia, 29 March 2002).

99 Commonwealth of Australia, *Parliamentary Debates*, House of Representatives, Second Reading Speech for the Fair Work Bill 2008 (Cth) (Julia Gillard, Minister for Workplace Relations).

100 According to the Explanatory Memorandum of the *Fair Work Act 2009* (Cth), abolishing the 100 employee exemption and replacing it with qualifying periods of six and twelve months (depending on the size of the employer) allowed many more employees to access unfair dismissal laws – estimated to be 6.7 million (or 80 per cent of employees) compared with 3.7 million (or 44 per cent of employees) under Work Choices.

101 A copy of the FDC can be found on the website of the Fair Work Commission: <www.fairwork.gov.au/ending-employment/unfair-dismissal>.

102 *Said v Jokar Holdings Pty Ltd* [2011] FWA 977 [6].

balances the needs of business (including small business) and the needs of employees[103] and establishing procedures for dealing with unfair dismissal that are quick, flexible and informal which address the needs of employers and employees.[104] The procedures intended to ensure a 'fair go all round' are accorded to both the employee and the employer concerned.[105] Under section 385(c) of the Act, a person has been unfairly dismissed if the commission is satisfied that 'the dismissal was not consistent with the Small Business Fair Dismissal Code'. Under section 388(2) of the Act, a person's dismissal is consistent with the code if 'immediately before the time of the dismissal or at the time the person was given notice of the dismissal (whichever happened first), the person's employer was a small business employer; and the employer complied with the [code] in relation to the dismissal'. The effect of these provisions is to deprive a dismissed employee of access to relief that is otherwise generally available to dismissed employees on the ground that the dismissal is harsh, unjust or unreasonable, in circumstances where the employer is a small business and has complied with the FDC.[106]

The FDC is intended to provide a fast-tracked dismissal process for small business employers seeking to fire a member of staff. All that is required is a meeting between the employer and employee where the latter is given a warning. The employee is allowed to bring a support person to the meeting. Dismissal is then permitted if an employee's performance does not improve. If the commission deems that the FDC is complied with, an employee is unable to continue with a claim of unfair dismissal before the commission. In this way, the design of the FDC is intended 'to provide small business employers and employees with clear guidelines to minimise the extent of unfair dismissal action'.[107] The FDC is accompanied by a checklist, which is not required to be completed by employers but rather is a guide regarding matters to be taken into account and can be used as evidence. In the case of serious misconduct, the employer can dismiss the employee without complying with the FDC. As such, the employee is not entitled to the other provisions of the FDC dealing with elements of procedural fairness, including the right to be given a valid reason why he or she is at risk of being dismissed, a warning that there is a risk of dismissal if there is no improvement, an opportunity to respond to the warning, a reasonable chance to rectify the problem and the choice to be represented in discussions in circumstances where dismissal is possible.[108] In situations of serious misconduct, there is no requirement that the employer has reported the situation to the police, just that the employer has reasonable grounds to suspect the employee of serious misconduct.

Despite the Labor government's intention that the FDC would result in more expedient processing of unfair dismissal claims for small businesses, in practice this has not occurred. The FDC does not act as a blanket barrier to external review

103 *Fair Work Act 2009* (Cth) s 381(1)(a).
104 S 381(1)(b).
105 S 381(2).
106 *Said v Jokar Holdings Pty Ltd* [2011] FWA 977 [6].
107 Fair Work Bill 2008, Explanatory Memorandum, xiix.
108 *Said v Jokar Holdings Pty Ltd* [2011] FWA 977 [6].

of an employer's dismissal decision. The commission can inquire into whether the dismissal has truly complied with the FDC and can make an order for a remedy if the employer failed to comply with the FDC and the dismissal was unfair.[109] In one case, where an employee was dismissed from her role as a property manager but was given no verbal or written warnings about her performance, the commission said her dismissal was clearly inconsistent with the FDC.[110] This removed the business's exemption from the general unfair dismissal system and the standard test of whether the dismissal was 'harsh, unjust or unreasonable' applied, resulting in the employee being awarded compensation of $3000.[111] In another case, which involved an employer relying on the summary dismissal provisions in the FDC to dismiss an employee, the commission looked at the former's conduct to determine that there were insufficient reasonable grounds for believing that the latter's conduct was sufficiently serious to warrant immediate dismissal.[112] Despite this, the commission did not make a finding of unfair dismissal because, when applying section 387, it was determined that the dismissal was not harsh, unjust or unreasonable.[113] Thus, it is insufficient for an employer merely to assert that it has complied with the FDC as the commission has shown its preparedness to assess the genuineness of compliance.[114]

One area where the FDC does provide for a lessened standard of fairness for small business employees is in the event of a summary dismissal.[115] The FDC stipulates that 'it is fair for an employer to dismiss an employee without notice or warning when the employer believes on reasonable grounds that the employee's conduct is sufficiently serious to justify immediate dismissal'.[116] It is implicitly irrelevant whether or not the allegation turns out to be well founded,[117] which is in contrast with the provisions of section 387(a) of the Act where the commission, in determining whether there was a valid reason for the dismissal, must find whether the conduct in fact occurred.[118] In one case, an employee's unfair dismissal claim was dismissed because the small business employer believed, on reasonable grounds, that the employee was stealing goods from the

109 See eg, *Clayworth v Vita Property Group Pty Ltd* [2012] FWA 5380; *Loughnan v ergonomic office (sic) Pty Ltd* [2012] FWA 3836 and on appeal: [2012] FWAFB 5864; *Hobbs v Achilleus Taxation* [2012] FWA 290; *Sedina Sokolovic v Modestie Fashion Australia Pty Ltd* [2011] FWA 3063; *Elton v Acupuncture Australia Pty Ltd* [2015] FWC 864.

110 *Clayworth v Vita Property Group Pty Ltd* [2012] FWA 5380 [35–36].

111 Ibid [51].

112 *Loughnan v Ergonomic Office (sic) Pty Ltd* [2012] FWA 3836 [30].

113 Ibid [44].

114 For example, between July and September 2013, of the 504 claims relating to a small business, only one was dismissed at a hearing based on compliance with the FDC: Fair Work Commission, 'Quarterly Report to the Minister' (July–September 2013) 6.

115 See O'Neill (n 34) 17–18.

116 The current Small Business Fair Dismissal Code can be found online: <www.fairwork.gov.au/termination/small-business-fair-dismissal-code/pages/the-code.aspx>accessed 12 December 2013.

117 For example, see *Peter John Harley v Rosecrest Asset Pty Ltd T/A Can Do International* [2011] FWA 3922. For academic commentary on this point, see Anna Chapman, 'Protections in Relation to Dismissal: From the Workplace Relations Act to the Fair Work Act' (2009) 32(3) UNSW LJ 746, 763.

118 *Harley v Rosecrest Asset Pty Ltd T/A Can Do International* [2011] FWA 3922.

business.[119] However, once the matter reached the commission, the evidence was clear that the employee had not taken the goods and, even if he had, he would have had permission to do so. Despite acknowledging that the employee had not in fact stolen the goods, Deputy President McCarthy stated:

> Considering all of these circumstances, I have come to the conclusion that Mr Nielsen believed, albeit erroneously, that the goods had been removed from the Respondent's premises without permission by the Applicant and that he had reasonable grounds for holding that belief. I therefore find that the Respondent believed on reasonable grounds that the Applicant's conduct was sufficiently serious to justify immediate dismissal. The Respondent thus complied with the Code and the dismissal was consistent with the Code.[120]

Thus, the standard of fairness set by the FDC for summary dismissals has been interpreted to be substantially lower than the general standard. With reference to dismissals for serious misconduct, the commission has confirmed that whilst employers should conduct investigations to arrive at a reasonable belief of misconduct, this need not involve communicating with the employee.[121] Further, employers are not required to substantiate allegations of misconduct provided that they reasonably believed that misconduct occurred.[122] This test that an employer must establish a reasonable basis for the belief was established in the Full Bench decision of *John Pinawin t/a Rose Hair, Face, Body v Edwin Domingo*.[123] Here, the Full Bench explained that the requirement to act reasonably does not dictate a particular course of action but may encompass a number of different responses or conclusions that an employer may legitimately reach.[124] Some of the factors the court will take into account is whether an employer carried out a reasonable investigation and reached a reasonable conclusion in all the circumstances, as well as the background, experience and resources of the small business employer concerned.[125]

When dismissals result from inadequate performance, warnings regarding performance need not be in writing. Thus in *Grigonis v Adelaide Coffee Company*,[126] although the employer had 'used the concept of warnings in its broadest sense', it was nonetheless sufficient to advise the employee informally that her work was slipping. Further, whilst employees must be afforded an opportunity to improve their performance, employers are not obliged to assist in this process.[127] Perhaps

119 Ibid.
120 Ibid [23]–[24].
121 *John Pinawin t/a Rose Hair, Face, Body v Edwin Domingo* [2012] FWAFB 1359, [29]–[30].
122 Ibid.
123 Ibid.
124 Ibid.
125 Ibid. See also, *Sandra McKenna v Home Theatre Group* [2012] FWA 9309.
126 [2011] FWA 1586 [70].
127 Joanna Howe, Submission to Fair Work Act Review Panel, *Fair Work Act Review*, 1.

the employee's performance in *Grigonis* could have improved if the employer had provided further training rather than merely asking her how she envisaged the problem being fixed.[128] Whilst the FDC has potential to assist employers to comply with their dismissal obligations, in its current format it is not a guarantee of fairness in dismissal.

So what does this review of the case law reveal about the impact of the FDC upon standards of fairness? Has the FDC assisted in the achievement of best practice? Has it had a transformative impact upon workplace culture in small businesses? Whilst it is arguably more efficient for an employer to be able to dismiss an employee summarily with a lesser standard of procedural fairness, as it less time-consuming when the employer only has to be concerned about a reasonable belief in the substance of their allegation, this does erode job security. Not only does the allegation not have to be true, dismissal can also be deemed fair even when an employer has made few attempts to put serious allegations to an employee for a response. The brevity of the FDC in requiring only a warning and a reasonable opportunity to improve performance hardly guarantees employees that their dismissal occurs according to a fair process, although it does provide a clear process for employers to follow. For example, the Council of Small Business of Australia has stated that their members appreciated the guidance provided by the code and the certainty and simplicity of its checklist approach,[129] and the Office of the Small Business Commission has stated: 'The information in the Code is easy to understand and the checklist provides practical steps to follow. In our opinion, the Code is a valuable resource which assists small business employers and should remain part of the workplace relations system.'[130]

Nonetheless, some employer groups are less certain of the code's ability to inoculate small business from unfair dismissal law, arguing that it still places an evidentiary burden on small business as 'the matters subject of the Code are still subjective and capable of challenge'.[131] In practice, the FDC affords only a limited protection to small business owners, as the code's content reflects the substantive and procedural issues an arbitrator would investigate through arbitration of an unfair dismissal claim. As this section's review of recent case law shows, the FDC does not preclude substantive review of an employer's dismissal decision and, according to the Productivity Commission, it should be abolished, as it is not 'a sufficient safeguard for small businesses against a claim of unfair dismissal, nor is the advice provided by the Code clear and concise'.[132] In this light, the

128 *Grigonis v Adelaide Coffee Company* [2011] FWA 1586 [45].

129 Cited in Productivity Commission (n 66) 224.

130 Office of the Small Business Commissioner, Submission No 119 to Productivity Commission, *Inquiry into the Workplace Relations Framework*, 2015, 8–9.

131 Housing Industry Association, Submission No 169 to Productivity Commission, *Inquiry into the Workplace Relations Framework*, 2015, 48; see also, Australian Chamber of Commerce and Industry, Submission No 161 to Productivity Commission, *Inquiry into the Workplace Relations Framework*, 2015, 109.

132 Productivity Commission (n 66) 239.

introduction of the FDC is indicative of Labor's willingness to accept the previous government's argument that the power balance between a small business owner and their staff is more evenly distributed. This resulted in Labor's acceptance of a limited form of regulatory tiering in the context of unfair dismissal law.

The endurance and resilience of Australian unfair dismissal law

Although Australian unfair dismissal law has certainly gone through a period of revision since its inception,[133] it still endures today and at the time of writing seemed to be very much entrenched as part of the fabric of federal labour law. This final section considers the evolution of federal unfair dismissal law since 1993 and examines how it has survived threats to its existence during this time.

Why did the Howard Coalition government choose not to abolish unfair dismissal law?

This question seems a reasonable one to ask given the Howard Coalition's vehement opposition to the unfair dismissal provisions in the *Industrial Relations Reform Act 1993* enacted by the Keating Labor government. Faced with a hostile Senate for most of its years in government, there was no possibility of abolishing unfair dismissal law until 2006, when the government had a majority in both Houses of Parliament after changes to the Senate's composition following the 2004 election. Prior to this, the combination of the Labor Party, the minor parties and independents in the Senate meant the Senate had been very reluctant to curtail unfair dismissal law and was only willing to canvass minor changes to the jurisdiction, such as watering down the procedural fairness test and introducing filing fees, time limits and disincentives for cases to proceed to arbitration. The minor parties in the Senate were unwilling to acquiesce to a more radical set of reforms, such as abolishing unfair dismissal rights or removing these rights for the employees of small business. When the Howard Coalition government finally possessed a majority in both Houses of Parliament after its 2004 election victory, it did choose to remove the unfair dismissal rights of a significant number of Australian workers through a combination of jurisdictional bars: the operational reasons exclusion and the 100 employee rule, but it stopped short of abolishing unfair dismissal law altogether.

Despite Work Choice's maintenance of federal unfair dismissal law to some extent, the operational reasons exclusion led some commentators to describe unfair dismissal protection as 'virtually dismantled'[134] and operating more as a 'legal

133 Chapman referred to the period prior to the passage of the *Fair Work Act 2009* (Cth) as one of 'contraction' or 'constriction': Anna Chapman, 'Unfair Dismissal Law and Work Choices: From Safety Net to Legal Privilege' (2006) 16(2) Eco & Lab Relations Rev 237.

134 Marilyn Pittard, 'Protection from Unfair Dismissal: Fairness and the Fair Work Act' in Clare Ozich (ed), *Employment Rights Now: Reflections on the Australian Charter of Employment Rights* (Hardie Grant, Richmond, Vic 2015).

privilege'[135] rather than as a safety net of broad application. The operational reasons exclusion prevented an employee from accessing the unfair dismissal jurisdiction if one of the reasons for termination of his or her employment included 'genuine operational reasons'.[136] If such reasons were asserted by an employer or were otherwise apparent to the AIRC, a hearing was held to deal with the issue before proceeding any further with assessing the substantive merits of the application. If satisfied that the operational reasons were genuine, the AIRC was required to dismiss the application. The operational reasons exclusion in section 649(1)(a) was given a wide reading by the AIRC and it was held permissible for an employee to be made redundant from his or her position and subsequently have the position advertised at a lower salary.[137] The test that the AIRC developed for assessing a genuine operational reason was set out in *Village Cinemas Australia Pty Ltd v Carter*,[138] where it was held to be irrelevant whether an employer might have taken another course of action rather than dismissing an employee. The key consideration was merely whether 'a reason for termination of the employment of a particular employee can be genuine in the sense that it is real, true or authentic, not counterfeit whilst it may not have been valid, meaning sound, defensible or well founded'.[139] At this preliminary proceeding, the AIRC was unable to investigate questions of fairness – either procedural or substantive. If a genuine operational reason was found to exist, even if its merits were dubious, this rendered the application jurisdictionally barred.[140]

Thus, although the Coalition stopped short of abolishing unfair dismissal law altogether, the Howard Coalition government's unfair dismissal reforms during its period in office illustrate its desire to dilute the regulatory burden of these laws on business, to exempt a large portion of the labour force from their application, and to discourage the making of unfair dismissal claims. Its *rhetoric* went even further, however, with a promise to take the 'unfair dismissal monkey off the back of business'[141] because of its belief that unfair dismissal law was a 'statutory on-cost' upon employers[142] and 'one of the greatest blots on the escutcheon of small business'.[143] Prime Minister Howard's speech during the second reading debates for the Workplace Relations Amendment (Work Choices) Bill 2005 (Cth) reflected his intention to dismantle unfair dismissal law altogether, as I noted earlier in this chapter.[144]

135 Chapman (n 134).
136 S 649(1)(a).
137 *Cruikshank v Priceline Pty Ltd* (2007) PR976793, Melbourne (17 April 2007, Eames C).
138 PR975821, Sydney (15 January 2007).
139 Ibid [26].
140 For more, see Chapman (n 134).
141 Commonwealth of Australia, *Parliamentary Debates*, House of Representatives, 2 November 2005 (Kevin Andrews).
142 See eg, Commonwealth of Australia, *Parliamentary Debates*, House of Representatives, 17 November 1993 (John Howard).
143 Howard (n 99).
144 Commonwealth of Australia, *Parliamentary Debates*, House of Representatives, 9 November 2005 (John Howard, Opposition Leader).

The (partial) restoration of unfair dismissal law under labor

After the Howard Coalition government's resounding election loss in 2007, the Rudd and Gillard Labor governments did not revert to the traditional justification of industrial justice for unfair dismissal regulation but continued the deregulatory trend of the previous government. This election of Labor to government in 2007 led to both some continuity with and some change from the deregulatory policies of the previous government, although this was within a paradigm of believing in the importance of some form of unfair dismissal protection. Upon decisively winning the federal election in 2007, the Labor government sought to reverse the Coalition government's operational reasons exemption and the 100 employee rule. These jurisdictional bars were removed, and access to the unfair dismissal system was reinstated for the majority of Australian employees. Nonetheless, as I have explained, the Labor government after 2007 reformed the statutory unfair dismissal scheme in a manner that diluted job security protection to some extent. Labor's rhetoric and policy outcomes post-2007 centred upon resolving disputes quickly and simply, and if possible without recourse to tribunal arbitration, encapsulated by their desire for the claims process to be 'faster, less costly and less complex for all'.[145] In many ways this represented a reformulation by Labor of its original vision for federal unfair dismissal law as a vehicle for achieving job security according to international norms. Labor in 2007, whilst still articulating a positive view of unfair dismissal law, was more prepared to canvass reforms that would increase managerial prerogative and allow an employer's decision to dismiss staff to be free from independent scrutiny or, if scrutinised, to be tested in a less rigorous fashion using conciliation by telephone and via lay conciliators. In addition to introducing the Fair Dismissal Code, Labor increased the qualifying period to 12 months for employees of small business. Thus, whilst Labor undoubtedly and importantly reinstated unfair dismissal rights for the majority of Australian employees and reversed some of the more radical oscillations in unfair dismissal policy of the previous government, many of Labor's ideas represent a continuation, rather than a departure, from the previous Coalition government's desire to deregulate unfair dismissal law.

Unfair dismissal law today and beyond

Remarkably after such an intense initial period of reform, revision and contestation around federal unfair dismissal law, following the changes ushered in by the *Fair Work Act 2009* (Cth), federal unfair dismissal law has entered a period of relative stability. The Abbott and Turnbull Coalition governments have not announced any reform to unfair dismissal law during their first term and although the Abbott government commissioned a Productivity Commission inquiry into

145 Rudd and Gillard (n 32). See also, Anna Chapman, 'The Decline and Restoration of Unfair Dismissal Rights' in A Forsyth and A Stewart (eds), *Fair Work: The New Workplace Laws and the Work Choices Legacy* (Federation Press, Sydney 2009) 207.

the workplace relations framework, the inquiry's final report presents a view that Australian unfair dismissal law is generally working as intended, although some tinkering in the form of minor reform has been forecast.[146] In particular, what is striking about the Productivity Commission's report is the conclusion that abolition of unfair dismissal law is unwise and 'unjustified', that this law provides 'important and needed protections for employees' and that there is no need for 'fundamental change' of federal unfair dismissal law.[147] This provides a clear normative basis in support of Australian unfair dismissal law and means that it is unlikely to be subject to significant revision during the remainder of the Coalition government's first term or as part of its re-election platform for a second term. Although the winds of change are never far away, it seems that, for now, Australia's unfair dismissal law is proving fairly resilient in spite of continuing calls for its operation to be simpler and more efficient.

146 These include recommendations to abolish the Small Business Fair Dismissal Code, changes to procedures for dealing with unfair dismissal claims 'on the papers' and rejecting the idea of reinstatement as the primary remedy: Productivity Commission (2015) ch 17.
147 Ibid 557.

6 United States of America – Part I

The origins of employment at will

Introduction

Unlike almost every other industrialised country and many developing countries including Australia and the United Kingdom, the United States, with the exception of one state, has never provided private sector employees with statutory protection against unfair dismissal.[1] Instead, the United States adopted the employment-at-will doctrine.[2] This allows dismissal 'for good cause, for no cause or even for cause morally wrong'[3] and 'at the pleasure of either party at any time'.[4] It is a default rule that courts apply when parties in an employment relationship have failed to specify the duration of that relationship.[5] It is founded upon a notion of free, contractual

1 Clyde Summers, 'Employment at Will in the United States: The Divine Right of Employers' (2000) 3(1) U Penn J Lab & Emp Law 65. Beck says that the job protection afforded to US workers is amongst the weakest of all industrialised nations even though the protection of other forms of property in the United States is amongst the broadest. See Matthias Beck, *The Elusive Search for Job Security: A Historical Inquiry into Dismissals in the United States Workplace* (Nova Science Publishers, New York 2012). A different comparative analysis is provided by Samuel Estreicher and Jeffrey Hirsch in their study of twelve countries' approach to regulating dismissal. They argue that the growth of judicial exceptions to at will, the size of pay-outs and the breadth of remedies render the US less of an exceptional case: Samuel Estreicher and Jeffrey Hirsch, 'Comparative Wrongful Dismissal Law: Reassessing American Exceptionalism' (2014) 92 NC L Rev 343.

2 There are some exceptions to this general American approach of employment at will, which I will explore in the following chapter. These include Montana's adoption of a Wrongful Discharge from Employment Act that extends similar protection to non-unionised workers; collective agreements that provide that an employee may only be dismissed for 'just cause', a matter on which an independent arbitrator can be asked to rule; and statutory protection against dismissal for certain reasons, notably those which are based on discriminatory factors such as gender, race or age or which relate to the exercise of collective bargaining rights. The at-will rule began to gain strength in the late 1800s and was adopted in nearly every state by the 1930s. For more, see Andrew P Morriss, 'Exploding Myths: An Empirical and Economic Reassessment of the Rise of Employment At-Will' (1994) 59 MLR 679.

3 *Payne v The Western Atlantic Rail Road Company* 81 Tenn 507 (1884). This case was overruled on other grounds by *Hutton v Watters* 132 Tenn 527 (1915).

4 *Adler v American Standard Corporation* 432 A2d 464, 467 (1981).

5 Richard Bales, 'Explaining the Spread of At-Will Employment as an Interjurisdictional Race to the Bottom of Employment Standards' (2008) 75 Tenn L Rev 453, 453. In this article Bales argues that the default rule spread due to under-industrialised states trying to attract capital.

economic exchange.[6] The rule, succinctly stated, is that 'absent a prior agreement, either the employer or the employee may terminate the employment relationship at any time for any lawful reason without notice'.[7] Whilst at-will is a default rule that the parties can contract out of, unlike an immutable rule like the US's minimum wage provision, contractual provision for just-cause dismissal is rare because of the power disparity that employees generally have in the workplace.

Undoubtedly, the United States employment-at-will approach seems harsh when viewed in light of the contrasting statutory unfair dismissal schemes existing in Australia and the United Kingdom.[8] On its face, the employment at will rule challenges the worker-protective normative ideal of job security.[9] The United States is also an outlier amongst developed countries more generally. Even though only thirty-four countries have ratified ILO Convention No 158, the labour laws in many more countries give effect to its basic principles.[10] Indeed, in the three decades since its promulgation, laws protecting against arbitrary dismissal have generally remained in place around the developed world, with the United States as a clear exception. Trying to understand why United States labour law has taken a different trajectory in regulating job security is best understood in light of the historical origins of employment at will and the reasons for its introduction – and to that I now turn.

Early approaches to regulating termination of employment

Employment at will was not always the dominant approach in the United States. In fact, historically, a fair degree of disorder characterised how different United States jurisdictions approached the issue of an employee's job security. Prior to 1877, laws regarding job security in America exhibited 'a confusion of principles and rules',[11] with early judicial decisions going in diverse directions.[12] In the

6 Jay Feinman, 'The Development of the Employment-at-Will Rule Revisited' (1991) 23 Ariz St LJ 733, 735.

7 Bales (n 5) 453. The definition of 'just cause' varies between jurisdictions as 'there is no single definition of what constitutes good cause for discharge': *Shapiro v Massengill* 105 Md App 743, 760, 661 A2d 202, 211 (1995) (citation omitted). See also, Roger I Abrams and Dennis R Nolan, 'Toward a Theory of "Just Cause" in Employee Discipline Cases' [1985] Duke LJ 594.

8 This chapter and the chapter which follows focus purely on describing the evolution of US law. Chapter 8 will include a comparative analysis of the divergent regulatory approaches of the UK, US and Australia in regulating dismissal for cause.

9 Freedland and Kountouris suggest that labour law rests on a number of normative commitments to do with the achievement of workers' dignity and capacity building, decent working conditions, stability in employment and maximising workers' access to labour markets. M Freedland and N Kountouris, *The Legal Construction of Personal Work Relations* (OUP, Oxford 2011) 372. I will engage with these ideas more thoroughly in Chapter 8.

10 Committee of Experts on the Application of Conventions and Recommendations, 'Report III (Pt 1A)', International Labour Conference, 98th Session (ILO, Geneva 2009) 537. See also: Joanna Howe, Esther Sanchez and Andrew Stewart, 'Job Loss' in Matthew Finkin and Guy Mundlak (eds), *Comparative Labor Law Handbook* (Elgar and Elgar, Cheltenham 2015).

11 Jay Feinman, 'The Development of the Employment at Will Rule' (1976) 20 Am J Leg Hist 118, 122.

12 Summers (n 1) 67.

early to mid-nineteenth century, the arrangements between a master and servant evolved from being status based, with customary duties and responsibilities, to being more contractual in nature. Historically, the master had quasi-parental duties such as to provide medical care, moral guidance, instruction on literacy and the administration of discipline, which could include corporal punishment.[13] Under this regime, employment relations were not of great importance in the law. The arrangement was not a matter of contract, but was imposed by the common law by way of public policy.[14] The law did not emphasise the subjective intent of the parties and what their relationship ought to be.[15]

There are differing views about what the arrangements changed to. At that time, many contracts of service in the United States followed the yearly hiring principle derived from the English law of the master and servant, a subcategory of the common law of contract.[16] That law was formulated and made prominent in a statement by Sir William Blackstone in 1765. He said:

> If the hiring be generally, without any particular time limited, the law construes it to be hiring for a year; upon a principle of natural equity, that the servant shall serve, and the master maintain him, throughout all the revolutions of the respective seasons, as well when there is work to be done as when there is not: but the contract may be made for any larger or smaller term.[17]

Blackstone's statement was designed in the shadow of earlier English statutes. For example, the Statute of Artificers 1563, the source for much of the English master and servant law, forbade employment for less than a year in order to restrict labour mobility.[18] Such restrictions were to lessen the impact of labour shortages.[19] In *Beeston v Collyer* the court implied a yearly hiring where there was no written contract, and the employee was paid monthly for the six years prior to his dismissal and was dismissed for no reason.[20]

13 Sanford Jacoby, 'The Duration of Indefinite Employment Contracts in the United States and England: An Historical Analysis' (1982) 5 Comp Lab Law 85, 89.
14 Henry Perritt Jr, *Employee Dismissal Law and Practice* (5th edn Aspen Publishers, New York 2014) 1–9.
15 Ibid.
16 Beck (n 1) 2.
17 Sir William Blackstone, *Commentaries on the Laws of England, Volume 1* (9th edn Garland Publishing, London 1978) 425.
18 Jacoby (n 13) 90.
19 The poor laws also had an influence. Because of the overabundance of labourers, healthy people who were old enough to work were forced to become servants. Those who were unable to get work became charges on the community. To avoid being responsible for these people, communities had the right to 'warn out' paupers who had not lived in the community for at least a year. See Deborah Ballam, 'The Traditional View on the Origins of the Employment-at-Will Doctrine: Myth or Reality?' (1995) 33 Am Bus LJ 1, 8.
20 (1827) 130 Eng Rep 786. For the importance of this case at the time in understanding the yearly hiring rule, see Robert Burn, *The Justice of the Peace and the Parish Officer* (26th edn Sweet & Maxwell, London 1831) vol 5, 360.

When the yearly hiring rule was adopted in the United States, the purpose was largely to provide job security to the agricultural workforce by preventing opportunism. Farmers, who worked long hours during the growing season, were at risk of being discharged after the harvest when they were not in such demand.[21] Interestingly, most courts levied forfeitures on a worker if he were fired, unless the dismissal was without just cause.[22] The regime provided job security and rigorous limits on dismissals for the period of a year.

The common law of England was influential in the early development of employment law in the United States. For example, Tapping Reeve's pioneering domestic relations treatise at mid-century stated the English presumption of yearly hiring but noted that no such rule existed in Connecticut.[23] Shortly thereafter Charles Manly Smith's *Treatise on the Law of Master and Servant*, the first devoted solely to the subject in the United States, was published in Philadelphia. Covering English law with reference to American cases, Smith identified a presumption that a general hiring was a yearly hiring for all servants, adding that the presumption was rebuttable by custom or other evidence and, in spite of yearly hiring, the relationship could be terminated on notice where that was customary.[24] Evidence of yearly hiring was also present in the case law at the time. In *Adams v Fitzpatrick*[25] the court said the general rule of hiring by the year applied absent other circumstances but found there was yearly hiring in that case because of an inference of fact from all of the circumstances and evidence. In another case, *Davis v Gorton*,[26] the English rule was adopted to cover servants who managed a farm and household, and in *Bascom v Shillto*[27] the court emphasised that the rules were not inflexible in America or in England. This statement acknowledged the rule's origins and the court in *Bleeker v Johnson*[28] unambiguously stated the 'English Rule is accepted as the law in this country'.

Under the yearly hiring rule, there was a focus on the duty of the servant to serve, so a master could bring a criminal action or seek either specific performance or damages if a worker failed to complete his or her service, though this was rare. Workers could seek unpaid wages if they were dismissed prematurely.[29] However, 'it is less clear whether a servant could recover damages from a master for premature or improper termination of the relationship'.[30] Perritt holds the

21 Bales (n 5) 456.
22 Katherine Stone, 'Revisiting the At-Will Employment Doctrine: Imposed Terms, Implied Terms and the Normative World of the Workplace' (2007) 36(1) Indust LJ 86.
23 Tapping Reeve, *The Law of Baron and Femme, of Parent and Child, Guardian and Ward, Master and Servant, and the Powers of the Court of Chancery* (Oliver Steele, New Haven, CT 1846) 347.
24 Charles Manley Smith, *A Treatise on the Law of Master and Servant* (6th edn Sweet & Maxwell, London 1906) 51.
25 26 NE 143 (1891).
26 16 NY 255 (1857). Though Ballam notes that no United States or New York cases support this proposition; the only citation was the treatise. See Ballam (n 19) 47.
27 37 Ohio St 431 (1882).
28 51 How Pr 380 (1876).
29 Jacoby (n 13) 89.
30 Perritt (n 14) 1–11.

view that some of the third party interference cases suggest that civil liability could have been imposed in an action by a plaintiff servant against a defendant master.[31]

It also seems that there was some use of the employment-at-will doctrine prior to 1877, which provided much less job security than the yearly hiring rule. Scholars such as Deborah Ballam go so far as to say there was no evidence of the colonies attempting to use the yearly hiring rule.[32] She says it was never adopted in America because the economy and market created conditions that were not conducive to it.[33] Her view is that with the exception of a brief period in early colonial times, employment at will has been the norm in the United States. The only change in the nineteenth century was that 'some Courts stopped interpreting fixed term agreements for payment of wages as an agreement to employ the worker for the same term'.[34] Her study, which was published in 1996, examined nine states and concluded that the employment at will doctrine was already a part of the common law prior to 1877 and had been established by economic imperatives arising from an agricultural economy characterised by labour scarcity during colonial times.[35] In an earlier study published in 1995, she considers evidence from four states which demonstrates that the annual hiring rule was not utilised and that the employment-at-will concept was not suddenly adopted in the late nineteenth century.[36]

Case law also provides evidence of the existence of employment at will at this time. *Butler v Smith*[37] and *Coffin v Landis*[38] both applied the employment-at-will rule. It was also included in the National Currency Act 1863 for bank officers as well as in earlier state banking statutes.[39]

Other scholars have acknowledged the presence of employment at will but had a different view to Ballam as to its prominence, instead depicting a diversity

31 Ibid. Whatever the method of hiring, Jacoby says that litigation in the United States prior to 1877 was less widespread than in England. He cites several reasons for this difference. Firstly, the American courts heard fewer settlement cases which had regard to the employment contract. Jacoby says that this was because over half of the original thirteen states no longer permitted settlement by hiring by 1810. Secondly, breach of the employment contract was rarely subject to criminal penalties. Before the Industrial Revolution, several of the colonies were reluctant to allow masters to bring criminal actions against their free workers. After the revolution, criminal proceedings of that sort were against the doctrines of personal liberty and equality under the laws that were adopted by at least the northern states. The United States never enacted its own version of the Master and Servant Acts which allowed this. See Jacoby (n 13) 104.

32 Ballam (n 19) 9.

33 Deborah Ballam, 'Exploding the Original Myth Regarding Employment-at-Will: The True Origins of the Doctrine' (1996) 17 Berk J Emp & Lab Law 91, 126.

34 Ibid 94.

35 Ibid 129.

36 Ballam (n 19) 49.

37 35 Miss 457 (1858).

38 46 Pa 426 (1864).

39 Morriss (n 2) 681.

of employment practices, some of which relied on employment at will and others which relied on the yearly hiring rule. For example, Jacoby, while acknowledging the impact of the English yearly hiring rule in some occupations, gave examples of textile mill employees who were effectively employed at will between 1820 and 1850. There was a labour shortage, so the mills required the employees to work one full year before they could receive an 'honourable discharge' and were required to give two to four weeks' notice of intention to leave. However, the employer could terminate them at will.[40] By the 1870s in that industry most contracts were indefinite.[41] Similarly, Feinman's view was that in the colonies day labourers tended to be employed at will, while agricultural labourers and domestic servants were usually hired on a yearly basis. He cites clear authorities which show that there was no consensus.[42] Morriss says that the rule was adopted in seven states before 1877.[43]

By way of contrast, Summers downplays the influence of the English yearly hiring rule, but for a reason other than the prevalence of employment at will. His view was that 'the United States largely followed the English common law, but the presumption of annual hiring was not generally adopted'.[44] Summers says there were divergent judicial approaches. On the one hand, there were cases that determined that where a contract stated that payment was for work done for a particular term, this could also be seen as identifying the duration of the hiring, whereas he also identifies other cases where the courts rejected the use of any presumption and determined whether the employee should be employed at will on the basis of the facts surrounding the contract.[45]

In both England and America, there was a state of confusion as to whether a 'servant', who was evolving through the development of labour law into an 'employee', was entitled to any measure of job security. The notions of yearly hiring and employment at will were both in existence at this time, but by the turn of the twentieth century different trajectories were taken in the two jurisdictions. For the English, the issue of what notice was required to terminate an employment contract moved to the fore,[46] and the idea of a statutory unfair dismissal law began to be canvassed. In the United States, there was a move to something entirely different, as employment at will, although still controversial, became generally accepted and embedded in that jurisdiction's labour laws.

Widespread adoption of employment at will

If the preceding section showed that the United States did initially follow English law, it did not do so for long, as the widespread acceptance of employment at will

40 Jacoby (n 13) 105.
41 Ibid 106.
42 Feinman (n 6) 122.
43 Morriss (n 2) 681.
44 Summers (n 1) 67.
45 Ibid.
46 Feinman (n 6) 121.

by the late nineteenth century gave a clean break by explicitly rejecting the yearly hiring rule.[47] Conventional narratives of American labour law depict Horace Wood's publication of *Master and Servant* in 1877 as the driving force behind the widespread adoption of the at-will rule.[48] Supposedly resolving the contradictions in American law, Wood wrote:

> [T]he rule is inflexible, that a general or indefinite hiring is prima facie a hiring at will, and if the servant seeks to make it out a yearly hiring, the burden is upon him to establish it by proof. . . . A hiring at so much a day, week, month, or year, no time being specified, is an indefinite hiring, and no presumption attaches that it was for a day even, but only at the rate fixed for whatever time the party may serve. . . . It is competent for either party to show what the mutual understanding of the parties was in reference to the matter; but unless their understanding was mutual that the service was to extend for a certain fixed and definite period, it is an indefinite hiring and is determinable at the will of either party.[49]

There were advantages of employment at will, particularly for unskilled workers. The yearly hiring rule was harsh for some workers. With employment at will, those workers now had the opportunity to be paid for the time worked if they wanted to quit or were dismissed. As they were able to resign without consequences, it gave them a larger degree of autonomy and freedom that they did not have when the yearly hiring presumption applied. They did lose some job security, but 'that was not something they had enjoyed in the first place'.[50]

There have been diverging views about Wood's contribution. Those who are of the view that the employment-at-will rule was already in existence at the time of Wood's treatise such as Ballam say that Wood did not actually invent the rule, but instead was only summarising what was already in existence[51] and generally accepted.[52] Even if Wood's treatise alone did not cause the change to employment at will, it is arguable that without it the rule would likely not have advanced as quickly and as uniformly as it did,[53] and in a way that was suited to America's developing society.

Another controversy surrounding Wood's contribution to the development and acceptance of the at-will rule is whether he correctly interpreted the law. Theodore

47 Jacoby (n 13) 112.

48 Horace Wood, *A Treatise on the Law of Master and Servant* (JD Parsons, Albany, NY 1877). For further discussion on the influence of Wood's treatise, see: Bales (n 5) 457; Jacoby (n 13) 111; Beck (n 1) 16; Morriss (n 2) 759.

49 Wood (n 48) 272.

50 Katherine Stone, 'Revisiting the At-Will Doctrine: Imposed Terms, Implied Terms and the Normative World of the Workplace' (UCLA School of Law, Public Law and Theory Research Paper Series, Research Paper No. 06–38, 2006) 5.

51 Bales (n 5) 457.

52 Mayer Freed and Daniel Polsby, 'The Doubtful Provenance of "Wood's Rule" Revisited' (1990) 22 Ariz St LJ 551, 556.

53 Feinman (n 6) 127.

St Antoine, for example, described employment at will as having 'sprung full-blown . . . from [Wood's] busy and perhaps careless pen'.[54] Most of the controversy stems from the four cases cited in Wood's footnote 4, which do not seem to have supported his analysis in favour of the at-will rule.[55] The allegations are that two of the cases were employee victories,[56] which gave weak support for a legal rule giving employers an unfettered power to fire at will; one of the cases did not involve an employment contract at all, but rather a contract between the United States Army and a private company for the transportation of goods,[57] and the final case concerned a bartender who lived on the employer's premises – when he was fired, he challenged his eviction rather than his discharge.[58] Thus, Feinman argues that Wood offered no policy grounds in support of the employment-at-will rule, rendering it an innovation wholly unsupported at the time of its supposed foundation.[59] On the other hand, Freed and Polsby state that 'these cases do indeed support the principle for which Wood cited them'.[60] Another view, articulated by Jacoby, is that there is enough support elsewhere in the treatise. Jacoby thought that 'Wood was neither as foolish nor disingenuous as his critics made him out to be' and notes that the cases cited by Wood supported his specific claims.[61]

Scholarly debate also ensued about the reasons for employment at will being introduced. For example, Feinman suggests that the rule was an 'adjunct to the development of advanced capitalism in America'.[62] He viewed employment at will as the 'ultimate guarantor of the capitalist's authority over the worker'.[63] The rule transformed long-term employment relationships into non-binding agreements terminable at will. He found that the participants in the litigation that resulted in the change to Wood's rule were mostly middle-level employees and their employers who wanted to apply the annual hiring rule to their situations.[64] This is significant because, at that time, they were a newly important economic group presenting a potential threat to the owners of capital, as they were becoming more important, prevalent and powerful. The employment-at-will rule made the employee's relationship with the employer precarious and ensured a clear division between owners and employees by allowing the former absolute control over their businesses, which could result in greater profits.[65] Also, it allowed

54 Theodore St Antoine, 'You're Fired' (1982) 10(1) Hum Rts 32, 33.

55 See J Peter Shapiro and James F Tune, 'Implied Contract Rights to Job Security' (1974) 26 Stanford L Rev 335, 341. See further, Bales (n 5) 458.

56 *Tatterson v Suffolk Mfg Co* 106 Mass 56 (1870) and *Franklin Mining Co v Harris* 24 Mich 115 (1871).

57 *Wilder v United States* 5 Ct Cl 462 (1869).

58 *De Briar v Minturn* 1 Cal 450 (1851).

59 Feinman (n 6) 739.

60 Freed and Polsby (n 52) 554.

61 Jacoby (n 13) 112.

62 Feinman (n 6) 131.

63 Ibid 132.

64 Ibid 131.

65 Ibid 133.

employers to hire and discharge workers as the economic conditions dictated; to 'minimize the costs of discharge by imposing a great part of the burden of capitalist crises on the workers, rather than on themselves'.[66]

Jacoby, in his study which considered the duration of indefinite contracts in both the United States and the United Kingdom, speculates that if American trade unions had been stronger they might have taken a more voluntarist approach to limiting unjust dismissals.[67] Jacoby argued that the weakness of the union movement and judicial hostility towards the collective organisation of employees allowed the at-will rule to be imposed on manual workers because they only relied on laws prohibiting 'discriminatory dismissals, yellow-dog contracts and collective bargaining agreements'.[68] He concludes that the at-will doctrine would not have become as salient an issue in the courts and might not have been so readily extended to the higher, white collar positions.[69] He argued that this was different from the situation in the United Kingdom, where the British courts sought to protect these employees by providing them with a higher degree of job security through notice periods. At the same time, British trade unions sought shorter contracts to prevent employers from obtaining criminal enforcement of duration and notice clauses.

Others suggested that the employment-at-will rule was developed due to the changing nature of the employment relationship. For example, Finkin suggests that the rule reflected the dominant pattern of employment when it was developed, which was characterised by short-term employment, with workers constantly changing jobs. He charts the bureaucratisation of work, coining the term 'administre' to describe the transformation of the worker's role. In Finkin's view, although the employment relationship continued to be a relationship of subordination, dominance and subservience, it became, at least in part, impersonal and rational, producing both rights and obligations for employees.[70] Stone's view of how the employment contract changed is somewhat different. According to her, in the latter half of the nineteenth century, employment contracts for an indefinite term became commonplace. With the rise of mass production and the factory system after the Civil War, immigration by rural Americans and Europeans to American cities to become factory workers prompted a reconception. These workers were hired for indefinite terms and hence did not fit naturally into the entire contract doctrine. Because factory workers were not hired for a specified term, if they quit they were not abandoning a contractual obligation that was fixed in time.[71]

66 Ibid 134.
67 Jacoby (n 13) 126. For more on 'voluntarism' see chapters 2 and 3.
68 Ibid.
69 Ibid.
70 Matthew Finkin, 'The Bureaucratization of Work: Employer Policies and Contract Law' (1986) Wisconsin L Rev 733, 751.
71 Stone (n 50) 4.

The spread of employment at will and its acceptance

Whatever the rule's origin, over time it became entrenched in the common law and spread across the nation until it was generally adopted.[72] After 1877, the courts could adopt one of four alternatives when making a decision regarding an employer's right to terminate an employee on an indefinite contract.[73] Firstly, the court could use the annual hiring rule; however, after 1877 nearly all cases that mentioned the rule preferred to rely on employment at will.[74] Secondly, the court could analyse the facts and circumstances of an individual's employment situation to determine its intended duration. Some courts after 1877 found in favour of the employee relying on this approach.[75] Thirdly, the court could use the rate of payment rule, which was accepted by many courts even as late as 1942, but almost exclusively this was limited as applying to employees on an annual salary.[76] Fourthly, the court could use the at-will presumption. This was the major development of the period: the 'widespread rejection of that rule in favour of a strict presumption of terminability at will'.[77]

While the spread of employment at will was not slow, states adopted it in their own time. For example, in *Adams v Fitzpatrick*[78] the New York Court of Appeal readily applied the pay period presumption, holding that if a contract stipulated a monthly amount, this supports a presumption that the hiring was on a monthly basis even if the contract is silent regarding its intended duration. Just four years later the same court in *Martin v New York Life Ins Co*,[79] quoting Wood's treatise, held that employees in a similar circumstance could have their contracts terminated without cause. Summers suggests that this evolution by the New York Court of Appeal was highly influential in embedding employment at will in the American common law and that by 1930 the rule had been 'accepted without question or discussion'.[80] Certainly, by 1913, Labatt's commentaries on master and servant concluded that the majority of American courts had rejected the English rule and substituted it with another presumption that a general hiring is to be construed as hiring at will.[81]

72 Morriss (n 2) 458.
73 These alternatives are helpfully outlined in Jacoby (n 13) 113.
74 Ibid 113.
75 Ibid 114.
76 Ibid.
77 Ibid 115.
78 26 NE 143 (1891).
79 42 NE 416, 417 (1895).
80 Summers (n 1) 68. For a description of when each state adopted employment at will, see Morriss (n 2) 701–2. Using maps, Morriss demonstrates that the rule primarily spread from the West to the South and Midwest and only moved into the industrialised North East after several decades. Ballam claims that Morris did not examine the historical developments of the states' labour markets to determine whether these decisions and statutes adopted new law or merely reflected the current law and practice. See Ballam (n 19) 3.
81 C Labatt, *Master and Servant* (1913) sec 160, 519.

States not only adopted the rule at different times, but they varied how they adopted it. For example, 'several states adopted a weak version of the rule as part of the general codification of the common law',[82] and there was also variation in the types of cases that set precedent for the rule, with not all cases relying upon a dispute between an employer and employee.

At the heart of the employment at will rule was a concern with the reciprocity and equality of obligations within the employment relationship. For example, in 1884 in the abovementioned *Payne v The Western & Atlantic Rail Road Company*, the Tennessee Supreme Court articulated its classic formulation of the rule:

> [Men] must be left, without interference to buy and sell where they lease, and to discharge or retain employees at-will for good cause or for no cause or even for bad cause without thereby being guilty of an unlawful act per se. It is a right which an employee may exercise in the same way, to the same extent, for the same cause or want of cause as the employer. . . . All may dismiss their employees at will, be they many or few, for good cause, for no cause or even for a cause morally wrong, without being thereby guilty of legal wrong.[83]

Embedded within the rule was a clear assumption that either an employer or an employee could act in a similarly callous fashion in deciding unilaterally to end the employment relationship. Deeper interrogation of whether this assumption was correct seemed absent from the court's analysis, as there was no recognition, like there was in Australia or the United Kingdom, of the differential resources of capital and labour, and the very personal costs of dismissal upon an employee's economic prosperity, including their existence, social connections and livelihood.[84]

Conclusion

This brief historical examination has shown how employment at will came to be embedded in American labour law. Evolving from a master and servant tradition and founded upon notions of contract law, the employment-at-will rule assumes an employment relationship which each party is equally free to end without cause. On its face, this rule seems harsh when compared with other countries like Australia and the United Kingdom, which provide the opportunity for an individual to query the fairness of her dismissal via an independent adjudicative mechanism. Many critics have suggested that the United States should reconsider its approach

82 Morriss (n 2) 697.
83 *Payne v The Western & Atlantic Rail Road Company* 81 Tenn 507, 519–20 (1884).
84 These different perspectives will be discussed in more detail in Chapter 8.

and abandon or modify employment at will.[85] Nonetheless, employment at will cannot be understood solely by looking at its history, purpose and content. The role of the exceptions to the employment-at-will default rule, the presence of the United States arbitration system and the existence of broader remedies suggest that a more nuanced analysis is required. In fact, there may be less substantive difference between employment at will and the unfair dismissal laws of Australia and the United Kingdom than might be first thought.[86] In order to interrogate this comparative issue, which will be the focus of the final chapter of this book, we now turn to a description of how employment at will operates in the United States today.

85 Beck (n 1) xii. See also, Kenneth G Dau-Schmidt, 'Promoting Employee Voice in the American Economy: A Call for Comprehensive Reform' (2011) 94 Marq L Rev 765, 826 ('America is unique in its adherence to the at-will rule.'); Kenneth A Sprang, 'Beware the Toothless Tiger: A Critique of the Model Employment Termination Act' (1994) 43 Am U L Rev 849, 890–91 ('The United States stands alone among the world's major industrialized nations in failing to protect employees from wrongful discharge through federal legislation. . . . The time has come for us to join the community of nations in protecting employees from wrongful termination' [footnotes omitted]); Theodore J St Antoine, 'A Seed Germinates: Unjust Discharge Reform Heads Toward Full Flower' (1988) 67 Neb L Rev 56, 68–69 ('The United States remains the last major industrial democracy that has not heeded the call for unjust dismissal legislation.').

86 This, for example, is the argument of Estreicher and Hirsch (n 1) 465.

7 United States of America – Part II

The evolution and erosion of employment at will

Introduction

Following the introduction and entrenchment of the American rule of employment at will in the nineteenth century, inequities resulting from the doctrine became more apparent.[1] Over time, this led both the legislature and courts to modify the doctrine so that the arbitrary exercise of managerial prerogative by employers in the context of dismissal was curtailed in certain circumstances. However, instead of creating a comprehensive statutory scheme to regulate unfair dismissal like in the United Kingdom and Australia,[2] wrongful dismissal law in the United States has evolved into a complex system composed of numerous strands that bear little relationship to one another.[3] These strands were introduced at different times and were diverse in both origin and purpose. Unlike Australia, which adopted a federal unfair dismissal law covering employees in each of the Australian states,[4] or the United Kingdom, which has only one statutory unfair dismissal system, in the United States laws regulating job security exist at both the federal and state levels. As such, exceptions to the default rule of employment at will have been adopted in some states or for some employees but not others.

To create the exceptions, the courts 'camouflaged' the terminology of familiar doctrines or principles of law by stretching and misshaping them.[5] As I will explain, civil service employees have an unfair dismissal regime and some protection under the Constitution, whilst most employees covered by collective

1 Kurt Decker, 'Pennsylvania's Whistleblower Law's Extension to Private Sector Employees: Has the Time Finally Come to Broaden Statutory Protection for all At-Will Employees?' (2000) 38(3) Duquesne L Rev 724, 733.

2 Early seminal articles calling for the development of a statutory scheme in the US include Clyde W Summers, 'Individual Protection Against Unjust Dismissal: Time for a Statute' (1976) 62 U Va L Rev 481; Lawrence Blades, 'Employment at Will vs Individual Freedom: On Limiting the Abusive Exercise of Employer Power' (1967) 67 Colum L Rev 1404.

3 Stephen Befort, 'Labor and Employment Law at the Millennium: A Historical Review and Critical Assessment' (2002) 43(2) Boston College L Rev 351, 378.

4 A few exceptions exist as public sector state employees are covered under state unfair dismissal law, but the vast majority of Australian employees are covered through federal unfair dismissal law.

5 Cornelius Peck, 'Penetrating Doctrinal Camouflage: Understanding the Development of the Law of Wrongful Discharge' (1991) 66 Wash L Rev 719, 734.

bargaining agreements have access to substantive and procedural fairness via arbitration in the event of an unfair dismissal. Legislation protects employees from certain types of retaliatory discharge. Additionally, judicial exceptions, although these differ significantly among the states, protect employees where termination offends public policy, is contrary to good faith and fair dealing and if just cause or employment security is implied in fact, although, as I will examine, good faith only exists in ten states and public policy means vastly different things in different states. Nevertheless, in the view of some US scholars, the result has been to produce a regulatory framework where the 'legal right to fire for bad reasons has been virtually decimated'.[6] Or as other US scholars have put it, 'the judicial conception of what "at will" really means is framed by the exceptions that derogate from it; and as these differ greatly from jurisdiction to jurisdiction, so too does the core conception against which these exceptions resonate'.[7]

Thus, it is possible that the exceptions ultimately 'could result in a system that is arguably more protective of employee rights and which serves as more of an impediment to employer discretion than [the systems of] most other countries'.[8] This is because 'the U.S. enforcement system may in fact impose higher costs on employers for noncompliance with employment laws than previously acknowledged'[9]; the evidence of this being the high settlement amounts and damages in the event of a successful claim. This is but one perspective, and the obvious counterargument is that in the US there are very few successful claims and settlements in comparison with the overall number of dismissals, although arguably even the threat of litigation provides an important disincentive against employers' poor behaviour with regard to dismissal of staff.[10] However, the answer to this question is a complex one and this chapter cannot possibly endeavour to answer it conclusively. In fact, enunciating laws regulating dismissal for cause in the United States is a Herculean task, with different states developing this law in different ways, in part based on the order of cases before them.[11] Further, despite efforts to codify American law on this point,[12] the governing common law principles are very much in a state of flux and still evolving.

6 Cynthia Estlund, 'Wrongful Discharge Protections in an At-Will World' (1995–96) 74 Tex L Rev 1655, 1655.

7 Matthew Finkin, Lea Vandervelde, William Corbett, Stephen F Befort, 'Working Group on Chapter 2 of the Proposed Restatement of Employment Law: Employment Contracts: Termination' (2009) 13(1) Em Rts & Emp Pol'y J 93, 97–98.

8 Samuel Estreicher and Jeffrey Hirsch, 'Comparative Wrongful Dismissal Law: Reassessing American Exceptionalism' (2014) 92 NC L Rev 343, 465.

9 Ibid 464.

10 For a discussion of the protective value of the threat of litigation for employees, see Jean Sternlight, 'Disarming Employees: How American Employers are Using Mandatory Arbitration to Deprive Workers of Legal Protection' (2015) 80(4) Brooklyn L Rev 1309.

11 Some scholars have called this path dependency. See eg, Michael J Gerhardt, 'The Limited Path Dependency of Precedent' (2005) 7 U Pa J Const L 903; Oona A Hathaway, 'Path Dependency in the Law: The Course and Pattern of Legal Change in a Common Law System' (2001) 86 Iowa L Rev 601, 604.

12 American Law Institute, 'Restatement of the Law, Third Employment Law, Proposed Final Draft' (18 April 2014).

So the purpose of this chapter is to provide an introduction to how American law has evolved since the entrenchment of employment at will in the nineteenth century. I will endeavour to trace the erosion of the at-will rule through both legislation and the common law, recognising the existence of the various state systems as 'multiple at-will hybrids' whose evolutionary story is far from settled.[13] Unlike in the United Kingdom and Australia, there is no dominant operative rule governing this area. Whereas the former determines unfair dismissal based on the range of reasonable responses test and the latter ascertains whether a dismissal was unfair, unjust or unreasonable, for American courts the process of identifying the legality of a dismissal is more challenging. Although the at-will rule *was* the traditional approach, it is no longer a pithy and accurate reflection of American law in this area. The contemporary legal reality is far more nuanced, and it is to this complexity and uncertainty I shall now turn.

Legislative incursions into employment at will

Erosion of the employment at will rule began with two defined groups of employees, one of those being civil service employees, and the other being union members.[14] For both of these, federal law developed to protect employees' job security, albeit for different reasons. For civil service employees, the motivation for legislative reform was largely political.[15] It was common practice at the time for civil service appointments to be based on political considerations; offices were used for partisan political activity and for kickbacks, with a percentage of employees' salaries returning to the political system.[16] Dissatisfaction with this approach to appointing civil servants motivated a number of political campaign reforms.[17]

This produced the Pendleton Civil Service Reform Act 1883, which provided protection for federal civil service employees.[18] This Act introduced appointment based on merit and fitness for service.[19] As it was focused only on hiring, the criticism that removals were unregulated and that arbitrary dismissals

13 Finkin et al. (n 7) 100.

14 Henry Perritt Jr, *Employee Dismissal Law and Practice* (5th edn Aspen Publishers, New York 2014) 1–17. See also Joseph Kelly, 'A Comparative Analysis of the Termination-at-Will Doctrine in the United States and Great Britain' (1989–90) 7(1) Ariz J Int & Comp Law 105.

15 H Manly Case, 'Federal Employee Job Rights: The Pendleton Act of 1883 to the Civil Service Reform Act of 1978' (1986) 29 Howard LJ 283, 305.

16 Ibid 287.

17 Ibid.

18 Perritt (n 14) 1–17.

19 'The Pendleton Act was designed for the classified civil service. It served to have implemented a system of competitive examinations administered and supervised under a three-member bipartisan board of commissioners. The tests were to be practical in nature and selection for appointment was made from the top competitors. The legislation was permissive in nature and positions were brought into the classified service by Executive Order. The legislation provided for a probationary period and forbid recommendations from senators or representatives not concerned with the applicant's character and residence.' Case (n 15) 288.

went unprotected remained.[20] Dismissal for cause was introduced in the Lloyd-LaFollette Act 1912.[21] Section 6 provided that 'no person in the classified service . . . shall be removed except for such cause as will promote the efficiency of said service'.[22] The Act also afforded procedural fairness such as notice for reasons in writing, a reasonable time to reply in writing and the opportunity to submit affidavits in support of the reply. There was no legislative requirement for a civil service employee to receive a hearing, except at the discretion of the officer making the removal.[23]

After some development in the law,[24] job protection and appeal rights of civil service employees were addressed in a comprehensive statute, the Civil Service Reform Act 1978. That Act prohibits dismissal of public employees covered by civil service law or regulation, again, except 'only for such cause as will promote the efficiency of the service'.[25] These words have been given content by the Civil Service Commission created by the 1883 Act and the Merit Systems Protection Board under the 1978 Act[26] and the courts.[27] In addition, the Act specifies in some detail the procedural steps that must occur before an employee can be terminated. These include advance notice of the proposed action, an opportunity for the employee to respond orally and in writing and to present evidence, representation by counsel, a written decision and reasons supporting it from the employing agency, a right of appeal and ultimately a right to judicial review of the administrative decision.[28] These protections now cover all civilian positions in the executive branch other than those appointed by the US president, therefore covering most federal employees.[29] Over time, these basic protections were gradually extended to virtually all state and most local government employees.[30] Even though the structure of the federal civil service is somewhat different from these systems, the underlying concepts regarding wrongful dismissal were adopted.[31]

20 Ibid 305.
21 Perritt (n 14) 1–17.
22 Case (n 15) 289.
23 Ibid.
24 For example, the provision of job protection rights for veterans: see Case, ibid 305–6.
25 Civil Service Reform Act 1978 s 7513. See also, Janice Linn, 'Job Security for the At Will Employee: Contractual Right of Discharge for Cause' (1981) 57(3) Chicago-Kent L Rev 697, 707.
26 Office of Personnel Management, 'Our Mission, Role & History' <www.opm.gov/about-us/our-mission-role-history/>.
27 US Merit Systems Protection Board, 'Judicial Review' <www.mspb.gov/About/review.htm>.
28 Perritt (n 14) 8–11.
29 Summers (n 2) 497.
30 Perritt (n 14) 1–17. There have been some legislative attempts to erode job security protection for civil service employees, for example, see a Bill which at the time of writing was being considered in Wisconsin, 2015 Assembly Bill 373 <https://docs.legis.wisconsin.gov/2015/proposals/ab373>accessed 8 December 2015.
31 Perritt (n 14) 8–10.

This introduction of job security protection for civil service employees was by no means insignificant. In 1976 an estimated 2,879,000 civilian employees of the federal government constituted about 3 per cent of all persons employed in the United States. Over 90 per cent of these were tenured and enjoyed the protections set out above. In the same year, there were approximately 12,170,000 state and local government employees, of whom 3,340,000 were state employees. Reliable information is not available regarding how many of these had civil service type job protection, but certainly more than half were protected.[32] Soon after the passage of the Civil Service Reform Act 1978, case law developed in a manner that would have been previously inconceivable had these employees still been covered by the at-will common law rule. For example, in *Hoska v United States Department of the Army*[33] the army revoked a petitioner's top secret security clearance because of alleged security violations, an unfavourable psychiatric evaluation, and several incidents of allegedly indiscreet behaviour. Because he no longer possessed the required security clearance, the army dismissed him. It was found that the army's revocation of the petitioner's clearance was not in accordance with the requirements of its own regulations, specifically its inherent nexus requirement to the 'efficiency of the service' under the Civil Service Reform Act 1978. In another case, the employee's grossly immoral off-duty misconduct was found not to be a sufficient basis for discharge because it did not adversely impact the efficiency of the postal service.[34]

Apart from civil service employees, the rise of organised labour meant that employment at will, as a contractual matter, was superseded by just cause provisions negotiated by unions as part of collective agreements. By the early twentieth century, labour interests were gaining political power and around that time industrial relations scholars such as Frank Taussig[35] and Albion Taylor[36] questioned the assumption that injustices in the labour market could be remedied through strengthening individual employment rights. They were of the view that a collective regime was necessary. Some judges at the time were also in support.[37] For example, Judge Oliver Wendell Holmes Jr in *Vegelahn v Guntner*[38] opposed bans on union activity on account of the fact that it merely counterbalanced the combined power of capitalists.

An alternative administrative system was created, in part to mitigate the effects of the perceived inadequacy of the employment-at-will rule.[39] Explicit legislative

32 Peck (n 5) 729–30.

33 677 F2d 131 (DC Cir 1982).

34 *Bonet v United States Postal Service* 661 F2d 1071 (5th Cir 1981).

35 Matthias Beck, *The Elusive Search for Job Security A Historical Inquiry into Dismissals in the United States Workplace* (Nova Science Publishers, New York 2012) 34. According to Beck, Frank Taussig was a Harvard economist who made the suggestion in his popular 1920s economic textbook *Principles of Economics* (4th edn Macmillan, New York 1921) 293.

36 According to Beck, Albion Taylor's influential monograph was *Labor Problems and Labor Law* (3rd printing Prentice Hall, New York 1940), first published in 1938.

37 Beck (n 35) 35.

38 167 Mass 92 (1896).

39 Paul Berks, 'Social Change and Judicial Response: The Handbook Exception to Employment-At-Will' (2000) 4 Em Rts & Emp Pol'y J 231, 245.

protection of those involved in union activity commenced as late as 1926 with the Railroad Labor Act, which required employers to bargain with unions and prohibited employers discriminating against union members.[40] Other legislation around that time gave unions and their members rights to bargain collectively and engage in other activities – for example, the Norris La Guardia Act 1932 and the National Industrial Recovery Act 1933.[41]

However, it was the passage of the National Labor Relations Act 1935 (NLRA) which represented the 'most sweeping limitation on employment at will'.[42] Relevantly, and broadly speaking, the NLRA prohibited employers from stymieing the formation of unions and from inhibiting employees from accessing collective bargaining, and protected employees from engaging in concerted activities for mutual aid and protection, such as strikes, pickets and boycotts. Sections 7 and 8 of the NLRA 'effectively tied the legal protection of employees from retaliatory discharges to the right of employees to organize collectively'.[43] Those sections stated:

> Sec. 7. Employees shall have the right to self-organization, to form, join, or assist labor organizations, to bargain collectively through representatives of their own choosing, and to engage in concerted activities, for the purpose of collective bargaining or other mutual aid or protection . . .
>
> Sec. 8. It shall be an unfair practice for an employer –
>
> 1) to interfere with, restrain, or coerce employees in the exercise of the rights guaranteed by section 7.
> 2) to dominate or interfere with the formation or administration of any labor organization or contribute financial or other support to it . . .
> 3) by discrimination in regard to hire or tenure of employment or any term or condition of employment to encourage or discourage membership in any labor organization . . .
> 4) to discharge or otherwise discriminate against an employee because he had filed charges or given testimony under this Act.
> 5) to refuse to bargain collectively with the representatives of his employees . . .[44]

These rights are enforced through administrative procedures. The NLRA established as its administrative enforcement mechanism a National Labor Relations Board (NLRB) which has two distinct functions. One branch of the NLRB investigates and prosecutes unfair labour practices and proceedings on behalf of unions, employees or employers. Independently, the NLRB has 'a five-member,

40 Beck (n 35) 36.
41 Although the National Industrial Recovery Act 1933 was found unconstitutional by the US Supreme Court, it and the Norris La Guardia Act 1932 (prohibiting most labour law–based court injunctions) provided a template for the National Labor Relations Act 1935.
42 Estlund (n 6) 1658.
43 Beck (n 35) 37.
44 Ibid.

quasi-judicial body [and] reviews the unfair labor practice decisions of administrative law judges'.[45]

Although section 9(a) of the NLRA mandated bargaining in collective agreements for pay, wages, hours of employment and other conditions of employment, it provided little guidance on the question of whether bargaining over 'other conditions of employment' included issues relating to job security.[46] However, 'when issues like redundancies, mass layoffs and mass discharges were at stake, the courts and the Board usually interpreted "other conditions of employment" to mean that union involvement in decisions about which workers were to be laid off or made redundant was mandatory'.[47] In any event, unions chose not to trade job security provisions in exchange for wage increases or other benefits, reflecting their recognition of its importance to employees.[48]

The form in which job security was provided varied. This could be done by unions negotiating an explicit guarantee of work or through achieving partial job security – for example, by instituting a seniority system.[49] More frequently, collective agreements provided for an employment relationship other than at-will employment through a 'just cause' limitation on discharge and other disciplinary decisions. Unions also negotiated a multi-step grievance procedure culminating in final, binding arbitration before a neutral decision maker jointly selected by the parties. Negotiators rarely attempted to include a comprehensive list of offences in the agreement, with the contractual language often simply prohibiting discipline or termination 'without cause' or 'without just cause'.[50]

There would also usually be a grievance procedure in the agreement that employees could use to protest against the discipline or termination. If the parties failed to resolve the grievance, the union could usually take the case to an impartial arbitrator for a final and binding resolution.[51] An arbitrator typically could order reinstatement and back pay. Arbitration decisions were subject to limited judicial review.[52] Unions brought an increasing number of cases before the NLRB during the seventies: 'from 1965 to 1980, the number of cases in which the NLRB offered reinstatement to workers roughly doubled with approximately twice the number of workers, about 10,000, being reinstated in 1980'.[53]

As union membership grew, and agreements came to control the terms and conditions of work for a substantial number of employees, so did arbitral

45 Befort (n 3) 359.
46 Beck (n 35) 38.
47 Ibid 45.
48 Harvard Law Review Association, 'Protecting at Will Employees against Wrongful Discharge: The Duty to Terminate Only in Good Faith' (1980) 93(8) Harv L Rev 1816, 1832.
49 Roger Abrams and Dennis Nolan, 'Toward a Theory of "Just Cause" in Employee Discipline Cases' [1985] Duke LJ 594, 599.
50 Ibid.
51 Ibid 602.
52 Befort (n 3) 360.
53 Beck (n 35) 74. For a comprehensive review of the arbitration system, see Kenneth May Patrick M Sanders, Michelle T Sullivan, *Elkouri and Elkouri: How Arbitration Works* (Bloomberg, Arlington, VA 2012).

principles governing dismissal.[54] These developed rules around management's right to manage, the right of employees to equal treatment and procedural fairness, and corrective discipline.[55] Although arbitration has the benefit of taking into account industrial realities, it does not create an appealable body of law, as it involves the private resolution of disputes.[56] As such, collective bargaining agreements are generally not interpreted according to the judicial principles governing common law employment contracts.[57] Despite the non-application of the doctrine of precedent,[58] arbitrators are usually aware of the pattern of decisions by other arbitrators and are reluctant to deviate far from them.[59]

A key benefit of union representation and collective bargaining afforded by the NLRA was that it allowed employees to avoid the risk and insecurity of employment because protective provisions could be agreed upon and included in collective bargaining agreements. Collective bargaining was seen as the best method for voluntarily obtaining job security during that time.[60] It was inextricably intertwined with the development and survival of the employment-at-will rule because it decreased the number of workers employed under it, which dampened the political opposition to the rule, thus reducing the impetus for common law change.[61]

In the years following the passage of the NLRA, union representation spread in rapidly growing basic industries and millions of employees exited the employment-at-will regime in favour of protections provided by collective agreements.[62] Union members accounted for 31.5 per cent of the non-agricultural workforce in 1950.[63] By 1954 it reached its all-time high of 35 per cent before it began to fall.[64] In the 1970s less than 28 per cent of the non-agricultural workforce was employed pursuant to the terms of an agreement,[65] with the vast majority of these agreements providing some limitation on the employer's power to discharge without just cause.[66] However by 2014, with unionism declining in America, as in the UK and Australia, collective agreements applied to less than 7 per cent of the private sector workforce.[67]

54 Berks (n 39) 236.
55 Summers (n 2) 501–8.
56 For a comparative critique, see Matthew Finkin, 'Privatization of Wrongful Dismissal Protection in Comparative Perspective' (2008) 37 Indust LJ 149.
57 Berks (n 39) 248.
58 Posner critiques the US model of arbitration as a product of a market-driven system that does not produce fully reasoned opinions with precedential value. See R Posner, 'What do Judges Maximize?' in R Posner (ed), *Overcoming Law* (Harvard UP, Cambridge, MA 1995) 109.
59 Summers (n 2) 501.
60 Sally Gertz, 'At-Will Employment: Origins, Applications, Exceptions and Expansions in the Public Service (2008) 31(5) Int J Pub Admin 489, 492.
61 Berks (n 39) 237.
62 Ibid 249.
63 Befort (n 3) 357.
64 Ibid 357, 361.
65 Peck (n 5) 729.
66 Rachel Arnow-Richman, 'Just Notice: Re-Reforming Employment at Will' (2010–11) 58 UCLA L Rev 1, 17.
67 Befort (n 3) 362–76; US Bureau of Labor Statistics, 'Economic News Release', USDL-14-0095 (2014) <www.opm.gov/about-us/our-mission-role-history/>.

Despite union decline, the NLRA had an effect on non-unionised workplaces too. In these workplaces, no grievance or bargaining procedures were specified, unless by voluntary agreement.[68] However, bargains struck in the union sector set the pattern for much of the non-union sector. Non-union firms, whether to keep up with the market and attract good workers or to dissuade employees from joining unions, often matched the job security provisions in the collective agreements of their union counterparts.[69]

Thus, the judiciary's wholehearted embrace of the employment-at-will rule towards the end of the nineteenth century gave way to legislative reform that saw its gradual erosion. Job security protection was developed for both civil service employees and union members under statute and this paved the way for employees outside of these groups to begin to expect some measure of protection against arbitrary dismissal. In the twentieth century, the maturation of the common law saw a growing acceptance that in certain circumstances the courts could limit an employer's power to discharge.

The emergence of common law exceptions to employment at will

Before we turn to examining the primary ways in which the common law came to erode the edifice of employment at will, it is important to allude briefly to the impetus for this development. One possible cause was that the courts were responding to union decline, as this greatly increased the number of workers with no job security.[70] Berks posits that the courts are willing to 'pick up the slack' when 'institutions separate from the formal judicial process no longer satisfy a recognizable legal demand'.[71] Declining union density meant that fewer workers could rely on collective agreements to provide them with a remedy for dismissal without just cause. It is also possible that there was increasing judicial acceptance that the at-will rule was less suitable to the conditions of contemporary society.[72] Although a laissez-faire approach had characterised judicial decisions in this area in the nineteenth century, the emergence of statutory protection of job security for civil service employees and union members evinced 'a legislative judgment that employee interests in employment deserved protection from the unhindered power of employers to discharge and that the interests of society would be better served by limiting that power even though it encumbered the freedom of employers to direct and manage businesses'.[73]

Widespread social change was also under way. This included the growth in large corporate employers and specialised job functions. Employment at will was seen as

68 Beck (n 35) 85.
69 Befort (n 3) 393.
70 Gertz (n 60) 492.
71 Berks (n 39) 279.
72 Peck (n 5) 732.
73 Ibid 727.

harsh and unbalanced, as employees were no longer typically employed in a transitory nature in smaller enterprises characterised by personal relationships amongst staff and management.[74] The emergence of the global economy forced employers to reduce costs in order to compete internationally and led to corporate restructuring, downsizing and a growing reliance on contingent workers.[75] Modern information and communication technology made capital considerably more mobile than labour and forced production facilities to move to locations with lower labour costs. This was seen as exacerbating the imbalance between employers and employees, thereby necessitating protection of employees' job security.[76] Finally, political support emanating from both liberal and conservative quarters,[77] coupled with the writing of academics, provided justification for eroding employment at will. A number of academics advocated the development of a tort remedy. For example, in 1894 Oliver Wendell Holmes formulated a broad cause of action for intentional torts. It is said to be the genesis of the prima facie tort concept (although this is not recognised in most states anymore) and the 'framework within which the public policy tort has been developed'.[78] In 1967 Professor Blades argued that the prima facie tort doctrine provided an avenue with which remedies could be developed for wrongful dismissal.[79] His seminal article has been frequently cited.

We now turn to an examination of certain categories of common law erosions to the default at-will rule. Whilst the universe of erosions is far larger than I have time to cover here, in this section I hope to provide a glimpse into the myriad ways employees can challenge their dismissal in the US courts.[80]

The public policy exception

Introduced in 1959, the public policy tort was the first judicial exception to employment at will. It allows recovery by a dismissed employee when the dismissal violates a clear public policy of the state without justification. The vast majority of states recognise public policy as a basis for limiting an employer's power to terminate an at-will employment relationship,[81] although some of these

74 Befort (n 3) 386.
75 Ibid.
76 Ibid 387.
77 Beck (n 35) 89.
78 See Perritt (n 14) 1–25. Perritt cites Oliver Wendell Holmes, 'Privilege, Malice and Intent' (1894) 8 Harv L Rev 1.
79 Peck (n 5) 724, referring to Blades (n 2).
80 In addition to the public policy, implied-in-fact and good faith exceptions, other exceptions exist. There are employment at will tort erosion other than public policy torts, including intentional infliction of emotion distress, and whistleblower common law claims and statutes. Similarly with contract erosions, in addition to implied-in-fact exceptions there are express oral and written exceptions, implied exceptions based on theories of additional consideration and promissory estoppel, and exceptions revolving around employee handbooks. For a full examination of these and other exceptions, see American Law Institute, *Restatement of the Law: Employment Law* (American Law Institute, Philadelphia, PA 2015) ch 2.
81 For a list of states that recognise the exception, see American Law Institute (n 12) 194–96.

states construe the exception rather narrowly,[82] and other states do not recognise it at all, such as New York,[83] Maine[84] and Alaska.[85] Another state that does not recognise this exception is Rhode Island, where a court held 'unequivocally' that it is 'not the role of the courts to create rights for persons whom the Legislature has not chosen to protect'.[86]

It is generally accepted that there are four elements of the public policy tort, each of which must be proved by the plaintiff: firstly, the existence of a clear and substantial public policy; secondly, jeopardy to that policy if employers are allowed to escape liability for terminating employees in circumstances like those that involve the plaintiff; thirdly, actual conduct by the employee that promotes the public policy, resulting in dismissal; and fourthly, lack of a legitimate employer interest (other than the employment-at-will rule) to justify the dismissal.[87] At the heart of the tort is a concern with 'societal or general third-party interests', as benefits accruing to employees are incidental.[88] This involves a careful balancing exercise between the default position, which is that the at-will rule represents 'society's interest in market forces as the best way to promote efficient enterprise', and a societal interest posited by the employee, which might be weightier than the former.[89] Distinguishing a societal interest can be difficult, and different states have varied in their approach. For example, the Supreme Court of Washington has been willing to examine whether employee conduct that does not fall into the usual understanding of 'societal interest' has 'socially redeemable aspects' nevertheless.[90] In most states, the tort of wrongful discharge in violation of public policy is also applicable in instances of constructive dismissal.[91]

The case of *Petermann v International Brotherhood of Teamsters*[92] introduced the exception. In that case, an employee was fired for refusing to perjure himself by making certain false and untrue statements in his testimony before a committee of the California legislature. In contrast to his employer's wishes, he answered all questions truthfully. The Court reasoned that it was not in the interests of the state to allow an employer to fire at will if such a dismissal contravened the

82 For example, Pennsylvania: *Geary v United States Steel Corporation* 319 A2d 174, 178 (1974); Wisconsin: *Ward v Frito-Lay Inc* 290 NW2d 536 (Wis 1980); *Jones v Keogh* 409 A2d 581 (Vt 1979).

83 *Weider v Skala* 609 NE2d 105 (NY 1992).

84 *Bard v Bath Iron Works* 590 A2d 152 (Me 1991).

85 *Reich v Holiday Inn* 454 So2d 982 (Ala 1984).

86 *Pacheco v Raytheon Co* 623 A2d 464, 465 (RI 35 1993).

87 Perritt (n 14) 7–6.

88 Jeffrey Harrison, 'The "New" Terminable-at-Will Employment Contract: An Interest and Cost Incident Analysis' (1994) 69 Iowa L Rev 327, 350.

89 Perritt (n 14) 7.

90 *Gardner v Loomis Armoured Inc* 913 P2d 377, 382 (Wash 1996).

91 See eg, *Colores v Bd of 12 Trs* 130 Cal Rptr 2d 347 (Cal Ct App 2003); *Flesner v Technical Commc'ns Corp* 575 NE2d 1107 (Mass 1991); *Karch v BayBank FSB* 794 A2d 763, 774–75 (NH 2002); *Pa State Police v Suders* 542 US 129, 142 (2004); *Krohn v City of Seattle* No. 42244-8-I, 2000 Wash App LEXIS 320 (Wash Ct App, 22 Feb 2000).

92 174 Cal App 2d 184 (1959).

state's own penal code which made perjury unlawful, as this would undermine public welfare. A unanimous decision was made by the court to break from the employment-at-will rule.

After the case of *Tameny v Atlantic Richfield Co*,[93] in which an employee had been discharged after fifteen years' service because he refused to participate in an illegal price-fixing scheme, it became clear that violating public policy warranted an action in tort, rather than in contract. The rule that public policy claims in all dismissal matters should be actions in tort was established in the 1986 case of *Koehrer v Superior Court*.[94] These decisions were significant because employees could use tort theories to avoid contract law defences such as lack of consideration or the statute of frauds. Also, tort actions 'hold the potential for a greater range of relief than contract actions'.[95]

Initially, most courts interpreted the public policy doctrine to imply that claims had to be based on the violation of a clearly stated public policy mandate. However, over time the law developed so that issues that could not be traced to a statute but were related to broadly accepted public policy principles could be the basis of claims. Such general public policy principles were 'particularly prominent in such areas as consumer protection and patient rights, where legal formalization of rules of conduct was in a state of flux'.[96] Some jurisdictions have even recognised that in appropriate cases non-statutory sources of public policy such as judicial decisions[97] and certain well-established principles of professional or occupational responsibility[98] can form a basis for the public policy exception. For example, *Dabbs v Cardiopulmonary Management Services*[99] involved a certified respiratory therapist who was terminated after she refused to work the night shift. Her action was in protest at the working conditions on the shift, since the employer required her to work with someone who was not qualified to handle the assigned work. She alleged she was terminated in retaliation for her refusal to continue working under conditions that would jeopardise 'the health, safety and physical well-being of the patients' and that this violated public policy. The court concluded that the allegations were sufficient to state a cause of action even though her employer had not violated a specific statute.

Although the public policy exception, in states where it is recognised, does represent an erosion of the at-will rule, it is by no means as far reaching as a general statutory right to just cause in dismissal. This is because the latter substantially limits employer discretion by requiring a proper reason for dismissal, whereas the

93 27 Cal 3d 167 (1980).
94 181 Cal App 3d 1155, 225 Cal Rptr 820 (1986).
95 Robin Foster, 'Employment at Will: When Must an Employer Have Good Cause for Discharging an Employee?' (1983) 48 Missouri L Rev 113, 128.
96 Beck (n 35) 93.
97 See eg, *Faulkner v United Tech Corp* 693 A2d 293 (Conn 1997); *Palmateer v Harvester Co* 421 NE2d 876, 877 (Ill 1981); *Hysten v Burlington N Santa Fe Ry Co* 108 P3d 437 (Kan 2004).
98 See eg, *Dynamics Corp v Super Ct* 876 P2d 487 (Cal 1994).
99 188 Cal App 3d 1437 (1987).

public policy exception only gives rise to damages in tort for a plaintiff who can prove that her dismissal violated an important public policy.[100]

Implied in fact contract exception

Another type of modification of the employment-at-will rule is an implied in fact contract exception.[101] This allows the default position of at-will employment to be rebutted by contrary evidence. In these cases, courts impose contractual liability on employers who give verbal or written promises of long-term or lifetime employment or foster a corporate culture that assures its employees they will not be fired without cause.[102] This approach requires courts to consider the facts and circumstances surrounding an at-will agreement and to ascertain whether there is any implied or express contractual provision which may alter the terms governing discharge.[103] To establish the presence of an implication in fact, a wide range of sources has been permitted to form part of the employment contract, such as employee handbooks, company policy and oral representations.[104] These statements, reasonably read in context, may establish limits on the employer's power to terminate the employment relationship at will. Like the public policy exception, the implied in fact exception operates in the vast majority of American jurisdictions.

To make out the exception, job security can be implied in a number of ways. Firstly, a promise of employment can be found in specific oral commitments to an individual employee. For example, in *Terrio v Millinocket Community Hospital*[105] an authorised agent of the employer made oral statements that the employee had 'nothing to fear' and that her job would be 'for the rest of her life'. These oral statements were accepted by the court because of the context of her long service in a position of substantial responsibility. In the oft-cited Supreme Court of Michigan's decision of *Toussaint v Blue Cross & Blue Shield of Michigan, Ebling v Masco Corporation*[106] one of the issues was the effect of oral statements made by the employer. The court held that employer statements that an employee would be with the company 'as long as [he] did [his] job' or that he would not be discharged if he was 'doing the job' can give rise to a contract of employment for an indefinite term, terminable only for cause.

Secondly, job security can also be derived from employer representations made to the workforce generally. Of particular interest is the implication of terms contained in an employer handbook. At issue here is whether promises employers

100 *Sheets v Teddy's Frosted Foods, Inc* 179 Conn 471 (1980).

101 For early cases which established and developed this exception, see: *Drzewiecki v H & R Block, Inc* 24 Cal App 3d 695 (1972); *Pugh v See's Candies, Inc* 116 Cal App 3d 311 (1981).

102 Katherine Stone, 'Dismissal Law in the United States: The Past and Present of At-Will Employment' (2009) UCLA School of Law, Law & Economics Research Paper Series No 09–03, 9.

103 *Bascom v Shillito* 37 Ohio St 431, 434 (1882).

104 *Mers v Dispath Printing Co* 483 NE2d 150, 154 (Ohio 1985).

105 379 A2d 135, 138 (Me 1977).

106 408 Mich 579, 292 NW2d 880 (1980).

make in handbooks or policy manuals can be construed as being implied into employment contracts. This issue became especially important during the late twentieth century as employers sought to induce employees to forgo union representation by promising in handbooks and similar documents to maintain or implement benefits, including job security, equal to those usually contained in collective bargaining agreements.[107] At present, thirty-nine out of fifty-one jurisdictions accept that unilateral employer policy statements can establish binding employer obligations.[108]

Courts have justified their decisions regarding the implication of employer handbooks in a few distinct ways. Some jurisdictions have held that an employer handbook may constitute a unilateral contract accepted through performance of the required job duties.[109] This approach eliminates the need to find an express mutual exchange of promises as a prerequisite to enforceability. A contract is formed when a party responds to a promissory offer by commencing performance of the desired task. There is no need for a prior or even an accompanying express reciprocal promise of performance, as the promise in the handbook is deemed to be accepted by the employee's continuing employment.[110] Other jurisdictions have relied on a theory of 'legitimate expectations', where the benefit conferred on the employer through the establishment of policies and procedures creates an equitable requirement that those procedures be enforced on behalf of employees as well.[111] Still another group of decisions scrutinise handbook statements in terms of equitable principles that resemble the doctrine of promissory estoppel.[112]

One common approach of the courts is to focus on the benefit that accrues to an employer when it establishes desirable personnel policies. In the aforementioned case of *Toussaint* the Michigan Court held that an employee's expectations grounded in statements in an employer's manual of personnel policies were contractually enforceable even though no pre-employment negotiations took place and there was no meeting of the parties' minds on the subject. The Court reasoned it was enough that the employer chose to create an environment in which employees believed that the employer's policies and practices were fair and applied consistently and uniformly. Similarly in *Woolley v Hoffman-La Roche Inc*[113] the New

107 Berks (n 39).
108 American Law Institute (n 12) 85.
109 See eg, *Asmus v Pacific Bel* 23 Cal 4th 1, 96 Cal Rptr 2d 179, 999 P2d 71, 76 (2000); *Birmingham Parking Authority v Wiggins* 797 So 2d 446, 448–49 (Ala 2001); *Thompson v City of Des Moines* 564 NW2d 839, 844, 845 (Iowa 1997); *O'Brien v New England Tel & Tel Co* 422 Mass 686, 664 NE2d 843, 848 (Mass 1996); *Toroysan v Boehringer Ingelheim Pharm* 234 Conn 1, 662 A2d 89, 92 (1995).
110 Berks (n 39) 269.
111 See eg, *Touissant v Blue Cross & Blue Shield of Michigan* 408 Mich 578, 292 NW2d 880 (1980); *Parts Depot Inc v Beiswenger* 170 SW3d 354, 362, 363 (Ky 2005); *Sisco v GSA Nat'l Capital Fed Credit Union* 689 A2d 52, 55, 57 (DC 1997).
112 See eg, *Jones v Central Peninsula General Hospital* 779 P2d 783 (Alaska 1989). See also: Stephen Befort, 'Employee Handbooks and the Legal Effect of Disclaimers' (1992) 13(2) Berkeley J Emp & Lab Law 343, 343.
113 491 A2d 1257 (NJ 1985).

Jersey Supreme Court adopted a reasonable expectations analysis. In this case the Court considered an employee manual that conferred benefits that were competitive with those found in collective bargaining agreements. It concluded that:

> [W]hen an employer of a substantial number of employees circulates a manual that, when fairly read, provides that certain benefits are an incident of the employment (including, especially, job security provisions), the judiciary, instead of 'grudgingly' conceding the enforceability of those provisions, should construe them in accordance with reasonable expectations of the employees.[114]

Furthermore, on occasion, a promise of indefinite employment has been implied because of a long period of service. In *Delzell v Pope*,[115] where evidence showed that the employer had intended the employee would be hired on a fixed term of a year but had in fact relied on his services for a long period of time, the Court said 'it would be most unreasonable to infer that he was employed on a month to month basis and was subject to dismissal on a moment's notice'.[116]

As this exemption is contractual in origin, courts have found that the term can be waived. Increasingly, employers have decided to make disclaimers. An example of this approach can be found in *Boll v Hyatt Corp*,[117] where the Illinois Appellate Court held that a statement signed by the employee saying 'I understand that my employment is terminable-at-will, and that the application is not, and is not intended to be a contract for continued employment' assisted in negating the reasonableness of the employee's beliefs that subsequently distributed documents created an implied commitment to dismissal only for cause.

Implied covenant of good faith and fair dealing

The implied covenant of good faith and fair dealing is the least accepted of the three judicial exceptions discussed in this chapter.[118] The obligation to act in good faith during contractual performance of employment contracts gained traction because of developments in contract law more generally. It was written into the Uniform Commercial Code and in 1981 it was inserted as a new section in the Restatement (Second) of Contracts.[119] Section 205 of the Restatement stipulates that every contract imposes upon the parties a duty of good faith and

114 Ibid.

115 294 SW2d 690 (1956).

116 Ibid.

117 614 NE2d 71, 74 (1993).

118 Examples of courts declining to recognise the exception or significantly limiting its scope include: *First Nat Bank of Omaha v Centennial Park LLC* 48 Kan App 2d 714, 303 P3d 705, 716 (2013); *Cramer v Fairfield Med Ctr* 182 Ohio App 3d 653, 663 (2009); *Brozo v Oracle Corp* 324 F3d 661, 668 (8th Cir 2003); *Miller v Mass Mutual Life Ins Co* 455 SE2d 799, 802 (WVa 1995).

119 James Brudney, 'Reluctance and Remorse: The Covenant of Good Faith and Fair Dealing in American Employment Law' (2010–11) 32 Comp Lab L & Pol'y J 773.

fair dealing in its performance and its enforcement. This section has led to many courts using various formulations to imply an employer's obligation not to discharge employees wrongfully.[120]

Breach of the good faith and fair dealing term occurs when 'one party to a contract performs an act that is not expressly barred by the contract in question but is contrary to the reasonable expectations of the other party'.[121] It is a subjective concept without precise meaning and encompasses, among other things, 'an honest belief, the absence of malice and the absence of design to defraud or to seek an unconscionable advantage'.[122]

Although good faith and fair dealing is potentially the most expansive judicial qualification of the employment-at-will doctrine,[123] the courts that have accepted the existence of a covenant agree that it cannot limit the prerogative of the employer to discharge an at-will employee, as a general proposition. It is widely held in those jurisdictions that, in at-will employment, the implied covenant must be understood so that it is consistent with the at-will nature of the relationship.[124]

Some courts have recognised that the implied duty protects against retaliatory discharge. For example, *Fortune v The National Cash Register Company*[125] involved a salesman who was barred from recovery of a commission allegedly due to him by the fact that he failed to follow a notice and grievance procedure set forth under the contract. He was fired just before the commission had become due and payable. The court found that the company's actions violated an implied covenant of good faith and fair dealing. However, the Court declined to speculate whether the good faith requirement is implicit in every contract for employment.

Length of service can be used to support a claim for breach of the implied term. For example, the California Court of Appeal has concluded that employment contracts in that jurisdiction, like all contracts, include an implied covenant of good faith and fair dealing. The court decided that an important factor in construing the covenant was the plaintiff's eighteen years of service: 'termination of employment without legal cause after such a period of time offends the implied in law covenant of good faith and fair dealing'.[126]

While good faith as an implied contractual term has been recognised by most American jurisdictions for at least the past several decades, in the employment setting the covenant has not fared nearly so well. Of the debates raging over the

120 *Wade v Kessler Institute* 172 NJ 327, 345, 798 A2d 1251 (2007); *Wieder v Skala* 80 NY2d 628, 637, 593 NYS2d 752, 756, 609 NE2d 105, 109 (1992); *Jones v Central Peninsula General Hospital* 779 P2d 783 (Alaska 1989).

121 Kim Sheehan, 'Has Employment-at-Will Outlived Its Usefulness? A Comparison of US and New Zealand Employment Law' (1997–98) 28 Cal Western Int LJ 323, 329.

122 Linn (n 25) 712, quoting *Black's Law Dictionary.*

123 Theodore St Antoine, 'A Seed Germinates: Unjust Discharge Reform Heads toward Full Flower' (1988) 67 Neb LJ 56, 63.

124 See eg, *Jenkins v Boise Cascade Corp* 108 P3d 380, 390 (Idaho 2005); *EI DuPont d Nemours & Co v Pressman* 679 A2d 436, 444 (Del 1996).

125 373 Mass 96 (1977).

126 *Cleary v American Airlines, Inc* 111 Cal App 3d 443 (1980).

implied covenant's existence, Finkin has said 'no question has produced quite so much confusion in the modern context of at-will employment',[127] and Brudney says that some states that have applied it have 'circumscribed the covenant's impact in what amount[s] to expressions of judicial remorse'.[128]

Statutory exceptions to employment at will: the case of Montana

Montana was the first jurisdiction of the United States to adopt a statutory dismissal regime.[129] Prior to the passage of the Wrongful Discharge from Employment Act 1987 (WDEA), employees in Montana were employed at will. However, unlike the majority of states, employment at will was conferred legislatively, rather than judicially.[130] This was subject to many exceptions. In 1982 Montana's Supreme Court recognised that employment contracts contain a covenant of good faith and fair dealing. In 1983, the Court found that the covenant was to be pursued as a tort claim.[131]

There were a number of possible reasons for the adoption of WDEA. Firstly (and the most likely reason), the legislation was introduced to counter the large amount of damages that were being awarded in unjust dismissal cases.[132] Damages awarded were in the millions.[133] Some, which resulted from a flood of lawsuits relating to downsizing in Montana's health and tourism industries, were not covered by employers' general liability insurance.[134] Employer and insurer groups objected to the uncertainty and expense created by the evolving common law and vigorously supported the introduction of unjust dismissal legislation.[135]

Secondly, between 1975 and 1985 union membership in Montana declined from nearly one third of the non-agricultural workforce to merely one fifth; a

127 Matthew Finkin, 'Second Thoughts on a *Restatement of Employment Law*' (2013) 7 U Penn J Bus Law 279.

128 Brudney (n 119) 774.

129 The United States Virgin Islands and Puerto Rico (which are unincorporated territories) also have wrongful discharge legislation. See Richard Lord, 'The At-Will Relationship in the 21st Century: A Consideration of Consideration' (2006) 58 Baylor L Rev 707, 711.

130 Ibid.

131 See *Gates v Life of Mont Ins Co* 638 P2d 1063, 1066–67 (Mont 1980). See also: William Corbett, 'Resolving Employee Discharge Disputes under the Montana Wrongful Discharge Act (MWDA), Discharge Claims Arising Apart from the MWDA, and Practice and Procedure Issues in the Context of a Discharge Case' (2005) 66 Montana L Rev 329, 332.

132 Estreicher and Hirsch (n 8) 466.

133 For example, in *Mildred Flanigan v Prudential Federal Savings* 720 P2d 257 (Mont 1986) an employee was awarded $1.3 million for punitive damage, $100,000 for emotional distress, and $94,170 for economic losses. In *Farrens v Meridian Oil* 852 F2d 1289 (unpublished disposition) the employee was initially awarded $2.5 million for economic losses. After appeal, the Ninth Circuit Court of Appeals upheld the liability claim but ruled that the evidence supported a $1.7 million award for economic damages.

134 Beck (n 35) 98.

135 Bradley Ewig, Charles North and Beck Taylor, 'The Employment Effects of a "Good Cause" Discharge Standard in Montana' (2005–06) 59 Indust & Lab Relations Rev 17, 20.

relative decline of 34 per cent.[136] It was the most significant decline of union density in any state. This increased the number of workers who were unable to bargain collectively for protection against unfair dismissal. The WDEA was a response to that problem which satisfied the demand.[137]

Thirdly, the WDEA was passed as a result of the significant deviations the common law had made from employment at will.

> A prediction of the political-compromise hypothesis is that in states where the employment-at-will doctrine had withered the most, employers would resist unjust-dismissal legislation least strongly and might even actively support such legislation, allowing unjust-dismissal legislation to gain enough support to be formally proposed in the state's legislature. The empirical evidence is largely consistent with this prediction, as legislation is far more likely to be proposed in states that have recognized exceptions to the employment-at-will doctrine, all else being equal.[138]

The Bill was reworked several times. For example, the early drafts were considered too pro-employer for employee rights advocates.[139] There were objections even after the WDEA was adopted. The constitutionality of the WDEA was challenged in three cases before the Montana Supreme Court. The primary challenge was from the plaintiffs' bar, who were opposed to the WDEA and brought an unsuccessful constitutional challenge.[140]

The WDEA is a 'peculiar combination of just cause and enumerated reasons'.[141] Under section 904, Montana employers are prohibited from terminating employees for three reasons. Firstly, if the discharge is retaliatory because of an employee's refusal to violate public policy or for reporting a violation of public policy[142]; secondly, if the discharge was not for good cause after the expiration of the employee's probationary period.[143] 'Good cause' is defined in the legislation as referring to 'reasonable job-related grounds for dismissal based on a failure to satisfactorily perform job duties, disruption of the employer's operation, or other

136 Berks (n 39) 278.

137 Ibid 279.

138 Jack Steiber and Richard Block, 'Communications: Unjust-Dismissal Legislation' (1991–92) 45 Indust & Lab Relations Rev 792, 796.

139 Ibid 792. Also see LeRoy Schramm, 'Montana Employment Law and the 1987 Wrongful Discharge from Employment Act: A New Order Begins' (1990) 51 Montana L Rev 94, 108 which describes the amendments made to the Bill.

140 See *Meech v Hillhaven W, Inc* 776 P2d 488, 498–91 (Mont 1989). See also, Leonard Bierman and Stuart Youngblood, 'Interpreting Montana's Pathbreaking Wrongful Discharge from Employment Act: A Preliminary Analysis' (1992) 53 Montana L Rev 53, 54.

141 Perritt (n 14) 11–60.

142 WDEA s 904(1). For example, see *Krebs v Ryan Oldsmobile* 843 P2d 312 (1992) (where an employee was terminated for reporting illicit drug activity of several co-employees and the Court held there was substantial evidence precluding summary judgment being granted for the employer).

143 WDEA s 904(2).

legitimate business reason'.[144] A third reason is where employers have expressly violated their personnel policy.[145]

The Act created an enforcement system which encourages arbitration and caps damages. In lieu of court action, parties can agree to final and binding arbitration;[146] however, a party cannot reject an offer to arbitrate without risk. A party who rejects a valid arbitration offer and subsequently loses the case may be required to pay legal fees arising after the offer.[147] An employee can only be awarded lost wages and fringe benefits for a period not exceeding four years from the date of the discharge plus interest.[148] Some other limitations exist, including: punitive damages are restricted to situations involving actual fraud or malice,[149] a time limit of one year exists for the filing of claims,[150] and an employer's internal dispute resolution process must be exhausted prior to filing a claim.[151]

Conclusion

With the promulgation of the at-will rule and its acceptance in every state other than Montana, American labour law has moved in an altogether different direction to countries it shares a common law heritage with, like the UK and Australia, which are the focus of this book. Yet, as this chapter has shown, the at-will rule does not preclude claims to protect employees' job security if the employee is exempted under statute or if a common law exception can be found. The at-will rule, therefore, is not the formidable edifice that an outside observer to the US jurisdiction might have thought at first glance, and in some cases employees can win larger compensation payments than in other jurisdictions with a just cause statute. Nonetheless, although the common law rules around at-will employment continue to evolve, American statutory labour law appears to have ossified, with little to suggest this will change.[152]

144 S 903(5). See eg, *Becker v Rosebud Operating Services, Inc* 981 P2d 275 (2008) where the Montana Supreme Court affirmed summary judgment for the employer, finding that good cause existed based on the employee's insubordination and profanity directed at his supervisor.

145 See eg, *Hager v JC Billion Inc* 184 P3d 340 (2008) where the employee alleged his employer failed to follow its own disciplinary procedures before it demoted him and reduced his wages. The matter was found in the employee's favour.

146 WDEA s 914.

147 Mont Code Ann Sections 39–2–915 (2011). See also: Jeffrey Hirsch, 'The Law of Termination: Doing More with Less' (2008) 68 Maryland L Rev 89, 102.

148 WDEA s 905(1).

149 S 905(2).

150 S 911(1).

151 Ss 911(2) and (3). See also *Casiano v Greenway Enterprises Inc* 47 P3d 432 (2002).

152 Cynthia Estlund, 'The Ossification of American Labor Law' (2002) 102 Colum L Rev 1527.

8 Conclusion

Future prospects for job security

Introduction

The focus of this book has been to interrogate the making and evolution of laws pertaining to protection of workers who lose their jobs in the United Kingdom, Australia and the United States. In all three jurisdictions, the importance of traditional labour law approaches in shaping future reform is apparent. Collective laissez-faire in the United Kingdom and conciliation and arbitration in Australia were embedded in the two systems' labour law heritages and acted as a constraining force upon the development of a statutory right not to be unfairly dismissed for individuals. Nonetheless, whilst the United Kingdom and Australia shared a common law tradition as the overarching legal principle for the two jurisdictions, this masked their highly divergent traditions in the area of labour law. The United Kingdom's collective laissez-faire system accorded the parties a substantial degree of industrial autonomy to determine the content of agreements. In contrast, Australia's labour law tradition of conciliation and arbitration was significantly more juridified, although the state transferred its power to regulate industrial relations to an independent commission to determine the outcomes of disputes through a system of awards developed via conciliation and arbitration. These two methods, voluntary collective bargaining in the United Kingdom and compulsory collective conciliation and arbitration in Australia, both sought to secure industrial peace. Moreover, when the two methods were regarded as failing in this objective, the labour law traditions of the United Kingdom and Australia were subject to near terminal stress and strain, and alternative labour law models were canvassed. By way of contrast, although various scholars called for alternative labour law models in the US, there was no widespread recognition of a need for wholesale change or an unfair dismissal statute. The American labour law tradition involved both the yearly hiring rule and the employment at will rule, with the latter ultimately becoming the dominant position at common law, particularly after its enunciation in the work of Horace Woods,[1] and more recently in its acceptance as part of the restatement project.[2]

1 Horace Wood, *A Treatise on the Law of Master and Servant* (JD Parsons, Albany, NY 1877).
2 American Law Institute, 'Restatement of the Law, Third Employment Law, Proposed Final Draft' (18 April 2014) ch 2.

Despite this initial divergence, the hypothesis developed in this final chapter is that there is less difference between the systems in practice than might be originally thought.[3] Drawing upon Estreicher and Hirsch, who say that the US has a 'defacto cause regime' because of the numerous statutory and common law exceptions to the at-will rule,[4] in this chapter I consider whether the contemporary regulation of laws pertaining to protection of job security in the United Kingdom, Australia and the US are really so different in practice.

I begin, however, by examining the role of labour law traditions in influencing the evolution and development of unfair dismissal laws in the United Kingdom and Australia. This gives way to a comparative analysis of the contemporary legal protection for workers who lose their jobs in the United Kingdom, Australia and the United States. The final part tests the hypothesis of a convergent evolutionary dynamic between the three jurisdictions and considers future directions for job security regulation.

The role of labour law traditions in the United Kingdom and Australia in constraining legal change

The United Kingdom and Australia's divergent labour law traditions were important in constraining the development of unfair dismissal law. My point of departure for this discussion in Chapters 2 and 4 was the pioneering work of Kahn-Freund in the United Kingdom and Higgins in Australia in establishing these traditions in theory and identifying the factors critical to their continuation. Higgins' contribution went beyond the theoretical realm, as his ideas about how Australia's conciliation and arbitration system should operate were influential in his decision making as president of the Commonwealth Court of Conciliation and Arbitration from 1907 until 1920. In this book, what began as an account of these labour law traditions became an analysis of how they operated to constrain the development of unfair dismissal law. In many regards, whilst the United Kingdom and Australia's labour law traditions were deeply divergent, they operated to stymie legal change according to a similar evolutionary dynamic.

First and foremost, both traditional systems prioritised the achievement of job security through union security. In order to secure industrial peace, it was regarded that the union movement needed placating in the form of the legitimisation of its

3 Although it is beyond the scope of this work, see other scholars who invoke legal origins theory or the concept of an 'inner relationship' to explain why laws develop in a similar way across jurisdictions. See eg, Peter Gahan, Richard Mitchell, Sean Cooney, Andrew Stewart and Brian Cooper, 'Economic Globalization and Convergence in Labor Market Regulation: An Empirical Assessment' (2012) 60 Am J Comp Law 703; Simon Deakin, Priya Lele and Mathias Siems, 'The Evolution of Labour Law: Calibrating and Comparing Regulatory Regimes' (2007) 146 Int Lab Rev 133; Bob Hepple and Bruno Veneziani, *The Transformation of Labour Law in Europe: A Comparative Study of 15 Countries from 1945–2004* (Hart, Oxford 2009) 11.

4 Samuel Estreicher and Jeffrey Hirsch, 'Comparative Wrongful Dismissal Law: Reassessing American Exceptionalism' (2014) 92 NC L Rev 343, 467.

role in industrial relations by the state. In the United Kingdom both unions and employers were opposed to the introduction of statutory unfair dismissal protection because of their attachment to the British tradition of voluntarism in industrial relations. Their reluctance can be identified both in the National Joint Advisory Committee's final report advocating the extension of voluntary methods to secure unfair dismissal protection and in their lukewarm support for statutory reform in their submissions to the Donovan Commission. Kahn-Freund's observation that collective laissez-faire accorded the industrial parties a substantial amount of autonomy provides a reason for the attachment of unions to retaining their control over industrial relations outcomes and their aversion to the juridification of labour law which would necessarily diminish this role. The preference of both British unions and employers for the extension of union coverage via collective bargaining can be seen as an attempt by the industrial parties to preserve their respective positions. The objective of British unions was to defend the traditional system and keep the courts out of industrial relations. They believed the position of workers would be strengthened through greater unionisation, not through statutory individual rights. British unions were highly suspicious of legal intervention and reluctant to support the enactment of statutory rights for individuals if this would involve the courts.

Australian unions exhibited similar protectiveness of their control over industrial relations. They were slow to canvass the development of statutory individual rights, with their central concern being to ameliorate the collective disadvantage faced by working people in Australia. Unlike in the United Kingdom, this reluctance exhibited by Australian unions was not because of a suspicion of the courts; for over one hundred years unions had operated in the highly juridified conciliation and arbitration system to determine the outcomes of disputes with employers. Nonetheless, their preference was to protect job security through the awards system, and they made significant advances through a test case during the 1980s recognising that the Metal Trades award could incorporate a clause that a dismissal must not be 'harsh, unjust or unreasonable' and that this clause could flow on to other federal awards.[5] So while Australian unions achieved their industrial agenda through state-sanctioned conciliation and arbitration, British unions attempted to secure their agenda through collective bargaining with only auxiliary support from the British state. I can conclude by observing that the traditional power structure existing within a legal system can operate as a powerful disincentive to legal change because groups which perceive their power to be threatened by the change will lobby for the status quo.

A second, related point is the role played by corporatist policies in both jurisdictions preceding the overturning of the labour law traditions of the United Kingdom and Australia in favour of statutory intervention. I rely here on the definition of corporatism provided by Crouch and Dore:

> An institutionalized pattern which involves an explicit or implicit bargain (or recurring bargaining) between some organ of government and private

5 *Termination, Change and Redundancy Case* (1984) 8 Indus R 34; 9 Indus R 115.

> interest groups (including those promoting 'ideal interests' – 'causes'), one element in the bargain being that the groups receive certain institutionalised or ad hoc benefits in return for guarantees by the groups' representatives that their members will behave in certain ways considered to be in the public interest.[6]

Again, whilst the United Kingdom's and Australia's labour law traditions were deeply divergent, a similar dynamic played out in bringing about legal change in the shape of statutory unfair dismissal law. In the 1960s in the United Kingdom, and in the 1980s in Australia, governments experimented with a form of corporatism in order to prop up the existing labour law tradition in the face of growing pressure to overturn it. In both jurisdictions the failure of these experiments and the mounting belief in an economic crisis brought about wholesale labour law reform. Now that this general point has been outlined, perhaps I can explore this similar dynamic, albeit occurring at different times in each system, in more detail. In the United Kingdom when Labour won government in 1964 it endeavoured to secure from the trade union movement a commitment to a permanent incomes policy in the form of state-mandated wage restraint. It was able to secure this commitment because it was sought in the context of explicit governmental undertakings to accelerate the rate of economic growth. This led to unions, employers and the government signing the National Plan. Similarly, in Australia, the Labor government formed an Accord among employers, unions and the government in the 1980s in an attempt to control spiralling wage demands in return for a commitment by the state to develop the welfare system and provide more aggressive tax breaks. Neither attempt at corporatism was successful and both unravelled in the face of spiralling inflation. These eleventh-hour corporatist reforms of governments in both systems ultimately gave way to wholesale labour law reform, occurring in 1971 in the United Kingdom with the enactment of the Industrial Relations Act, and in 1993 in Australia with the similarly titled *Industrial Relations Act*.

Another factor critical to prompting the overturning of the United Kingdom and Australia's divergent legal traditions was the strengthening desire of the state to control industrial relations outcomes directly. In the United Kingdom, successive governments had acquiesced to the collective laissez-faire tradition by a policy of abstentionism in industrial relations. While governments had enacted legislation facilitating the development of wages councils, Order 1305 and the modernisation statutes in the 1960s, successive British governments had refrained from legislating directly and comprehensively over industrial relations. This changed in 1971 with the enactment of the Industrial Relations Act, which as Wedderburn observed resulted in the substantial juridification of industrial relations because of the influence of a 'phantom draftsman' he described as 'a

6 Colin Crouch and Ronald Dore, 'Whatever Happened to Corporatism?' in Colin Crouch and Ronald Dore (eds), *Corporatism and Accountability: Organized Interests in British Public Life* (OUP, Oxford 1990) 3.

Conservative lawyer imbued above all else with doctrines of individual rights, often without regard to the shop-floor problems of collective bargaining'.[7]

Whilst the Australian labour law tradition was more highly juridified because of the complex system of awards which developed over time, it is possible to argue that this system was created through deferring state power over industrial relations to an independent commission. This commission was empowered to exercise compulsory powers of final and binding interest arbitration to prescribe terms and conditions of employment. In this way, the Australian labour law tradition was highly juridified: the law was central to the development of awards. Yet, this system largely bypassed the operation of the common law courts and federal Parliament in determining industrial relations outcomes. Quite obviously, this can largely be attributed to section 51(xxxv) in the Australian Constitution, which provided that the Parliament could make laws with respect to 'conciliation and arbitration for the prevention and settlement of industrial disputes extending beyond the limits of any one state'. It was this constitutional power that enabled the Australian government to enact federal labour laws that had as their centrepiece first a labour court and later an industrial relations commission. Thus, in both the United Kingdom and Australia, their respective labour law traditions held a minimalist role for the government in regulating industrial relations. Nonetheless, once the taboo on the use of statute to regulate the employment relationship directly had been broken, in 1971 in the United Kingdom and in 1993 in Australia, it was more readily accepted that a more juridified labour law would ensue, ultimately producing a national unfair dismissal law.

Thus, it was the breakdown of the United Kingdom and Australia's labour law traditions which ultimately gave way to new labour laws, an essential component of which recognised a statutory right not to be unfairly dismissed. Whilst certain aspects of the United Kingdom's and Australia's labour law traditions operated to inhibit this legal change, the unravelling of these traditions allowed new ideas for labour law to be considered. In both systems this involved a direct role for national governments to regulate industrial relations, the juridification of labour law and enactment of statutory protection against unfair dismissal as part of a new individual employment law.

Key themes animating reform of unfair dismissal law in the United Kingdom and Australia

The need for greater efficiency in the operation of the law

A key difference between the three jurisdictions examined in this book is that in the United Kingdom and Australia a special legal apparatus distinct from the common law was prevailed upon to resolve disputes relating to unfair dismissal. The US, by contrast, chose to rely upon the common law courts to resolve disputes pertaining to dismissal, although a private arbitration system did emerge

7 KW Wedderburn, 'Labour Law and Labour Relations in Britain' (1972) 10 BJIR 270, 282.

to resolve disputes of employees covered by collective bargaining agreements. However, as we pointed out in Chapter 7, arbitration does not create an appealable body of law, as it involves the private resolution of disputes. Much of the contemporary reform to unfair dismissal law in the United Kingdom and Australia can be attributed to a desire to achieve greater efficiency in the administration of justice. There is now considerable pressure for employment tribunals in the United Kingdom and the Fair Work Commission in Australia to resolve unfair dismissal disputes quickly, simply and with minimal cost to the parties.

Both the United Kingdom and Australia relied upon pre-existing adjudicative mechanisms to some degree. The United Kingdom's tripartite employment tribunals were chosen as the avenue for dispute resolution of unfair dismissal claims, although this has evolved into most unfair dismissal claims being heard by a single judge in the present day. In Australia, a combination of the pre-existing Conciliation and Arbitration Commission (as it then was called) and the newly created Industrial Relations Court were used to adjudicate claims. The Court's lifespan was fairly short, as it was abolished three years later, but the commission's role has proved fairly enduring, although its name and role have changed over time.

Increasingly, in both jurisdictions there has been concern about the caseload of these bodies, the associated costs and the legalistic and time-consuming nature of the disputes. This has led to reforms to their composition, their ability to hear claims and procedures for accessing them in the first place. For example, in Australia unfair dismissal claims now involve application fees[8] and have to be brought within the twenty-one-day time limit,[9] and the commission can make costs orders against either the parties and/or their legal representatives.[10] In the United Kingdom, there is no longer a requirement of tripartitism, as a single judge can hear unfair dismissal claims,[11] and substantial filing fees, hearing fees and fees for appeals have been introduced.[12] In both jurisdictions there is a concern with resolving unfair dismissal claims more efficaciously and with less cost to employers, which is an ironic reversal of one of the original justifications for the tribunals' and commission's existence as a low-cost alternative to the common law courts aimed at increasing access and justice for employees. In the United Kingdom, at least, there now appears to be less of a concern with the need for specialist labour courts, as the recent reforms to employment tribunals render them more like the civil courts,[13] giving credence to the argument that unfair dismissal law in that country is somewhat converging upon an employment-at-will situation. There is also considerable pressure for employment tribunals, as part of

8 *Fair Work Act 2009* (Cth) s 395.
9 S 394(2)(a).
10 S 400A.
11 Employment Tribunals Act 1996 (Tribunal Composition) Order 2012 SI 2012/988.
12 Employment Tribunals and the Employment Appeal Tribunal Fees Order 2013 SI 2013/1893.
13 See Susan Corby and Paul L Latreille, 'Employment Tribunals and the Civil Courts: Isomorphism Exemplified' (2012) 41(4) ILJ 387.

HM Courts and Tribunals Service, to resolve cases simply, quickly and cheaply, and in some cases without hearings.[14]

Another parallel development in the United Kingdom and Australia is the renewed efforts to resolve unfair dismissal disputes at the conciliation stage so as to eliminate the need for dispute resolution via tribunals or, in the case of Australia, via arbitration. Whilst ACAS conciliation in the United Kingdom and conciliation by the commission in Australia has always been a feature of both countries' unfair dismissal systems, the subsequent evolution of unfair dismissal law has been to preference conciliation rather than legally binding tribunal resolution or arbitration. The reforms to conciliation in both the United Kingdom and Australia typify the intention of policymakers to resolve unfair dismissal disputes as quickly and cheaply as possible, whilst avoiding legalism. In the United Kingdom this objective has manifested in the policy of facilitating pre-claim conciliation, which encourages employees and employers to ring an ACAS hotline to arrange mediation in the workplace between the parties in dispute. This is to prevent most unfair dismissal applications from ever reaching a tribunal by resolving disputes early and seeking to maintain the parties' relationship under the contract of employment. In addition, a recent British reform by the Coalition government is that prior to submitting a tribunal claim, a prospective claimant must report the details to ACAS.[15] During the period of conciliation, an ACAS officer must endeavour to promote settlement of the dispute; however, conciliation is not mandatory, as either party can refuse to participate.[16] The government believes that fostering greater reliance on conciliation can reduce the number of tribunal claims by 12,000 a year and remedy the present situation where only one third of claimants attempt conciliation before proceeding to the tribunal.[17]

Whilst conciliation has had a more embedded role in the Australian unfair dismissal system, the recent introduction of telephone conciliation is intended to empty the conciliation process of legal rules of procedure, formal submissions and lengthy proceedings. In Australia conciliation by telephone was introduced on the basis that it would efficaciously settle disputes whilst deterring applicants from proceeding to the more costly, time-consuming and legalistic process of arbitration. Both pre-claim conciliation in the United Kingdom and telephone conciliation in Australia can be critiqued on the basis that the emphasis is on resolving disputes expediently and cheaply at the expense of facilitating the achievement of justice in the individual case. Collins has criticised conciliation of unfair dismissal disputes because there is no duty for the conciliation officer to ensure that the settlement is fair to the employee, as the central duty of the

14 Natalie Ceeney, 'A Modernized Court and Tribunal Services' (speech to the Westminster Legal Policy Forum, 14 October 2015).

15 Enterprise and Regulatory Reform Act 2013 s 7, adding s 18A to the Employment Tribunals Act 1996.

16 Department for Business, Innovation and Skills, 'Ending the Employment Relationship: Government Response to Consultation' (BIS, January 2013) [108].

17 Department for Business, Innovation and Skills, 'Resolving Workplace Disputes: A Consultation' (BIS, January 2011) 21–22.

conciliator is to prevent applications proceeding to trial.[18] Whilst there might be many additional pressures to achieve that settlement, including costs and time on the parties, and it might be hard to disentangle those pressures from the role of the conciliator in procuring settlement, it is certainly true that the conciliator's role is influential.

Reducing the regulatory burden on business, particularly small business

A key theme animating contemporary reform of unfair dismissal law in both the United Kingdom and Australia is the need to minimise its regulatory burden on business, predicated on a belief that these laws impede a country's economic prosperity. This driver is by no means unique to the United Kingdom and Australia. For example, at a Tripartite Meeting of Experts convened in April 2011 to examine the International Labour Organization's standards on termination of employment, the spokesperson for the employer representatives present noted that 'strict employment protection regulation [of the type] encouraged by Convention No 158 increases the costs of hiring workers, and also hits hardest the weakest groups in the labour market'.[19] While acknowledging the need for constraints on 'abusive and arbitrary dismissal' and for workers to be afforded notice of termination, he stressed the need to ensure that any protections 'do not unduly burden employers and hence their ability and willingness to hire'.[20] In essence, this argument hinges upon a belief that unfair dismissal law deters job creation and business expansion as employers have to manage the risk of unfair dismissal claims.

Views of this kind find support in a neoclassical approach to labour economics that treats such laws as an interference with the efficient operation of the labour market. Richard Epstein, for example, claims that statutory unfair dismissal protection interferes with the efficient incentive structures provided by the law of contracts.[21] He suggests that the US model of employment at will produces efficient labour markets by reducing the costs and the stakes of disputes over dismissal. This in turn 'protects' dismissed employees as it promotes a free labour market in which jobs are frequently created and readily available. At the microeconomic level, unfair dismissal regulation of the type conceived by ILO Convention No 158 is said to create a disincentive for employees to work

18 Hugh Collins, *Justice in Dismissal: The Law of Termination of Employment* (Clarendon Press, Oxford 1992) 138.

19 International Labour Organization, 'Final Report. Tripartite Meeting of Experts to Examine the Termination of Employment Convention, 1982 (No. 158), and the Termination of Employment Recommendation, 1982 (No. 166)' (ILO, Geneva 2011) 10.

20 Ibid. The meeting concluded without any consensus on the future of the ILO termination of employment standards. The government and worker representatives supported them but this was countered by employer demands that they be abrogated or at least substantially reviewed.

21 Richard Epstein, 'In Defense of the Contract at Will' (1984) 51 U Chicago L Rev 947.

productively. In part, this is because it is difficult for an employer who wishes to replace a capable but relatively unproductive employee to establish inadequacy of performance as a good reason for dismissal.[22] More commonly, however, critics of employment protection laws focus on their macro effects. For example, they assert that by making job shedding more costly, unfair dismissal laws reduce the overall demand for labour.[23] They also assert that employment protection laws may encourage employers to prefer contingent work relationships that are not covered by labour regulations.[24]

The assumption that dismissal regulation is essentially onerous in nature is reflected in the data produced by the World Economic Forum, which ranks countries according to their 'global competitiveness'.[25] Countries with greater statutory protection against unfair dismissal are deemed less competitive on the index, indicating a belief that the laws are prohibitive to job creation and business efficiency. Similar assumptions underlie both the Employment Protection Index of the Organisation for Economic Co-operation and Development and the much-debated Employing Workers Index that appears in the World Bank's Doing Business Reports.

This perspective has influenced contemporary unfair dismissal reform in the United Kingdom and Australia. In the former, the Thatcher government's introduction of a two-year qualifying period for small business was a clear indication of a new argument that the particular case of small employers required special solicitude from the law. This two-year qualifying period was later rolled out to all businesses and, despite it being halved during the New Labour years, the Cameron government recently reinstated it as a measure to reduce the regulatory burden on business of unfair dismissal law. This perspective also saw the Cameron government consider and ultimately reject a proposal to remove unfair dismissal law for micro businesses.[26] Additionally, the introduction of substantial filing and hearing fees for unfair dismissal applicants is intended to reduce the number of claims based on a rationale of reducing business burdens. The British Ministry of Justice stated in its report of 14 December 2011: 'business tells us that the fear

22 Ann-Sophie Vandenberghe, 'Employment Contracts' in Kenneth G Dau-Schmidt, Seth D Harris and Orly Lobel (eds), *Labor and Employment Law and Economics* (Edward Elgar, Cheltenham 2009) 70. See also Guy Davidov, 'In Defence of (Efficiently Administered) "Just Cause" Dismissal Laws' (2007) 23 Int J Comp Lab Law & Indust Relations 117, 129, arguing that an efficient unfair dismissal law would militate against this potential inefficiency by mandating a standard of 'incapability' that would allow employers to discharge employees who are less productive than what is reasonably expected.

23 Richard A Posner, 'Hegel and Employment at Will: A Comment' (1989) 10 Cardozo L Rev 1625, 1634.

24 David H Autor, 'Outsourcing at Will: The Contribution of Unjust Dismissal Doctrine to the Growth of Employment Outsourcing' (2003) 21 J Lab Eco 1.

25 World Economic Forum, 'The Global Competitiveness Report 2014–2015' (World Economic Forum, Geneva 2015).

26 Department for Business Innovation and Skills, 'Dealing with Dismissal and "Compensated No Fault Dismissal" for Micro Businesses, Government Response' (BIS, September 2012).

of high awards being made against them creates uncertainty and can put them off taking on new staff'.[27]

In Australia, Prime Minister Howard was particularly proactive in seeking to protect small business owners from the statutory unfair dismissal laws, stating emphatically: 'we will not weaken or tire in our efforts to secure the passage through the Senate of further reforms of the unfair dismissal laws. They remain to me one of the greatest blots on the escutcheon of small business.'[28] The Howard government made multiple attempts to exempt small business from the unfair dismissal system. Between 1997 and 1998, six Bills were passed through the House of Representatives seeking to extract businesses with fewer than 15 employees from the unfair dismissal laws, and between 2001 and 2004 the government attempted on five further occasions to pass laws exempting businesses with more than 20 employees from the unfair dismissal system.[29] These Bills did not become law because they failed to pass the Senate.[30] The Howard government finally succeeded in its ambition to inoculate small business from unfair dismissal law in its Work Choices reforms, which removed unfair dismissal protection for workers in businesses with fewer than 100 employees. A key justification for these reforms was that they would stimulate job creation.[31] Although the subsequent Labor government removed this exemption entirely, its introduction of a Fair Dismissal Code and its preoccupation with expedient resolution of unfair dismissal disputes indicate its acceptance of the need for special regulatory solicitude towards small business and the need to remove the regulatory burden of unfair dismissal law overall.

Fair treatment for working people

Despite the general tenor of contemporary unfair dismissal reform being one of deregulation resulting in a diminution of job security protection, it must be acknowledged that in both the United Kingdom and Australia unfair dismissal law has proved fairly robust. At a fundamental level there does appear to be support for its existence from both sides of the political spectrum, albeit to varying degrees.

In the United Kingdom, unfair dismissal law has survived a number of suggestions that it be abolished. The first came in 1986 when the Thatcher government announced its intention to abolish the unfair dismissal jurisdiction.[32] This threat never eventuated, although the government did raise a new argument of principle against unfair dismissal law, observing that 'the most significant worry'

27 Ministry of Justice, 'Charging Fees in the Employment Tribunals and the Employment Appeal Tribunal' (14 December 2011).

28 John Howard, 'The Challenges Facing Small Business' (Speech to the Council of Small Business Organisations of Australia, 29 March 2002).

29 See further, Marilyn Pittard, 'Unfair Dismissal Law: The Problem of Application to Small Business' (2006) 19 Aust J Lab Law 255.

30 Ibid.

31 Anna Chapman, 'Protections in Relation to Dismissal: From the Workplace Relations Act to the Fair Work Act' (2009) 32 UNSW LJ 746.

32 Department of Employment, 'Building Businesses . . . Not Barriers' (Cmnd 9794, 1986).

in terms of employment protection regulation was unfair dismissal claims leading to industrial tribunal proceedings.[33] Nonetheless, the Thatcher government did not abolish unfair dismissal law altogether, preferring to reduce access to, and the quality of, the right to unfair dismissal in the United Kingdom during their years in elected office. The Cameron government has followed a similar trajectory with its initial tentative steps to replace unfair dismissal law with no-fault dismissal.[34] The Cameron government commissioned the Beecroft Report, which advocated replacing unfair dismissal law with a schedule of monetary payments which an employee would receive following termination, modified according to their length of service. The report's author, Adam Beecroft, a venture capitalist, wrote of the 'terrible impact of the current unfair dismissal rules on the efficiency and hence competitiveness of our businesses, and on the effectiveness and cost of our public services'.[35] Following the leaking of the Beecroft Report in the media, the Coalition government distanced itself from the no-fault dismissal proposal. The impact assessment for the Department of Business Innovation and Skills' January 2011 consultation on workplace disputes stated that 'a complete end to enabling employees to bring a case for unfair dismissal on any grounds, as some business commentators have suggested, was not considered as it could have had a significant impact on employee protection'.[36] Even the government's consideration of the compensated no-fault dismissal proposal for micro firms with ten employees or less[37] was ultimately scuttled because of significant opposition to the proposal,[38] with only lukewarm support from the business lobby.[39] Like the Thatcher government before it, the Cameron government reversed its original intention of a full-frontal assault on unfair dismissal law, favouring reform which reduces access to the system and the quality of job security protection it offers. The upshot is that unfair dismissal law has proved a fairly enduring addition to the corpus of British labour law since 1971 with a seemingly broad level of community and political support.

This is even more the case in Australia. Despite federal unfair dismissal law's shorter pedigree, being introduced only in 1993, the state unfair dismissal systems were around for much longer. Although the Liberal and National Coalition was opposed to the introduction of federal unfair dismissal law in Australia in 1993, unlike in the United Kingdom, where it had bipartisan political support, the Coalition did not abolish unfair dismissal law in 2004 when it had an opportunity to do so because its election victory gave the Coalition a majority in both houses

33 Department of Employment, 'Employment: The Challenge for the Nation' (White Paper, Cmnd 9474, 1985) 21.

34 Department for Business Innovation and Skills, 'Dealing with Dismissal and "Compensated No Fault Dismissal" for Micro Businesses' (BIS, May 2012).

35 Adam Beecroft, 'Report on Employment Law' (24 October 2011) 4–5.

36 Department for Business Innovation and Skills and Tribunals Service, 'Resolving Workplace Disputes: A Consultation – Impact Assessment' (BIS, 2011) 147.

37 HC Deb col 26WS (23 November 2011).

38 Department for Business Innovation and Skills (n 27).

39 See Chapter 3, n 139.

of Parliament. Instead, the Howard government's Work Choices reforms reduced access to the unfair dismissal system through a combination of exemptions which excluded large swathes of workers. As in the United Kingdom, Australian unfair dismissal law escaped a full-frontal assault. By 2007 the Howard government had lost the election, in no small part due to public opposition to its Work Choices reforms, and the ensuing Labor government restored access to federal unfair dismissal law, albeit with some modifications. Unlike in the United Kingdom, the subsequent election of a conservative government has not seen a return to a political agenda of abolishing or undermining unfair dismissal law, with no indication that this law will be reformed. The Abbott government commissioned an inquiry into the workplace relations framework by the Australian Productivity Commission and, unlike the Beecroft Report in the United Kingdom, its report provided resounding support for unfair dismissal law and rejection of the no-fault dismissal concept. In particular, what is striking about the Productivity Commission's report is its conclusion that abolition of unfair dismissal law is unwise and 'unjustified', that this law provides 'important and needed protections for employees' and that there is no need for 'fundamental change' of federal unfair dismissal law.[40] This provides a clear normative basis in support of Australian unfair dismissal law and means that it is unlikely to be subject to significant revision during the remainder of the Coalition government's first term or as part of its re-election platform for a second term. Although the winds of change are never far away, it seems that, for now, Australia's unfair dismissal law is proving fairly resilient in spite of continuing calls for its operation to be simpler and more efficient.

Thus, in both the United Kingdom and Australia, at a fundamental level, there appears to be widespread support for unfair dismissal law, even if there is disagreement about the level of protection this law should afford and continuing efforts to improve its efficiency and simplicity. This reflects the basic proposition in the United Kingdom and Australia that there should be some independent check on an employer's power to dismiss arbitrarily.

Comparing the legal protection of job security in the United Kingdom, Australia and the United States: a summary

Despite the regulatory convergence upon an unfair dismissal law that resolves disputes quickly, cheaply and has regard to reducing the burden on business whilst maintaining a skeletal framework of job security protection, in the United Kingdom and Australia there are some notable differences in the practical operation of unfair dismissal law (Table 8.1).

First, the two jurisdictions rely on a different test to ascertain whether a dismissal is unfair, although in both the United Kingdom and Australia the test does take into account the size and administrative resources of the business in

40 Productivity Commission, 'Inquiry into the Workplace Relations Framework' (Inquiry Report, Commonwealth of Australia 2015) 557.

Table 8.1 Comparison of unfair dismissal law in the United Kingdom[41] and Australia,[42] 2014–2015

	United Kingdom	*Australia*
Statute	Employment Rights Act 1996 (UK)	Fair Work Act 2009 (Cth)
Test for unfair dismissal	The determination of the question whether the dismissal is fair or unfair (having regard to the reason shown by the employer) (a) depends on whether in the circumstances (including the size and administrative resources of the employer's undertaking) the employer acted reasonably or unreasonably in treating it as a sufficient reason for dismissing the employee, and (b) shall be determined in accordance with equity and the substantial merits of the case.[a]	In considering whether it is satisfied that a dismissal was harsh, unjust or unreasonable, the FWC must take into account: (a) whether there was a valid reason for the dismissal related to the person's capacity or conduct; and (b) whether the person was notified of that reason; and (c) whether the person was given an opportunity to respond to any reason related to the capacity or conduct of the person; and (d) any unreasonable refusal by the employer to allow the person to have a support person present to assist at any discussions relating to dismissal; and (e) if the dismissal related to unsatisfactory performance by the person – whether the person had been warned about that unsatisfactory performance before the dismissal; and (f) the degree to which the size of the employer's enterprise would be likely to impact on the procedures followed in effecting the dismissal; and

(*Continued*)

41 All statistics regarding fees and outcomes relating to employment tribunals, unless otherwise stated, are found in the Tribunals and Gender Recognition Certificate Statistics Quarterly, April to June 2015 (Ministry of Justice, 10 September 2015) and are applicable for claims made in 2014–2015. All statistics regarding conciliation of unfair dismissal disputes are found in ACAS, *Annual Report 2014–2015* (ACAS, 2015).

42 All statistics, unless otherwise stated, are found in the annual report of the Fair Work Commission and are applicable for claims made in 2014–2015: Fair Work Commission, *Annual Report 2014–2015* (FWC, 2015).

Table 8.1 (Continued)

	United Kingdom	*Australia*
		(g) the degree to which the absence of dedicated human resource management specialists or expertise in the enterprise would be likely to impact on the procedures followed in effecting the dismissal; and (h) any other matters that the FWC considers relevant.[b]
Employer size threshold for claims	No threshold	No threshold, although small businesses are subject to the Small Business Fair Dismissal Code. Small business is defined as employing fewer than fifteen workers on a head count basis.
Qualifying period of service for making a claim	2 years	6 months but 12 months for small businesses
Time limit to lodge claims	3 months	21 days from the date the dismissal takes effect
Fees for lodging a claim	£250 at lodgement £950 for cases going to arbitration	$70 AUD
Remedies	Reinstatement or re-engagement Compensation	Reinstatement is the primary remedy. Compensation is capped at either half the high income threshold (which at 1 July 2015 was equal to $68,350 AUD) or 26 weeks' remuneration)
Number of claims	18,387 59% of all applications received for ACAS conciliation from the Employment Tribunal Service (ETS)[c] 30% of all applications made to the ETS	14,624 42.8% of all applications made to the FWC
Incidence of reinstatement at conciliation	Information not available.	0.6% of all applicants were reinstated.
Incidence of reinstatement at arbitration	0.1% of all applicants were reinstated in 2014–15.	1.5% of all applicants were reinstated.

	United Kingdom	*Australia*
Outcomes at conciliation	Information not available.	Settled: Monetary 1750 Settled: Monetary + non-monetary = 5147 Settled: non-monetary = 1820 Settled: reinstatement = 47 Settled: reinstatement + monetary = 15 Settled: reinstatement + non-monetary = 4 Settled: reinstatement, monetary + non-monetary = 5 Total settled matters = 8788 Not settled matters = 2337
Amount of monetary settlement at conciliation	Information not available.	Over 50% of settlements are for an amount of $4,000 or less.[d]
Remedies awarded at tribunal hearing/arbitration for cases upheld	Compensation = 1129 Reinstatement = 4 Remedy left to the parties = 439 No award made = 1082	Compensation =141 Reinstatement = 12 Reinstatement and lost remuneration = 15 No remedy awarded = 1
Amount of compensation awarded at tribunal hearing/arbitration	43% of applicants received less than £4,900. 41% received between £5,000 and £20,000. 16% of applicants received between £20,000 and a maximum award of £238, 216 The average award was £12,362.	57% of applicants received less than $10,000. Only 2 applicants received between $40,000 and the maximum amount.
% of claims resolved prior to tribunal resolution/ arbitration	Information not available.	90% were resolved prior to arbitration by conciliation, triage and case management or where persons withdrew their applications.[e]
Time taken to resolve claims	For the ETS the average clearance time of a single claim was 30 weeks, 8 weeks less than in the same period last year. The average clearance time for multiple claim cases was 188 weeks, up from 140 weeks in the previous year.[f]	Median time taken to resolve a claim from lodgement of an application to finalisation of an unfair dismissal conciliation is 28 days (dropping from 46 days in 2013–14) Median time taken to resolve a claim from lodgement of an application to finalisation is 35 days (dropping from 51 days in 2013–14)

(*Continued*)

Table 8.1 (Continued)

	United Kingdom	*Australia*
Success rates for unfair dismissal claimants[g]	50.7% of claims successful at hearing	54% of claims successful at arbitration

a Employment Rights Act 1996 (UK) s 98(4). At common law, it is well established that 'the function of the [employment] tribunal, as an industrial jury, is to determine whether in the particular circumstances of each case the decision to dismiss the employee fell within the band of reasonable responses which a reasonable employer might have adopted': *Iceland Frozen Foods Ltd v Jones* [1982] IRLR 549 (EAT) (Browne-Wilkinson J).
b *Fair Work Act 2009* (Cth) s 387.
c ACAS (n 42).
d Productivity Commission (n 41) 211.
e Fair Work Commission (n 43) 70.
f These statistics are reported on a quarterly basis and apply to the period April–June 2015. They are for all claims made to the ETS and are not only for unfair dismissals as this statistic is not available.
g The plaintiff success rate is the sum of compensation and reinstatement outcomes divided by the total number of cases substantively arbitrated according to the merits of the dismissal.

question. Second, whilst in the United Kingdom access to the jurisdiction is enlarged because an applicant has much more time to make an unfair dismissal claim, the qualifying period is also significantly longer, which means a former employee has to have been employed for two years prior to making a claim. Third, fees for making a claim are substantially higher in the United Kingdom in order to address an alleged problem of vexatious litigation, to assist in covering the public cost associated with resolving unfair dismissal claims and to dissuade claims reaching a tribunal hearing. These fees could indeed be prohibitive for a former employee who is without employment and the associated income. In both jurisdictions, reinstatement is rarely awarded and compensation is the likely outcome of a successful unfair dismissal claim. The amount usually awarded, however, is not high, although the absence of a cap in the British system means that there is still the possibility of a much higher pay-out, with the largest award in 2014–15 amounting to £238,216, a figure that would not be possible in the Australian system. The Australian system, with its much lesser caseload, is more efficacious in resolving unfair dismissal claims quickly, and this could be attributed to the recent introduction of telephone conciliations, although it must be noted that the timeline for processing an unfair dismissal claim has remained fairly consistent over the years. A final observation is that not only are the prospects of success fairly limited for applicants in both systems, the large majority of successful applicants receive only a relatively small sum, although in the United Kingdom average pay-outs tend to be somewhat higher.

The picture we are left with is a rather pared back unfair dismissal law in the United Kingdom and Australia, where the prospects of success for applicants are fairly limited, as are the monetary amounts that are awarded. But how does this compare with the United States? Although there is no federal or state unfair dismissal law in the US (except in Montana), the data do suggest that where an employee is successful in making a common law claim against termination, the awards are significantly higher. There are at least a couple of reasons why the average amount of monetary damages in the US far exceeds those in other countries. Firstly, while most countries allow for back pay of economic damages, only a few permit compensatory and punitive damages like the US does.[43] Secondly, damages in the United States are not limited by maximum allowable caps.[44] There is a high degree of variability and uncertainty in awards in US employment termination cases, although the amount of awards tends to be far higher than in Australia and the United Kingdom. For example, one study examining 2004–10 US jury awards found that in wrongful termination cases the median award was $292,233 and the mean award was $887,106.[45] Although the courts do not usually order reinstatement for breach of contract cases, it is regularly an outcome in arbitration and it is a presumptive entitlement in discrimination cases.[46] Although the quality of the remedy tends to be better in the US, it should be borne in mind that in the US there are very few successful claims and settlements in comparison with the overall number of dismissals.

According to Estreicher and Hirsch, the US legal system is 'expensive and formal' and it is highly challenging for unrepresented employees to navigate it.[47] There are some structural advantages to the US system in that the losing party usually will not be required to pay the other side's costs, contingency fee arrangements make it easier to get representation, there is a possibility of class actions and civil juries potentially lead to a higher award at trial.[48] However, this is offset by the very low success rates for US employees at trial, with one recent study finding that employment discrimination plaintiffs win just over 10 per cent of all cases initiated in federal district and appellate courts.[49] Claims also take far longer to process through the courts than in Australia, with one study of US employment cases finding that the median time required to resolve the initial phase of a case was 613 days for federal employment discrimination matters, although arbitrations tend to be much shorter, averaging between 215 and 350 days.[50]

Conclusion

This chapter began by identifying the view of some scholars that the United States has a 'defacto cause regime' which they believe to be comparable to the

43 Estreicher and Hirsch (n 4) 457.
44 Ibid.
45 Ibid 462.
46 OECD, 'Detailed Description of Employment Protections in OECD and Selected Non-OECD Countries' (2008) 17 <www.oecd.org/employment/emp/42740165.pdf>.
47 Estreicher and Hirsch (n 4) 454.
48 Ibid 455.
49 Kevin M Clermont and Stewart J Schwab, 'Employment Discrimination Plaintiffs in Federal Court: From Bad to Worse?' (2009) 3 Harv Law & Policy Rev 103.
50 Theodore Eisenberg and Elizabeth Hill, 'Arbitration and Litigation of Employment Claims: An Empirical Comparison' (2004) 58 Disp Resol J 44, 51; see also Estreicher and Hirsch (n 4) 456.

contemporary unfair dismissal laws of other jurisdictions. In this final section I consider this view in terms of both theory and practice.

In theory, there is a significant difference between the United Kingdom's and Australia's statutory unfair dismissal systems and the United States' rule of employment at will. The former seeks to afford an independent review of an employer's dismissal decision. If there is a finding of unfair dismissal, then an employee should be able to receive a monetary amount that compensates him or her for the loss of the job, or the opportunity of returning to his/her previous position. In theory, these remedies are aimed at achieving industrial justice for the unfairly dismissed employee. In contrast, employment at will enables an employer simply to dispense with an employee's services. This approach aims to achieve an efficient termination system with minimal costs and security of outcome for the employer. Whilst unfair dismissal law and employment at will are worlds apart in theory, questions remain as to whether the outcomes are similar in practice.

This book has shown how employment at will in its purest form fails to achieve job security. Nonetheless, a similar accusation can be levelled at the current operation of unfair dismissal law. Many critics of unfair dismissal law in both the United Kingdom and Australia argue that this law does not achieve Njoya's vision of drawing attention to the 'true value involved when the job was lost' because of the limited remedies which can be awarded.[51] Reinstatement is very much the exception,[52] and compensation pay-outs are capped in both jurisdictions, with both the average and the median payment well below the cap. In Australia, the great majority of unfair dismissal cases are settled without ever proceeding to a tribunal hearing, and they are settled on the basis of an unofficial 'tariff' whereby the employer pays what is colloquially referred to as 'go-away' money. Very few cases proceed to arbitration and, of those that do, most result in payment of a modest amount of compensation, with the upper limit for compensation capped at six months' pay. Similarly in the United Kingdom, whilst there were over 40,000 unfair dismissal claims before the tribunal in 2014–15, only four cases concluded with orders reinstating or re-engaging the claimant.[53] Renton identifies similar problems with the remedy of compensation:

> The median award made by way of compensation for unfair dismissal was just 4,591 pounds in 2010–11,[54] or roughly double the amount that the average claimant spends on legal fees (2,493 pounds).[55] At Tribunal, only around

51 Wanjuru Njoya, *Property in Work* (Ashgate, Aldershot 2007) 363.

52 In Australia between 2010 and 2011 only 25 reinstatement orders were made out of 517 unfair dismissal applications which proceeded to arbitration: Fair Work Australia, *Annual Report 2010–2011* (FWA, 2011) 15.

53 Ministry of Justice, 'Employment Tribunals and EAT Statistics, 2010–2011' (2011) 8.

54 Ibid 10.

55 Department of Trade and Industry, 'Better Dispute Resolution: A Review of Employment Dispute Resolution in Great Britain' (DTI, London 2007) 22.

> half of claims succeed. This suggests that the half of all Tribunal claimants who win will have achieved a net gain of 2000 pounds, while many of the other half who have lost will have to pay their own legal fees equivalent to around 10% of the average wage.[56]

Given this, perhaps the starkest difference between the ideas of employment at will and unfair dismissal is that there is no acknowledgement in the former system that there was no good reason for dismissal. All dismissals are treated equally with a failure to account for procedural and substantive differences between the terminations of various workers. Renton suggests that there are three 'victories' a claimant may set out to achieve in launching an unfair dismissal claim: first, the vindication from the tribunal that the dismissal should never have occurred and was unfair; second, the opportunity to return to one's old job, and third, compensation for economic losses suffered since the dismissal.[57] Nonetheless, given the limited nature of the remedies, neither the second or third 'victories' are achieved in any great measure in either the United Kingdom or Australia. Only the first 'victory' can be hoped for, but herein lies the crucial difference between employment at will and unfair dismissal law in its contemporary manifestation: with the latter there is the potential for some acknowledgement by an independent body that the employee should never have been dismissed in the first place. This provides satisfaction to the claimant and, combined with the opportunity for a remedy (however limited), provides an incentive for employers to dismiss their workers according to a fair process and with a valid reason. The presence of unfair dismissal law provides a check on managerial prerogative and provides employees with a greater sense of security about their jobs. Without unfair dismissal law, or with a system of employment at will, an employee could be dismissed for no good reason and be powerless to challenge the employer's decision.

But the problem with the preceding analysis is that the counterfactual to the United Kingdom's and Australia's unfair dismissal laws is not an Epsteinian or Hayekian version of pure employment at will but the contemporary United States approach in which employment at will is modified through a mosaic of statutory and common law exceptions. As I have shown, this produces a much more complex reality whereby United States employees are able to challenge their dismissal either through arbitration if that is available as part of their contract or via the courts. Moreover, the opportunities for reinstatement tend to be far higher via the United States arbitration system and the amounts of compensation far greater via the courts. This is why Estreicher and Hirsch say that the United States has a 'defacto cause regime'. I think there is some merit in their argument, as the diluted unfair dismissal protection afforded by the statutory schemes in the United Kingdom and Australia can be considered as almost on par with the modified version of employment at will currently present in each of

56 David Renton, *Struck Out: Why Employment Tribunals Fail Workers and What Can be Done* (Pluto Press, London 2012) 18.

57 Ibid.

the US states with the exception of Montana. In neither the United Kingdom nor Australia is contemporary unfair dismissal law realising its normative vision of industrial justice. Equally, however, the United States approach of employment at will has been diluted and is far from realising its normative vision of economic efficiency. It is more accurate, then, to think of the three jurisdictions as offering some protection against arbitrary dismissal according to a spectrum rather than an either/or binary.

Using the data from the preceding part, Table 8.2 illustrates that each system has its strengths and weaknesses in terms of the protection afforded to employees. The primary strength of the United States model is the quality of its remedy, as where employees are successful in arbitration cases reinstatement is the norm and in the courts the awards are significantly larger given the absence of statutory caps and the ability to award not only back pay economic damages but compensatory and punitive damages as well. However, bringing an employment termination case in the United States is considerably more expensive than in the United Kingdom and Australia, takes far longer to resolve and success rates are lower. The barriers to access in the United States are considerable and few employment termination claims end up reaching the courts. In contrast, the Australian unfair dismissal model is far more efficient in resolving claims quickly, enabling employees to access the jurisdiction, although the quality of the remedy is fairly poor. In contrast, whilst the United Kingdom permits higher awards than in Australia, the presence of filing fees constrains access to the tribunal system, and the United Kingdom system is only moderately effective in resolving unfair dismissal disputes quickly, with success rates for applicants on par with the Australian system.

Using Table 8.2 and awarding scores of 3 for high, 2 for moderate and 1 for low, the Australian system receives a score of 10 out of 15, the United Kingdom system 9 out of 15 and the US system 8 out of 15. This bears out my initial hypothesis that the regulatory approaches of the United Kingdom, Australia and the United States evince a convergent evolutionary dynamic upon an

Table 8.2 Comparison of job security protection in the United Kingdom, Australia and the United States

Jurisdiction	*Possibility of reinstatement*	*Size of awards*	*Efficiency of processing claims*	*Success rate of employees at court/ tribunal/ arbitration*	*Ability to access independent adjudication of employer's dismissal decision*
United Kingdom	Low	Moderate	Moderate	Moderate	Low
Australia	Low	Low	High	Moderate	High
United States	Moderate	High	Low	Low	Low

employment-at-will situation or a much diluted version of unfair dismissal law. It is possible to say, in agreement with Estreicher and Hirsch, that the United States approach with its at-will rule and common law remedies is less of an outlier, and actually part of a 'relatively narrow continuum of employment laws found in advanced economies'.[58]

This is not to say, however, that this regulatory convergence should go without challenge. The strong normative position of this work has been to argue in favour of job security protection with regard to dismissal. Real and important differences exist between the theoretical conceptions of employment at will and unfair dismissal law which need to be recognised. Even a diluted version of the latter is better than a trumped-up version of the former because of its starting point: unfair dismissal law recognises the more vulnerable position of the employee in the employment relationship. Even the mere presence of unfair dismissal law (albeit in its pared back contemporary iteration) makes a difference to the ongoing power balance in the employment relationship, not just at the time of the dismissal. It is not just about the remedy an unfairly dismissed employee is able to achieve after dismissal but also the powerful educative function of unfair dismissal law and its impact upon employer behaviour during the ongoing employment relationship.

Although in neither the United Kingdom nor Australia has reinstatement or meaningful compensation been generally achieved, a statutory right not to be unfairly dismissed provides a worker with acknowledgement by an independent body that the dismissal was unfair. This provides satisfaction to the worker and – combined with the opportunity for a remedy (however limited) – provides an incentive for employers to dismiss their workers according to a fair process and with a valid reason. The presence of unfair dismissal law provides an important check on managerial prerogative and accords workers a greater sense of security about their jobs. Without unfair dismissal law a worker is employed at will and is reliant on trying to mould a legal case to fit a statutory or common law exception in order to gain redress. The statutory right protecting against unfair dismissal is vital given the more vulnerable position of an employee in unfair dismissal disputes. After all, it is a worker's livelihood that is at stake, whereas in most instances an employer can readily replace one worker with another.

In the United Kingdom and Australia unfair dismissal law must now achieve both economic efficiency and the reduction of regulatory burdens on business, but this should not be without recognising its core purpose of industrial justice or, said differently, the fair treatment of working people. As this comparative work shows, each jurisdiction can learn from the strengths and weaknesses of the other, but this should be with a goal of drilling down to the most worker-protective model. The purpose of this law is to encourage better employer practices around termination, to protect employees from arbitrary dismissal and to achieve a more efficient, fairer termination review system.

58 Estreicher and Hirsch (n 4) 351.

Bibliography

Abel-Smith, Brian and Robert Stevens, *In Search of Justice* (Penguin, London 1968).
Abrams, Roger I and Dennis R Nolan, 'Toward a Theory of "Just Cause" in Employee Discipline Cases' [1985] Duke LJ 594.
ACAS, 'Making More of Alternative Dispute Resolution' (Policy Discussion Paper No 1, 2005).
ACAS, 'Response to the Government Consultation: Resolving Disputes in the Workplace' (ACAS, 2007).
ACAS, *Annual Report 2014–2015* (2015).
ACAS Research and Evaluation Section, 'Evaluation of the First Year of ACAS' Pre-Claim Conciliation Service' (Research Paper by ORC International, 2011).
Acton, Jennifer, 'Where Have All the Cases Gone? Voluntary Resolution of Unfair Dismissal Claims' (ALLA National Conference, Adelaide, November 2010).
American Law Institute, 'Restatement of the Law, Third Employment Law, Proposed Final Draft' (18 April 2014).
American Law Institute, *Restatement of the Law: Employment Law* (American Law Institute, Philadelphia, PA 2015).
Arnow-Richman, Rachel, 'Just Notice: Re-Reforming Employment at Will' (2010–11) 58 UCLA L Rev 1.
Arthurs, Harry, 'Developing Industrial Citizenship: A Challenge for Canada's Second Century' [1967] Canadian Bar Rev 786.
'Australia: Strikes and Legislation' [December 1912] *Round Table* 152.
Australian Bureau of Statistics, *Award Coverage, Australia, May 1990* (Cat no 6315.0, 1990).
Australian Bureau of Statistics, *Trade Union Statistics December 1995* (Cat no 6323.0. 40.001, 1995).
Australian Bureau of Statistics, *Characteristics of Small Business* (Cat no 8127.0, 2004).
Australian Industrial Relations Commission, *Annual Report 2008–2009* (AIRC, 2009).
Autor, David H, 'Outsourcing at Will: The Contribution of Unjust Dismissal Doctrine to the Growth of Employment Outsourcing' (2003) 21 J Lab Eco 1.
Bachelard, Michael, 'Burned by IR, Howard's Battlers Exact Revenge' *The Age* (Melbourne 26 November 2007).
Bales, Richard, 'Explaining the Spread of At-Will Employment as an Interjurisdictional Race to the Bottom of Employment Standards' (2008) 75 Tenn L Rev 453.
Ballam, Deborah, 'The Traditional View on the Origins of the Employment-at-Will Doctrine: Myth or Reality?' (1995) 33 Am Bus LJ 1.

Ballam, Deborah, 'Exploding the Original Myth Regarding Employment-at-Will: The True Origins of the Doctrine' (1996) 17 Berk J Emp & Lab Law 91.

Barbalet, JM, *Citizenship Rights, Struggle and Class Inequality* (University of Minnesota Press, Minneapolis, MN 1988).

Barrow, Charles, *Industrial Relations Law* (Taylor & Francis, London 2000).

Beck, Matthias, *The Elusive Search for Job Security: A Historical Inquiry into Dismissals in the United States Workplace* (Nova Science Publishers, New York 2012).

Bedford, N and Robin Creyke, *Inquisitorial Processes in Australian Tribunals* (Australian Institute of Judicial Administration, Melbourne 2006).

Beecroft, Adam, 'Report on Employment Law' (24 October 2011).

Befort, Stephen, 'Employee Handbooks and the Legal Effect of Disclaimers' (1992) 13(2) Berkeley J Emp & Lab Law 343.

Befort, Stephen, 'Labor and Employment Law at the Millennium: A Historical Review and Critical Assessment' (2002) 43(2) Boston College L Rev 351.

Bennett, L, 'The American Model of Labour Law in Australia' (1992) 5 Aust J Lab Law 135.

Bennett, L, *Making Labour Law in Australia: Industrial Relations, Politics and the Law* (LBC, Sydney 1994).

Bercussion, Brian, 'Employment Protection' in Charles D Drake and Brian Bercussion (eds), *The Employment Acts 1974–1980 with Commentary* (Sweet and Maxwell, London 1981).

Berks, Paul, 'Social Change and Judicial Response: The Handbook Exception to Employment-At-Will' (2000) 4 Em Rts & Emp Pol'y J 231.

Bierman, Leonard and Stuart Youngblood, 'Interpreting Montana's Pathbreaking Wrongful Discharge from Employment Act: A Preliminary Analysis' (1992) 53 Montana L Rev 53.

Birrell, Ian, 'The Employment Act 2008' (Institute of Employment Rights, 2009).

Blackstone, William, *Commentaries on the Laws of England, Volume 1* (9th edn Garland Publishing, London 1978).

Blades, Lawrence, 'Employment at Will vs Individual Freedom: On Limiting the Abusive Exercise of Employer Power' (1967) 67 Colum L Rev 1404.

Bogg, Alan, *The Democratic Aspects of Trade Union Recognition* (Hart, Oxford 2009).

Boland, Roger, 'In Defence of Industrial Tribunals' (Paper presented to the National Conference of the Industrial Relations Society of Australia, Sydney, May 2010).

Bongiorno, Frank, 'Howard's End: The 2007 Australian Election' (2008) 97(397) The Round Table 589.

Bosniak, Linda, 'Citizenship' in Peter Crane and Mark Tushnet (eds), *The Oxford Handbook of Legal Studies* (OUP, Oxford 2003).

Bramble, Tom, *Trade Unionism in Australia: A History from Flood to Ebb Tide* (CUP, Cambridge 2008).

Brett, Judith, 'Exit Right: The Unravelling of John Howard' (2007) 28 Quarterly Essay.

Briggs, Chris, 'Australian Exceptionalism: Australian Trade Unions in the Emergence of Enterprise Bargaining' [2001] JIR 27.

British Chambers of Commerce, 'Employment Regulation: Up to the Job' (BCC, 2010).

Brock, William A and David S Evans, 'The Economics of Regulatory Tiering' (1985) 16(3) Rand J Eco 398.

Brudney, James, 'Reluctance and Remorse: The Covenant of Good Faith and Fair Dealing in American Employment Law' (2010–11) 32 Comp Lab L & Pol'y J 773.

Burn, Robert, *The Justice of the Peace and the Parish Officer* (26th edn Sweet & Maxwell, London 1831).

Business Council of Australia, 'Enterprise-Based Bargaining Unit: A Better Way of Working' (Report to the Business Council of Australia by the Industrial Relations Study Commission, 1989).

Butler, Eamonn, *Hayek* (Temple Smith, London 1983).

'Car Men to Strike if DEP Rejects £2 Rise' *The Guardian* (London 12 April 1969).

Carr, Robert, 'Britain's Urgent Need of a Code for Industrial Relations' *The Times* (London 30 July 1968).

Case, H Manly, 'Federal Employee Job Rights: The Pendleton Act of 1883 to the Civil Service Reform Act of 1978' (1986) 29 Howard LJ 283.

CBI/Harvey Nash, 'Facing the Future: CBI/Harvey Nash Employment Trends Survey 2012' (2012).

Ceeney, Natalie, 'A Modernized Court and Tribunal Services' (speech to the Westminster Legal Policy Forum, 14 October 2015).

Chapman, Anna, 'Termination of Employment under the Workplace Relations Act 1996 (Cth)' (1997) 10 Aust J Lab Law 89.

Chapman, Anna, 'Unfair Dismissal Law and Work Choices: From Safety Net to Legal Privilege' (2006) 16(2) Eco & Lab Relations Rev 237.

Chapman, Anna, 'The Decline and Restoration of Unfair Dismissal Rights' in A Forsyth and A Stewart (eds), *Fair Work: The New Workplace Laws and the Work Choices Legacy* (Federation Press, Sydney 2009).

Chapman, Anna, 'Protections in Relation to Dismissal: From the Workplace Relations Act to the Fair Work Act' (2009) 32(3) UNSW LJ 746.

Clay, Henry, *The Problem of Industrial Relations* (Macmillan & Co, London 1929).

Clermont, Kevin M and Stewart J Schwab, 'Employment Discrimination Plaintiffs in Federal Court: From Bad to Worse?' (2009) 3 Harv Law & Policy Rev 103.

Collins, Hugh, 'Capitalist Discipline and Corporatist Law – Part I' (1982) 11 ILJ 78.

Collins, Hugh, *Justice in Dismissal: The Law of Termination of Employment* (Clarendon Press, Oxford 1992).

Collins, Hugh, 'Regulating the Employment Relation for Competitiveness' (2001) 30 ILJ 17.

Collins, Hugh, 'Is There a Third Way in Labour Law?' in Joanne Conaghan, Richard Fischi and Karl Klare (eds), *Labour Law in an Era of Globalization* (OUP, Oxford 2002).

Committee of Experts, 'Termination at the Initiative of the Employer' (International Labour Conference, 68th Session, 1982).

Committee of Experts on the Application of Conventions and Recommendations, 'Report III (Pt 1A)', (International Labour Conference, 98th Session, ILO, Geneva 2009).

Conroy, Diarmaid, 'Do Applicants Need Advice or Representation?' (Conference on the Future of Administrative Tribunals, edited transcript of proceedings of a conference held at Institute of Judicial Administration, University of Birmingham, April 1971).

Conservative Political Centre, *Fair Deal at Work* (Conservative Political Centre, London 1968).

Corbett, William, 'Resolving Employee Discharge Disputes under the Montana Wrongful Discharge Act (MWDA), Discharge Claims Arising Apart from the MWDA, and Practice and Procedure Issues in the Context of a Discharge Case' (2005) 66 Montana L Rev 329.

Corby, Susan and Paul L Latreille, 'Employment Tribunals and the Civil Courts: Isomorphism Exemplified' (2012) 41 ILJ 387.

Corby, Susan and Paul L Latreille, 'Tripartite Adjudication – An Endangered Species' (2012) 43 IRJ 94.

Creighton, WB, 'Trade Unions, the Law and the New Right' in K Coghill (ed), *The New Right's Australian Fantasy* (McPhee Gribble/Penguin, Melbourne 1987).

Creighton, B and A Stewart, *Labour Law* (1st edn Federation Press, Sydney 1990).

Creighton, B and A Stewart, *Labour Law* (2nd edn Federation Press, Sydney 1994).

Creighton, B and A Stewart, *Labour Law* (3rd edn Federation Press, Sydney 2000).

Creighton, B and A Stewart, *Labour Law* (4th edn Federation Press, Sydney 2010).

Crouch, Colin, *The Strange Non-Death of Neoliberalism* (Polity Press, Cambridge 2011).

Crouch, Colin and Ronald Dore, 'Whatever Happened to Corporatism?' in Colin Crouch and Ronald Dore (eds), *Corporatism and Accountability: Organized Interests in British Public Life* (OUP, Oxford 1990).

Dabscheck, B, *Australian Industrial Relations in the 1980s* (OUP, Melbourne 1989).

Dabscheck, B, 'The Slow and Agonising Death of the Australian Experiment with Conciliation and Arbitration' [2001] JIR 277.

Dau-Schmidt, Kenneth G, 'Promoting Employee Voice in the American Economy: A Call for Comprehensive Reform' (2011) 94 Marq L Rev 765.

Davidov, Guy, 'In Defence of (Efficiently Administered) "Just Cause" Dismissal Laws' (2007) 23 Int J Comp Lab Law & Indust Relations 117.

Davidson, AP, 'Reinstatement of Employees by State Industrial Tribunals' (1980) 54 Aust LJ 706.

Davies, Paul and Mark Freedland, *Labour Legislation and Public Policy* (Clarendon Press, Oxford 1993).

Davies, Paul and Mark Freedland, *Towards a Flexible Labour Market: Labour Legislation and Regulation since the 1990s* (OUP, Oxford 2007).

Deakin, Simon and Gillian Morris, *Labour Law* (4th edn Hart, Oxford 2006).

Deakin, Simon and Gillian Morris, *Labour Law* (5th edn Hart, London 2009).

Deakin, Simon, Priya Lele and Mathias Siems, 'The Evolution of Labour Law: Calibrating and Comparing Regulatory Regimes' (2007) 146 Int Lab Rev 133.

Decker, Kurt, 'Pennsylvania's Whistleblower Law's Extension to Private Sector Employees: Has the Time Finally Come to Broaden Statutory Protection for all At-Will Employees?' (2000) 38(3) Duquesne L Rev 724.

Department for Business, Innovation and Skills, 'Findings from the Survey of Employment Tribunal Applications 2008' (Employment Relations Research Series No 107, 2010).

Department for Business, Innovation and Skills, 'Consultation on Implementing Employee-Owner Status' (BIS, 2012).

Department for Business, Innovation and Skills, 'Dealing with Dismissal and "Compensated No Fault Dismissal" for Micro Businesses' (BIS, 2012).

Department for Business, Innovation and Skills, 'Dealing with Dismissal and "Compensated No Fault Dismissal" for Micro Businesses, Government Response' (BIS, 2012).

Department for Business, Innovation and Skills, 'Employment Law Review: Annual Update 2012' (BIS, 15 March 2012).

Department for Business, Innovation and Skills, 'Ending the Employment Relationship: Consultation' (BIS, 2012).

Department for Business, Innovation and Skills, 'Facilitating Settlement Agreements: Impact Assessment' (BIS, 2012).

Department for Business, Innovation and Skills, 'Flexible, Effective, Fair: Promoting Economic Growth Through a Strong and Efficient Labour Market' (BIS, 2011).

Department for Business, Innovation and Skills, 'Implementing Employee Owner Status: Government Response to Consultation' (BIS, 2012).

Department for Business, Innovation and Skills, 'Latest Developments' (2012).

Department for Business, Innovation and Skills, 'Resolving Workplace Disputes: A Consultation' (BIS, 2011).

Department for Business, Innovation and Skills, 'Unfair Dismissal Compensatory Awards: Impact Assessment' (BIS, 2012).

Department for Business, Innovation and Skills, 'Ending the Employment Relationship: Government Response to Consultation' (BIS, 2013).

Department for Business, Innovation and Skills and Tribunals Service, 'Resolving Workplace Disputes: A Consultation – Impact Assessment' (BIS, 2011).

Department of Employment, 'Proposed Amendments to the Employment Protection Legislation' (Working Paper, 1979).

Department of Employment, 'Employment: The Challenge for the Nation' (White Paper, Cmnd 9474, 1985).

Department of Employment, 'Building Businesses . . . Not Barriers' (Cmnd 9794, 1986).

Department of Employment, 'Resolving Employment Rights Disputes: Options for Reform' (Consultation Paper, Cmnd 2707, 1994).

Department of Trade and Industry, 'Fairness at Work' (White Paper, Cmnd 3968, 1998).

Department of Trade and Industry, 'Routes to Resolution' (DTI, 2001).

Department of Trade and Industry, 'Review of the ERA 1999: Government Response to the Public Consultation' (DTI, 2003).

Department of Trade and Industry, 'Better Dispute Resolution: A Review of Employment Dispute Resolution in Great Britain' (DTI, London 2007).

Dickens, Linda, 'Individual Statutory Employment Rights Since 1997: Constrained Expansion' (2001) 24 ER 619.

Dickens, Linda, Brian Weekes, John Lloyd, and Michael Mellish, *Dismissed: A Study of the Unfair Dismissal and the Industrial Tribunal System* (Blackwell, Oxford 1985).

Drago, Robert, Mark Wooden and Judith Sloan, *Productive Relations? Australian Industrial Relations and Workplace Performance* (Allen & Unwin, Sydney 1992).

Earnshaw, Jill and Stephen Hardy, 'Assessing an Arbitral Route for Unfair Dismissal' (2001) 30 ILJ 289.

Eisenberg, Theodore and Elizabeth Hill, 'Arbitration and Litigation of Employment Claims: An Empirical Comparison' (2004) 58 Disp Resol J 44.

'Electricians' Strikes Holds Up Magazine Production' *The Guardian* (London 12 April 1969).

Elias, Patrick, 'Fairness in Unfair Dismissal: Trends and Tensions' (1981) 10 ILJ 201.

Epstein, Richard A, 'In Defense of the Contract at Will' (1984) 51 U Chicago L Rev 947.

Epstein, Richard A, 'The Common Law and the Labour Market' (HR Nicholls Society, 2001).

Estlund, Cynthia, 'Wrongful Discharge Protections in an At-Will World' (1995–96) 74 Tex L Rev 1655.

Estlund, Cynthia, 'The Ossification of American Labor Law' (2002) 102 Colum L Rev 1527.

Estreicher, Samuel and Jeffrey M Hirsch, 'Comparative Wrongful Dismissal Law: Reassessing American Exceptionalism' (2014) 92 NC L Rev 343.

Ewig, Bradley, Charles North and Beck Taylor, 'The Employment Effects of a "Good Cause" Discharge Standard in Montana' (2005–06) 59 Indust & Lab Relations Rev 17.

Ewing, K and J Hendy, 'Unfair Dismissal Law Changes – Unfair?' (2012) 41 ILJ 115.

Fair Work Act Review Panel, 'Towards More Productive and Equitable Workplaces: An Evaluation of the Fair Work Legislation' (2 August 2012).

Fair Work Australia, 'Unfair Dismissal Conciliation Research' (TNS Social Research, 2010).

Fair Work Australia, *Annual Report 2010–2011* (FWA, 2011).

Fair Work Commission, 'Quarterly Report to the Minister' (July–September 2013).

Fair Work Commission, *Annual Report 2014–2015* (FWC, 2015).

Falconer, Kirsten and Fadil Pedic, 'Small Talk – Group Discussions with Small Business about Paper and Compliance Burden' (Small Business Deregulation Task Force, 1996).

Federation of Small Businesses, 'Regulatory Reform: Where Next?' (FSB, 2012).

Feinman, Jay, 'The Development of the Employment at Will Rule' (1976) 20 Am J Leg Hist 118.

Feinman, Jay, 'The Development of the Employment-at-Will Rule Revisited' (1991) 23 Ariz St LJ 733.

Finkin, Matthew, 'The Bureaucratization of Work: Employer Policies and Contract Law' (1986) Wisconsin L Rev 733.

Finkin, Matthew, 'Privatization of Wrongful Dismissal Protection in Comparative Perspective' (2008) 37 Indust LJ 149.

Finkin, Matthew, 'Second Thoughts on a *Restatement of Employment Law*' (2013) 7 U Penn J Bus Law 279.

Finkin, Matthew Lea Vandervelde, William Corbett, Stephen F Befort, 'Working Group on Chapter 2 of the Proposed Restatement of Employment Law: Employment Contracts: Termination' (2009) 13(1) Em Rts & Emp Pol'y J 93.

Flanders, Allan, *Industrial Relations: What Is Wrong with the System?* (Faber & Faber, London 1965).

Flanders, Allan, 'The Tradition of Voluntarism' (1974) 12 BJIR 352.

Foenander, Orwell, *Towards Industrial Peace in Australia* (Melbourne University Press, Melbourne 1937).

Foenander, Orwell, *Industrial Conciliation and Arbitration in Australia* (Law Book Company of Australasia, Sydney 1959).

Foster, Robin, 'Employment at Will: When Must an Employer Have Good Cause for Discharging an Employee? (1983) 48 Missouri L Rev 113.

Fredman, Sandra, *The Ideology of New Labour Law* (Hart, Oxford 2004).

Freed, Mayer and Daniel Polsby, 'The Doubtful Provenance of "Wood's Rule" Revisited' (1990) 22 Ariz St LJ 551.

Freedland, M, 'The Burden of Proof in Claims of Unfair Dismissal' [1972] ILJ 20.

Freedland, M and N Kountouris, *The Legal Construction of Personal Work Relations* (OUP, Oxford 2011).

Fryer, RH, 'Redundancy, Values and Public Policy' (1973) 4 IRJ 2.

Fudge, Judy, 'After Industrial Citizenship: Market Citizenship or Citizenship at Work?' [2005] IR 631.

Gahan, Peter, Richard Mitchell, Sean Cooney, Andrew Stewart and Brian Cooper, 'Economic Globalization and Convergence in Labor Market Regulation: An Empirical Assessment' (2012) 60 Am J Comp Law 703.
Gerhardt, Michael J, 'The Limited Path Dependency of Precedent' (2005) 7 U Pa J Const L 903.
Gertz, Sally, 'At-Will Employment: Origins, Applications, Exceptions and Expansions in the Public Service' (2008) 31(5) Int J Pub Admin 489.
Gibbons, Michael, 'Better Dispute Resolution: A Review of Employment Dispute Resolution in Great Britain' (Department of Trade and Industry, 2007).
Gillard, Julia and Kevin Rudd, *Forward with Fairness – Policy Implementation Plan* (Canberra: ALP, 2007).
'Give Firms Freedom to Sack Unproductive Workers, Leaked Downing Street Report Advises' *Daily Telegraph* (London 25 October 2011).
Haining, Sarah and Jan Schapper, 'Unfair Dismissal: Perception and Reality' (Monash University, 2006) <http://pegsnet.pegs.vic.edu.au/studentdownloads/Economics/Students/Year%2012%20Folder/Microeconomics/unfair-dismissal%20laws.pdf> accessed 10 January 2011.
Hancock, Keith, 'The First Half Century of Australian Wage Policy' (1979) 21 J Indust Relations 129.
Hancock, Keith and Sue Richardson, 'Economic and Social Effects' in Joe Isaac and Stuart Macintyre (eds), *The New Province for Law and Order* (CUP, Sydney 2004).
Harley, Bill, 'Managing Industrial Conflict' in Joe Isaac and Stuart Macintyre (eds), *The New Province for Law and Order* (CUP, Sydney 2004).
Harrison, Jeffrey, 'The "New" Terminable-at-Will Employment Contract: An Interest and Cost Incident Analysis' (1994) 69 Iowa L Rev 327.
Harvard Law Review Association, 'Protecting at Will Employees against Wrongful Discharge: The Duty to Terminate Only in Good Faith' (1980) 93(8) Harv L Rev 1816.
Hathaway, Oona A, 'Path Dependency in the Law: The Course and Pattern of Legal Change in a Common Law System' (2001) 86 Iowa L Rev 601.
Henderson, Gerard, 'Industrial Relations Club' *Quadrant* (September 1983).
Hepple, Bob, 'A Right to Work' (1981) 10 ILJ 65.
Hepple, Bob, 'Individual Labour Law' in GS Bain (ed), *Industrial Relations in Britain* (Blackwell, Oxford 1983).
Hepple, Bob, 'Back to the Future: Employment Law under the Coalition Government' (2013) 42 ILJ 203.
Hepple, Bob and Bruno Veneziani, *The Transformation of Labour Law in Europe: A Comparative Study of 15 Countries from 1945–2004* (Hart, Oxford 2009).
Higgins, Henry Bourne, 'A New Province for Law and Order' [1915] Harv L Rev 13.
Higgins, Henry Bourne, 'The Future of Industrial Tribunals' *The New Outlook* (Sydney 8–9 April 1922).
Higgins, Henry Bourne, *A New Province for Law and Order* (Constable & Co, London 1922).
Higgins, Henry Bourne, 'Industrial Arbitration' (address in Chapter House of St Paul's Cathedral, Melbourne, 22 March 1926).
Hirsch, Jeffrey, 'The Law of Termination: Doing More with Less' (2008) 68 Maryland L Rev 89.
Holmes, Oliver Wendell, 'Privilege, Malice and Intent' (1894) 8 Harv L Rev 1.

Honore, Tony, *The Quest for Security: Employees, Tenants, Wives* (Stevens & Sons, London 1982).
Howard, John, 'The Challenges Facing Small Business' (Speech to the Council of Small Business Organisations of Australia, 29 March 2002).
Howard, John, 'Workplace Reform: The Next Logical Step' (Address to the Sydney Institute, Four Seasons Hotel, Sydney 2005).
Howard, John, 'The Challenge of Economic Management' (Canberra: Menzies Research Centre, 2007).
Howe, Joanna, Esther Sanchez and Andrew Stewart, 'Job Loss' in Matthew Finkin and Guy Mundlak (eds), *Comparative Labor Law Handbook* (Elgar and Elgar, Cheltenham 2015).
HR Nicholls Society, *Arbitration in Contempt* (HR Nicholls Society, Melbourne 1986).
International Labour Organization, 'Final Report. Tripartite Meeting of Experts to Examine the Termination of Employment Convention, 1982 (No. 158), and the Termination of Employment Recommendation, 1982 (No. 166)' (ILO, Geneva 2011).
Jacoby, Sanford, 'The Duration of Indefinite Employment Contracts in the United States and England: An Historical Analysis' (1982) 5 Comp Lab Law 85.
Jenkins, Peter, *The Battle of Downing Street* (Charles Knight & Co, London 1970).
Jordan, E, AP Thomas, JW Kitching and RA Blackburn, 'Part A: Employer Perceptions and the Impact of Employment Regulation' (Employment Relations Research Series 123, BIS, 2013).
Jukes, M, 'Reply: Tribunals – Justice for All?' (1968) 60 Industrial Society 5.
Kahn-Freund, Otto, 'Legal Framework' in Allan Flanders and Hugh Clegg (eds), *The System of Industrial Relations in Great Britain* (Blackwell, Oxford 1954).
Kahn-Freund, Otto, 'Comparative Law as an Academic Subject' (1966) 82 LQR 40.
Kahn-Freund, Otto, *Labour Law: Old Traditions and New Developments* (Clark, Irwin & Co, Toronto 1968).
Kahn-Freund, Otto, 'Retrospect and Prospect' (1969) 7 BJIR 301.
Kahn-Freund, Otto, *Labour and the Law* (2nd edn Stevens, London 1977).
Kahn-Freund, Otto, *Selected Writings* (Stevens & Sons, London 1978).
Karvelas, Patricia, 'Tony Abbott Signs Contract on Work Choices but Muddles Message on Workplace Laws' *The Australian* (Sydney 19 July 2010).
Kelly, Joseph, 'A Comparative Analysis of the Termination-at-Will Doctrine in the United States and Great Britain' (1989–90) 7(1) Ariz J Int & Comp Law 105.
Kirby, Michael and Breen Creighton, 'The Law of Conciliation and Arbitration' in Joe Isaac and Stuart Macintyre (eds), *The New Province for Law and Order* (CUP, Sydney 2004).
Kirk, Eleanor, Morag McDermont and Nicole Busby, 'Employment Tribunal Claims: Debunking the Myths' (Policy Report 1, PolicyBristol Hub, Bristol 2015).
Kymlicka, Will, *Contemporary Political Philosophy* (2nd edn OUP, Oxford 2002).
Labatt, C, *Master and Servant* (1913).
Labour Party, 'In Place of Strife' (Cmnd 3888, 1969).
Lansbury, Russell and Mark Wescott, 'Collective Bargaining, Employment and Competitiveness: The Case of Australia' [2000] IJES 102.
La Porta, Rafael, Florencio Lopez-de-Silanes and Andrei Schleifer, 'Corporate Ownership Around the World' (1999) 54 J Finance 471.
La Porta, Rafael, Florencio Lopez-de-Silanes, Andrei Schliefer and Robert Vishny, 'Legal Determinants of External Finance' (1997) 52 J Finance 1131.

La Porta, Rafael, Florencio Lopez-de-Silanes, Andrei Schleifer and Robert Vishny, 'Law and Finance' (1998) 106 J Pol Eco 1113.

Liberal-National Coalition, 'The Coalition's Policy to Improve the Fair Work Laws' (Canberra, May 2013).

Linn, Janice, 'Job Security for the at Will Employee: Contractual Right of Discharge for Cause' (1981) 57(3) Chicago-Kent L Rev 697.

Lord, Richard, 'The At-Will Relationship in the 21st Century: A Consideration of Consideration' (2006) 58 Baylor L Rev 707.

Macintyre, Stuart, 'Neither Capital nor Labour: The Politics of the Establishment of Arbitration' in Stuart Macintyre and Richard Mitchell (eds), *Foundations of Arbitration: The Origins and Effects of State Compulsory Arbitration, 1890–1914* (OUP, Melbourne 1989).

Macintyre, Stuart, 'Arbitration' in Graeme Davison, John Hirst and Stuart Macintyre (eds), *The Oxford Companion to Australian History* (OUP, Melbourne 2001).

Mahoney, James, 'Qualitative Methodology and Comparative Politics' (2007) 40 Comp Pol Stud 122.

Mantouvalou, Virginia (ed), *A Right to Work* (Hart, Oxford 2014) Chapter 14.

Markey, R, 'Trade Unions, the Labor Party and the Introduction of Arbitration in New South Wales and the Commonwealth' in Stuart Macintyre and Richard Mitchell (eds), *Foundations of Arbitration: The Origins and Effects of State Compulsory Arbitration* (OUP, Melbourne 1989).

Marshall, TH, *Class, Citizenship and Social Development* (Anchor, New York 1965).

Martin, R and RH Fryer, 'The Myths of the Redundancy Payments Act' (1973) 2 ILJ 1.

May, Kenneth, Patrick M Sanders, Michelle T Sullivan, *Elkouri and Elkouri: How Arbitration Works* (Bloomberg, Arlington, VA 2012).

McCallum, Ron, 'The New Millennium and the Higgins Heritage: Industrial Relations in the 21st Century' [1996] JIR 294.

McCallum, Ron, 'Crafting a New Collective Labour Law for Australia' [1997] JIR 405.

McCallum, Ron, 'Citizenship Theory and Labour Law' (Citizenship at Work? An International Colloquium Theorising Citizenship at Work, University of Laval, Quebec, June 2004).

McCrystal, Shae, *The Right to Strike in Australia* (Federation Press, Sydney, 2010).

Mellish, Michael and N Collis-Squires, 'Legal and Social Norms in Discipline and Dismissal' (1977) 6 ILJ 164.

Meyers, Frederick, *Ownership of Jobs: A Comparative Study* (UCLA Press, Los Angeles 1964).

Ministry of Justice, 'Charging Fees in the Employment Tribunals and the Employment Appeal Tribunal' (14 December 2011).

Ministry of Justice, 'Employment Tribunals and EAT Statistics, 2010–2011' (2011).

Ministry of Labour, 'White Paper on the International Labour Conference' (Cmnd 2548, 1964).

Ministry of Labour, 'Dismissal Procedures' (Report of a Committee of the National Joint Advisory Council, 1967).

Mitchell, Richard, 'State System of Conciliation and Arbitration: The Legal Origins of the Australasian Model' in Stuart Macintyre and Richard Mitchell (eds), *Foundations of Arbitration* (OUP, Melbourne 1989).

Morriss, Andrew P, 'Exploding Myths: An Empirical and Economic Reassessment of the Rise of Employment At-Will' (1994) 59 MLR 679.

Morris, Richard, 'Mr Justice Higgins Scuppered: The 1919 Seamen's Strike' [1972] LH 52.

Muir, Kathie, *Worth Fighting for: Inside the Your Rights at Work Campaign* (UNSW Press, Sydney 2008).

Napier, Brian, 'Dismissals: The New ILO Standards' (1983) 12 ILJ 17.

Niland, J, 'Transforming Industrial Relations in New South Wales: A Green Paper' Vol 1 (NSW Government Printing Office, Sydney 1989).

Njoya, Wanjuru, *Property in Work* (Ashgate, Aldershot 2007).

'Nurses May Strike Over Meal Row' *The Times* (London 12 April 1969).

O'Donovan, J, 'Reinstatement of Dismissed Employees by the Australian Conciliation and Arbitration Commission: Jurisdiction and Practice' (1976) 50 Aust LJ 636.

OECD, 'Detailed Description of Employment Protections in OECD and Selected Non-OECD Countries 2008' (2009) 19 <www.oecd.org/employment/emp/42740165.pdf>.

Office of Personnel Management, 'Our Mission, Role & History' <www.opm.gov/about-us/our-mission-role-history/>.

O'Neill, B, 'General Manager's Report into the Operation of the First Three Years of the Fair Work Act 2009 (Cth) Unfair Dismissal System' (Commonwealth of Australia, December 2012).

O'Neill, Steve, 'Unfair Dismissal and the Small Business Exemption' (Parliament of Australia Library, 2008).

Ontiveros, Maria L, 'To Help Those Most in Need: Undocumented Workers' Rights and Remedies Under Title VII' (1993–94) 20 NYU Rev L & Soc Change 607.

Orr, Graeme, 'The Fair Work Act and Other Names of Shame' (2009) 16 Aust J Lab Law 74.

Osborne, George, 'Party Speech 2012' (Conservative Party Conference, Birmingham, 8 October 2012).

Owens, Rosemary, Joellen Riley and Jill Murray, *The Law of Work* (OUP, Melbourne 2011).

Oxnam, DW, 'The Incidence of Strikes in Australia' in JE Isaac and GW Ford (eds), *Australian Labour Relations Readings* (2nd edn Sun Books, Melbourne 1973).

Peck, Cornelius, 'Penetrating Doctrinal Camouflage: Understanding the Development of the Law of Wrongful Discharge' (1991) 66 Wash L Rev 719.

Peetz, David, 'Coming Soon to a Workplace Near You – The New Industrial Relations Revolution' (2005) 31 Aust Bull Lab 90.

Perritt Jr., Henry, *Employee Dismissal Law and Practice* (5th edn Aspen Publishers, New York 2014).

Pittard, Marilyn, 'Back to the Future: Unjust Termination of Employment under the Work Choices Legislation' (2006) 19 Aust J Lab Law 225.

Pittard, Marilyn, 'Unfair Dismissal Law: The Problem of Application to Small Business' (2006) 19 Aust J Lab Law 255.

Pittard, Marilyn, 'Fair Process in Unfair Dismissal Claims: Changing Landscape under the Fair Work Act' (2010) 17 Aust J Admin Law 199.

Pittard, Marilyn, 'Protection from Unfair Dismissal: Fairness and the Fair Work Act' in Clare Ozich (ed), *Employment Rights Now: Reflections on the Australian Charter of Employment Rights* (Hardie Grant, Richmond, Vic 2015).

Plowman, DH, 'Forced March: The Employers and Arbitration' in Stuart Macintyre and Richard Mitchell (eds), *Foundations of Arbitration: The Origins and Effects of State Compulsory Arbitration* (OUP, Melbourne 1989).

Pollock, George, 'Title?' *The Times* (London 30 April 1964).
Portus, John, *Australian Compulsory Arbitration, 1900–1970* (2nd edn Hicks Smith & Sons, Sydney 1971).
Posner, Richard A, 'Hegel and Employment at Will: A Comment' (1989) 10 Cardozo L Rev 1625.
Posner, Richard A, 'What do Judges Maximize?' in R Posner (ed), *Overcoming Law* (Harvard UP, Cambridge, MA 1995).
Prassl, Jeremias, 'Employee Shareholder "Status"? Dismantling the Contract of Employment' (2013) 42 ILJ 307.
Productivity Commission, 'Inquiry into the Workplace Relations Framework' (Inquiry Report, Commonwealth of Australia 2015).
'Protecting Against Unjustified Dismissal' *The Times* (London 15 March 1965).
Raz, Joseph, *The Morality of Freedom* (Clarendon Press, Oxford 1986).
Reeve, Tapping, *The Law of Baron and Femme, of Parent and Child, Guardian and Ward, Master and Servant, and the Powers of the Court of Chancery* (Oliver Steele, New Haven, CT 1846).
Reich, Charles A, 'The New Property' (1964) 73 Yale LJ 734.
Reith, Peter, Shadow Minister for Industrial Relations, 'Better Pay for Better Work' (Coalition Industrial Relations Policy, 1996).
Renton, D, *Struck Out: Why Employment Tribunals Fail Workers and What Can be Done* (Pluto Press, London 2012).
Renton, D and A Macey, *Justice Deferred: A Critical Guide to the Coalition's Employment Tribunal Reforms* (IER, Liverpool 2013).
Report of the Royal Commission on Trade Unions and Employers' Associations (Cmnd 3888, 1969).
Rickard, John, *HB Higgins: The Rebel as Judge* (Allen & Unwin, Sydney 1984).
Rigby, Elizabeth, 'Workplace Proposals are a Step too Far' *The Financial Times* (London 26 October 2011).
Riley, Joellen, 'Good Faith Performance' in Mordy Bromberg and Mark Irving (eds), *The Australian Charter of Employment Rights* (Hardie Grant Books, Melbourne 2007).
Rimmer, Malcolm, 'Unions and Arbitration' in Joe Isaac and Stuart Macintyre (eds), *The New Province for Law and Order* (CUP, Sydney 2004).
Rowse, Tim, 'Elusive Middle Ground: A Political History' in Joe Isaac and Stuart Macintyre (eds), *The New Province for Law and Order* (CUP, Sydney 2004).
Royal Commission on Trade Unions and Employers' Associations, Minutes of Evidence of 22 March 1966 (Her Majesty's Stationery Office, 1966).
Royal Commission on Trade Unions and Employers' Associations, Minutes of Evidence of 23 November 1965 and 7 December 1965 (Her Majesty's Stationery Office, 1966).
Royal Commission on Trade Unions and Employers' Associations, Minutes of Evidence of 1 February 1966 (Her Majesty's Stationery Office, 1967).
Royal Commission on Trade Unions and Employers' Associations, Minutes of Evidence of 29 November 1966 and 31 January 1967 (Her Majesty's Stationery Office, 1967).
Royal Commission on Trade Unions and Employers' Association, Minutes of Evidence of 12 December 1967 (Her Majesty's Stationery Officer, 1968).
Rudd, Kevin and Julia Gillard, *Forward with Fairness: Labor's Plan for Fairer and More Productive Australian Workplaces* (ALP, Canberra 2007).
Saunders, Astrid, 'Expanding the "No Difference" Rule in the Law of Unfair Dismissal' (2007) 36(3) ILJ 355.

Saunders, Astrid, 'Part One of the Employment Act 2008: "Better" Dispute Resolution?' (2009) 38 ILJ 30.
Schramm, LeRoy, 'Montana Employment Law and the 1987 Wrongful Discharge from Employment Act: A New Order Begins' (1990) 51 Montana L Rev 94.
Schregle, Johannes, 'Comparative Industrial Relations: Pitfalls and Potential' (1981) 120 Int Lab Rev 15.
Selznick, Philip, *Law, Society and Industrial Justice* (Russell Sage Foundation, New York 1969).
Shapiro, J Peter and James F Tune, 'Implied Contract Rights to Job Security' (1974) 26 Stanford L Rev 335.
Sheehan, Kim, 'Has Employment-at-Will Outlived Its Usefulness? A Comparison of US and New Zealand Employment Law' (1997–98) 28 Cal Western Int LJ 323.
Sherman, MR, 'Unfair Dismissal and the Remedy of Re-employment' (1989) 31 J Indust Relations 212.
Simpson, Bob, 'British Labour Relations in the 1980s: Learning to Live with the Law' (1986) 49 MLR 796.
Singleton, Gwynneth, *The Accord and the Labour Movement* (MUP, Melbourne 1990).
Small Business Deregulation Task Force, 'The Bell Report, Time for Business, Report of the Small Business Deregulation Task Force' (Small Business Deregulation Task Force, 1996).
Smith, Charles Manley, *A Treatise on the Law of Master and Servant* (6th edn Sweet & Maxwell, London 1906).
Spence, William, *Australia's Awakening: Thirty Years in the Life of an Australian Agitator* (The Worker Trustees, Sydney 1909).
Sprang, Kenneth A, 'Beware the Toothless Tiger: A Critique of the Model Employment Termination Act' (1994) 43 Am U L Rev 849.
St Antoine, Theodore J, 'You're Fired' (1982) 10(1) Hum Rts 32.
St Antoine, Theodore J, 'A Seed Germinates: Unjust Discharge Reform Heads Toward Full Flower' (1988) 67 Neb L Rev 56.
Steiber, Jack and Richard Block, 'Communications: Unjust-Dismissal Legislation' (1991–92) 45 Indust & Lab Relations Rev 792.
Sternlight, Jean, 'Disarming Employees: How American Employers are Using Mandatory Arbitration to Deprive Workers of Legal Protection' (2015) 80(4) Brooklyn L Rev 1309.
Stewart, Andrew, 'The New Unfair Dismissal Jurisdiction in South Australia' (1986) 28(3) J Indust Relations 367.
Stewart, Andrew, *Unfair Dismissal in South Australia* (Corporate and Business Law Centre, Adelaide 1988).
Stewart, Andrew, 'Employment Protection in Australia' [1989] CLL 27.
Stewart, Andrew, 'A Quiet Revolution: Unfair Dismissal in New South Wales' (1992) 5 Aust J Lab Law 69.
Stewart, Andrew, 'And (Industrial) Justice for All? Protecting Workers Against Unfair Dismissal' (1995) 1 Flinders J Law Reform 85.
Stone, Katherine VW, 'The New Psychological Contract: Implications of the Changing Workplace for Labor and Employment Law' (2001) 48 UCLA L Rev 519.
Stone, Katherine VW, 'Revisiting the At-Will Doctrine: Imposed Terms, Implied Terms and the Normative World of the Workplace,' (UCLA School of Law, Public Law and Theory Research Paper Series, Research Paper No. 06–38, 2006).
Stone, Katherine VW, 'Revisiting the At-Will Employment Doctrine: Imposed Terms, Implied Terms and the Normative World of the Workplace' (2007) 36(1) Indust LJ 86.

Stone, Katherine VW, 'Dismissal Law in the United States: The Past and Present of At-Will Employment' (UCLA School of Law, Law & Economics Research Paper Series No 09–03, 2009).

'Strike Hits Welsh Steel Plant's Output' *The Financial Times* (London 11 April 1969).

Summers, Clyde W, 'Individual Protection against Unjust Dismissal: Time for a Statute' (1976) 62 U Va L Rev 481.

Summers, Clyde W, 'Employment at Will in the United States: The Divine Right of Employers' (2000) 3(1) U Penn J Lab & Emp Law 65.

Sutcliffe, James, *A History of Trade Unionism in Australia* (2nd edn Macmillan, Melbourne 1971).

Taussig, Frank, *Principles of Economics* (4th edn Macmillan, New York 1921).

Taylor, Albion, *Labor Problems and Labor Law* (3rd printing Prentice Hall, New York 1940).

'Textile Unions' Militant "No" to Pay Offer: Steel Row Continues' *The Times* (London 12 April 1969).

Theret, Bruno, 'Theoretical Problems in International Comparisons' in Marc Maurice and Arndt Sorge (eds), *Embedding Organizations: Societal Analysis of Actors, Organizations and Socio-Economic Context* (John Benjamins, Amsterdam 2000).

Torode, John, 'Wilson Brushes off TUC Plea against Reform' *The Guardian* (London 12 April 1969).

Trades Union Congress, 'Government Squandered Reform of Work Dispute System' (media release, 16 December 2003).

Trades Union Congress, 'Trading Rights for Shares' (TUC, 2012).

Treasury, 'The Economic Implications of Full Employment' (Cmd 9725, 1956).

Treasury, 'Full and Fulfilling Employment: Creating the Labour Market for the Future' (2002).

'Unofficial Strike Halts London Freightliners' *The Financial Times* (London 11 April 1969).

US Bureau of Labor Statistics, 'Economic News Release', (USDL-14–0095, 2014) <www.bls.gov/news.release/union2.nr0.htm>.

US Merit Systems Protection Board, 'Judicial Review' <www.mspb.gov/About/review.htm>.

Vandenberghe, Ann-Sophie, 'Employment Contracts' in Kenneth G Dau-Schmidt, Seth D Harris and Orly Lobel (eds), *Labor and Employment Law and Economics* (Edward Elgar, Cheltenham 2009).

'Walk Out by 1,500 at Ipswich Factory' *The Financial Times* (London 11 April 1969).

'Warning of Destruction by Unofficial Strikes' *The Times* (London 12 April 1969).

Watson, Alan, *Legal Transplants: An Approach to Comparative Law* (Scottish Academic Press, Edinburgh 1974).

Wedderburn, KW, *The Worker and the Law* (1st edn Penguin, Harmondsworth 1965).

Wedderburn, KW, 'Labour Law and Labour Relations in Britain' (1972) 10 BJIR 270.

Wedderburn, KW, *The Worker and the Law* (3rd edn Penguin, Harmondsworth 1986).

Wedderburn, KW, 'Labour Law: From Here to Autonomy' (1987) 16 ILJ 1.

Weekes, Brian, John Lloyd, Linda Dickens and Michael Mellish, *Industrial Relations and the Limits of the Law: The Industrial Effects of the Industrial Relations Act 1971* (Blackwell, Oxford 1975).

Whiteley, Geoffrey, 'Strike by 1,500 Dockers' *The Guardian* (London 12 April 1969).

Whitley Committee, 'Interim Report on Joint Standing Industrial Councils' (Cd 8606, 1917).

Wood, Horace, *A Treatise on the Law of Master and Servant* (JD Parsons, Albany, NY 1877).
Wood, Karen and Ron McCallum, 'Crafting the Law: The High Court and Superannuation as an Industrial Matter' (1995) 8 Aust J Lab Law 121.
Woodward, Dennis, 'WorkChoices and Howard's Defeat' (2010) 69 AJPA 274.
World Economic Forum, 'The Global Competitiveness Report 2014–2015' (World Economic Forum, Geneva 2015).
Zweigert, Konrad and Hein Kotz, *An Introduction to Comparative Law* (3rd edn Clarendon Press, Oxford 1998).

Index

For Product Safety Concerns and Information please contact our EU
representative GPSR@taylorandfrancis.com
Taylor & Francis Verlag GmbH, Kaufingerstraße 24, 80331 München, Germany

www.ingramcontent.com/pod-product-compliance
Ingram Content Group UK Ltd.
Pitfield, Milton Keynes, MK11 3LW, UK
UKHW022133190926
475702UK00013B/1780
9781138363557